MW00817666

A MARXIST PHILOSOPHY OF LANGUAGE

Historical Materialism Book Series

Haymarket Books is proud to be working with Brill Academic Publishers (http://www.brill.nl) and the journal *Historical Materialism* on the Historical Materialism Book Series. In September, Haymarket Books will release paperback editions of the full Historical Materialism series, including:

Alasdair MacIntyre's Engagement with Marxism: Selected Writings 1953–1974
Edited by Paul Blackledge

Althusser: The Detour of Theory, Gregory Elliott

The Capitalist Cycle, Pavel V. Maksakovsky,
Translated with introduction and commentary by Richard B. Day

The Clash of Globalisations: Neo-Liberalism, the Third Way and Anti-globalisation, Ray Kiely

Critical Companion to Contemporary Marxism, Edited by Jacques Bidet and Stathis Kouvelakis

Criticism of Heaven: On Marxism and Theology, Roland Boer

Exploring Marx's Capital: Philosophical, Economic, and Political Dimensions, Jacques Bidet

Following Marx: Method, Critique, and Crisis, Michael Lebowitz

Globalisation: A Systematic Marxian Account, Tony Smith

Impersonal Power: History and Theory of the Bourgeois State
Heide Gerstenberger, translated by David Fernbach

Making History: Agency, Structure, and Change in Social Theory, Alex Callinicos

Marxism and Ecological Economics: Toward a Red and Green Political Economy, Paul Burkett

Utopia Ltd.: Ideologies of Social Dreaming in England 1870–1900, Matthew Beaumont

Previously published titles in the Historical Materialism series include:

Between Equal Rights: A Marxist Theory of International Law, China Miéville

The German Revolution: 1917–1923, Pierre Broué

Lenin Rediscovered: What Is to Be Done? In Context, Lars T. Lih

The Theory of Revolution in the Young Marx, Michael Löwy

About the series

More than ten years after the collapse of the Berlin Wall and the disappearance of Marxism as a (supposed) state ideology, a need for a serious and long-term Marxist book publishing program has risen. Subjected to the whims of fashion, most contemporary publishers have abandoned any of the systematic production of Marxist theoretical work that they may have indulged in during the 1970s and early 1980s. The Historical Materialism book series addresses this great gap with original monographs, translated texts and reprints of "classics."

Editorial board: Paul Blackledge, Leeds; Sebastian Budgen, London; Jim Kincaid, Leeds; Stathis Kouvelakis, Paris; Marcel van der Linden, Amsterdam; China Miéville, London; Paul Reynolds, Lancashire.

A MARXIST PHILOSOPHY OF LANGUAGE

JEAN-JACQUES LECERCLE
TRANSLATED BY GREGORY ELLIOTT

Haymarket Books
Chicago, Illinois

First published in 2005 by Brill Academic Publishers, The Netherlands
© 2006 Koninklijke Brill NV, Leiden, The Netherlands

Published in paperback in 2009 by
Haymarket Books
P.O. Box 180165
Chicago, IL 60618
773-583-7884
www.haymarketbooks.org
ISBN: 978-1-608460-26-7

Trade distribution:
In the U.S., Consortium Book Sales, www.cbsd.com
In the UK, Turnaround Publisher Services, www.turnaround-psl.com
In Australia, Palgrave Macmillan, www.palgravemacmillan.com.au
In all other countries, Publishers Group Worldwide, www.pgw.com

Cover design by Ragina Johnson. Cover image by Nadezhda Udaltsova, 1933.

Printed in Canada with union labor.

This book was published with the generous support of the Wallace Global Fund.

10 9 8 7 6 5 4 3 2

Library of Congress Cataloging-in-Publication Data is available.

In memory of my father, active Communist

Contents

Chapter One

'Chirac est un ver'

A not so bright *Sun*

In the run-up to the war of imperialist aggression against Iraq, the *Sun* – a newspaper known for its xenophobic and, in particular, anti-French campaigns – published an edition of several hundred copies in French attacking Jacques Chirac and distributed it free of charge in Paris. The front page featured a photomontage representing a rather dilapidated hexagon from which an enormous, spiralling earthworm emerged whose head was replaced by an unflattering photograph of Jacques Chirac. An enormous headline ran across the page:

CHIRAC EST UN VER [Chirac is a worm]

The accompanying text was the usual mixture of half-truths and barefaced lies.

As a French speaker, I have a problem with this headline. I am well aware that it contains an insult (the headline does not read: *Chirac est un lion*). But I cannot understand the precise import of the insult. If the headline read: *Chirac est un chien, une larve* [grub], *un serpent* [snake], *un dinosaure*, I would have no problem understanding what was involved, since each of these animals, in its own way, is of ill repute. If it said: *Chirac est un pou* [louse], I would not get it straight away, but I would be able to extrapolate, since lice are not natural objects of sympathy. But earthworms are a different matter: in French, they are neither obviously harmful, nor even altogether repugnant. People do say *le ver est dans le fruit* [the rot has already set in], but they also say *nu comme un ver* [as naked as the day she was born], where the main characteristic of the earthworm, as inscribed by commonsense – i.e. the language – is that it is defenceless, the humblest of God's creatures. For my earthworm to be dangerous, inspiring fear or disgust, it must be solitary or plural, like the worms that devour corpses. The result of all this is that the French reader does not immediately grasp how *Chirac est un ver* constitutes an insult.

Everything changes if I translate (I should say retranslate) the headline into English:

CHIRAC IS A WORM

In fact, the earthworm as seen by the English – i.e. through the prism of the English language – is an animal that is both contemptible and repellent. It is not humble; it is humiliated. The employee who has just been publicly humiliated by her superior might exclaim: 'He made me feel like a worm' (the closest French translation of this sentence would doubtless be: *il m'a traité comme un chien* [he treated me like a dog]). The kid who sulks might be mocked by her little friends with the help of the following nursery rhyme:

> Nobody loves me.
> Everybody hates me.
> Going into the garden,
> To eat worms.

And we should not forget that an archaic meaning of 'worm', still present in the titles of fairy stories, is 'dragon'.

The import of the insult is now clear. Chirac is both contemptible and repellent; and his opposition to the imperialist coalition roundly denounced. The *Sun*'s operation is not notable for its subtlety, but the insult is at least intelligible.

The problem is that my opening utterance is not in English, but in French. Or rather: *even though it has been formulated with French words, it is still in English*. Since provocation is the order of the day, I want to yell: 'And what's more, these idiots don't even know French!'. But this is precisely where the problem becomes interesting. Why on earth didn't the *Sun* get hold of a competent translator? In truth, however, the translator is not the problem: the article accompanying the headline is written in correct French. We must therefore look further or deeper for an explanation – to a philosophy of language, with its theoretical and political stakes. This book is devoted to elucidating it. I shall formulate it rapidly in two provisional theses: (1) the *Sun*'s antics exhibit an *implicit conception of language* that has disastrous consequences, and which unfortunately is dominant – not only among third-rate scribblers, but in the media, among politicians, a fair number of philosophers, and even some linguists; (2) English is the language of imperialism.

I am going to add a few words on each of these theses, which will serve as a guiding thread throughout the book.

A conception of language

The *Sun*'s translation is correct but naïve. It is correct, because the statement *Chirac est un ver* is impeccably grammatical; and both the common noun and the proper noun that it contains do indeed designate their referents: the photomontage attests to this. For this is indeed a worm and that is our revered president. But it is naïve. The translator has mentally opened an English-French dictionary at the word 'worm'. Robert-Collins gives: '1. ver; 2. minable [wretched]'. But if he had done the converse, the problem would have emerged, because the same Robert-Collins gives for 'ver': '1. worm; 2. grub; 3. maggot', without indicating any pejorative metaphorical extension. We can see what the naïveté consists in: the operation assumes that the word denotes its referent or the clause its state of affairs without further ado – that is, without metaphor intervening, without everything that we understand today by connotation. It was against this naïve conception that modern thinking about language, starting with Saussure's conception of *langue*, was constructed, introducing the intermediary level of the meaning or the signified between the sign and its referent. In short, for the *Sun*, there are no connotations, only denotations. Yet the utterance 'Chirac is a worm' derives its meaning from its connotations. And it is because these connotations are specific to the English language that the utterance *Chirac est un ver* does not mean much. A fine example of the biter getting bitten: the contempt rebounds on the authors of the insult.

This conception of language, which makes a language a *lingua franca*, a transparent instrument of communication (there are things which are sometimes said in French, sometimes in English, with different words, but the same things are said in both languages) completely ignores what a natural language is: the fact that, named thus in order to distinguish it from artificial languages, it is in reality a cultural construct. Understanding languages through the optic of connotations is to appreciate that a language is also a history, a culture, a conception of the world – not merely a dictionary and a grammar.

An example will illustrate the point. It has the advantage of approximating to my opening utterance. Readers may remember Sartre's phrase: *un anticommuniste est un chien*. The English translation (which is a genuine translation and does not carry on speaking French in English) reads: 'an anti-communist is a rat'.[1] Why this change of animal, which we already come across in my translation of 'he made me feel like a worm'? Because culturally the word 'dog', which denotes man's best friend, does not have the same negative connotations as the word *chien*. 'A dirty dog' is a nasty piece of work, 'a lucky dog' a jammy so-and-so, 'a gay dog' a likely lad. By contrast, in English and French alike no one has a good word to say about rats. What the authors of the French edition of the *Sun* do not realise is that translation, even in the simplest case (one can scarcely imagine a less problematic utterance than 'Chirac is a worm'), is a process which employs a conception of language as a combination of grammar, history and culture.

This lack of awareness is ubiquitous. It is even the source of a politics. In April 2003 Charles Clarke, British education minister and notionally a Labourist, declared that public funds should no longer be devoted to 'ornamental subjects' like mediaeval history or classical literature. Such provocations, too deliberate and insistent not to intimate a policy, earned him some epithets from the scholarly communities concerned ('philistine mobster', 'intolerant yahoo' – the latter being an allusion to Gulliver's travels, whereby literature takes its revenge on those who scorn it). In themselves, these attacks did not directly concern language: neither linguistics (which still enjoys a vague scientific aura), nor even philosophy (which Mr. Clarke had the good grace to exclude from his attacks), are directly implicated. But to attack the history-culture nexus, the cultural past that is inscribed in the English language, out of which the English language is made, presupposes a conception of language as tool and *lingua franca*, a simple instrument for the transmission of information

---

[1] I owe this example to Gregory Elliott.

and knowledge, without depth or past. This emerges even more clearly when we consider a second aspect of British national education.

The percentage of British pupils who take an exam in a living language at A-level is under ten per cent and continuing to fall. This does not mean that ninety per cent of young Britons have never learnt a foreign language (there is no obligatory programme for the English equivalent of the French *baccalauréat*, but multiple choice). It does mean that they have given it up much earlier than their continental counterparts. In Great Britain, notwithstanding worthy proclamations by the government of the need for it (accompanied by an insistence on 'freedom of choice' for parents and pupils which produces the opposite effect from the one proclaimed), study of foreign languages is not essential for two related reasons. What counts is content (a language is simply a transparent vehicle, not a subject of interest or study in itself). But, above all, a single language suffices – the language spoken by the whole world because it is the language of globalisation and empire: those who have the good fortune, or the privilege, to speak English as their mother tongue do not need to learn a second language, unlike the unfortunate natives of secondary languages and dominated cultures. Or, going even further: you need to know English, and there is no need to learn another language, because English is the language of imperialism.

English, language of imperialism

Since this formulation has a slightly provocative, if not insulting, aspect to it (but my starting-point prompts strong reactions), I shall begin by explaining the position I am speaking from. I am an Anglicist and have devoted my life to the English language, which I love with a passion (I take the title of Milner's *L'amour de la langue* seriously).[2] I am not only an Anglophile but an Anglomaniac. And loving the English language entails a passionate attraction to the grammar of this language, its sounds, its history, the literature that it sustains, the culture that is inscribed and sedimented in it. In short, I think I can claim that I am not an Anglophobe. However, it is clear that English has become the global language and the language of globalisation because it is the language

---

[2] See Milner 1978.

of empire, whose practices are ever more explicitly imperialist. To those who doubt the relevance of the old Marxist concept of imperialism in a world markedly different from that of the First World War, the recent war in Iraq will have come as a revelation. Thanks to George Bush, Lenin and Luxemburg are rising from their graves to haunt us.

But to say that English is the language of imperialism is not only to utter an insult or a slogan, but to give a name to a much more complicated situation.

Stage left, English, the language of globalisation, is an instrument of imperialism. A form of linguistic imperialism clearly exists. Anyone who uses a computer is immediately conscious of the fact. English is invading the media, either directly (American series broadcast in the original language – in this regard, France is still an island of resistance, but try watching Swedish or Dutch television during peak hours); or indirectly, when programmes, in French in the text, are copies of American programmes (here we find the cultural equivalent of the process of translation à la Sun: Loft Story is a cultural 'translation' of Big Brother). Naturally, it is invading teaching (not so long ago a French education minister declared that English was the second French language). And, by contamination, it is invading everyday language – and not only via music. Readers may be aware of the controversy over franglais. And the most common graffiti on the walls of my banlieue is an aggressive 'Fuck you!', which indicates that pupils, even the most deprived among them, benefit from the teaching they receive. To describe this situation, linguists have coined the concept of glottophagy, or the devouring of one language by another: it at least has the advantage of linking linguistic change to wider social change.[3] Obviously, I am not claiming that, in the short term, the French language risks being replaced by English. But I am registering an obvious trend whose effects are accelerating (a sign of this is the development of English at the expense of French in European institutions, despite the lack of enthusiasm for the EU on the part of British governments). Taken to the extreme, the domination of one language over another results in the death of languages: they are dying out more rapidly than species in danger of extinction and linguists argue that a language dies every fortnight. Of the five thousand languages currently spoken in the world, half will have disappeared before the end of the century.[4] English is certainly not the cause

---

[3] See Calvet 1974.
[4] See Crystal 2000; Dalby 2003; and Nettle and Romaine 2000.

of this extinction, which is not only that of an idiom, but of a culture, a specific way of conceiving the world: a voice has faded out. At least it is not always the cause (the fate of the Amerindian languages immediately springs to mind). And I would like readers to note that my lamentation presupposes a broader conception of language than that habitually entertained by linguists: I am not treating language as an innate characteristic of the human species (in which case the oblivion of some parameters – i.e. some terms or grammatical tools – would be of little consequence), but as the result of a specific history, the inscription of a culture, an irreplaceable perspective on the world.

In linguistics, however, imperialism is not only exploitation and domination: there is a stage right. Language of empire, English finds itself in a similar position to that once occupied by Latin. Accordingly, it will possibly experience the same fate. The issue is controversial, but it preoccupies all those who are interested in English as the language of globalisation.[5] For the language of empire is not only in a position of strength, but also in a position of weakness: there is a linguistic equivalent of the class struggle and the dominant language does not dominate absolutely, even if the empire that it serves, inscribes and diffuses, continues to dominate. A language possesses autonomy – i.e. an autonomous temporality – vis-à-vis the social structures in which it appears. Thus, Latin long survived the Roman empire, but its linguistic domination never went unchallenged (one thinks of the relations between Latin and Greek); and it slowly dissolved to give rise to the Romance languages.[6]

In the case of English, what is called standard English is caught up in a linguistic struggle with the national dialects, registers, idioms and languages with which it comes into contact: the result is not a simple domination, a simple glottophagy of other languages by the dominant English language. The outcome of this struggle between languages might be described as follows.

English has expanded significantly, to the point where it covers the whole surface of the globe. What is relevant here is not so much the number of speakers (there any many fewer native English speakers than Chinese speakers) as the concentric structure of diffusion of English. At the centre we find native speakers (English as a first language); in the second circle there are secondary speakers (English as a second language), for whom English is not their mother tongue but a compulsory language – the language of culture, administration,

---

[5] Cf. McArthur 1998.
[6] See Waquet 2001.

and so on; and, finally, at the periphery, we find the speakers of English as a living language learnt at school (English as a foreign language). At the centre we have standard English and at the periphery English as a *lingua franca*: these are not precisely the same language and will soon not be the same language at all.

This 'soon' is an exaggeration, for the imperial domination of English, relayed by contemporary technology, produces centripetal effects. When we consider that standard English is no longer the language of Shakespeare (or Tony Blair) but that of George Bush, we will note that the global diffusion of American TV series in the original is a powerful factor of linguistic unification: this is how the village is becoming global. And it is scarcely necessary to recall that English is the language of the world-wide web and the language of economics – that is, the language of neoliberal globalisation: here, the English language is the direct instrument of imperialism.

But these centripetal trends are, if not counter-balanced, then at least attenuated by centrifugal trends. The English of the centre – national English – is undergoing rapid diversification: American and English dialects are diverging and the same is true of Australian English. In the second circle, English is proliferating, with the emergence of what are today called New Englishes. The English of Singapore, for example, is different from that of the former metropolis not only phonetically (the first and most notable difference is that of accents), but also in its vocabulary and syntax. At the furthest stage of this development, we arrive at pidgins and Creoles, fruits of the contact between English and other national languages. Transformed into a *lingua franca*, globalised English is diverging rapidly from standard English. This involves a contradictory process of impoverishment (lexical and syntactical) and enrichment, with the emergence of contact dialects and literatures: I am thinking of what Dylan Thomas, an English writer of Welsh extraction, and Amos Tutuola, the first novelist to have dared to write in the English of Nigeria, do to the language of Shakespeare, to its considerable benefit.

Linguistic imperialism therefore involves a mixed picture, a position of strength that is at the same time one of weakness. The centripetal forces are massively present: globalised media and the web; Anglo-American universities being established throughout the world via subsidiaries; compulsory bilingualism for a significant percentage of the global population. But their effectiveness is often contradictory. Thus, the paradox of teaching a foreign language and not teaching the mother tongue means that foreigners who have been through school sometimes write a more 'correct' English – i.e. one closer to standard English – than the mass of native speakers; while the domination of English explains why refugees refuse to stop at Sangatte: they have not learnt French.

And, as we have seen, there are centrifugal forces. This is not restricted to the dissociation between the two main dialects of English, American and British. Within British English, dialects are diverging from one another and from standard English, which increasingly appears to be a paedagogical myth and ideological constraint. A gauge is required if the language of imperialism is to expand throughout the whole world and it is therefore accepted that 99 per cent of native English speakers speak a very different language – phonetically, lexically and syntactically – from the English diffused by the British Council or the BBC. It is enough to see a film by Ken Loach – *Sweet Sixteen*, for example – to be convinced of this. This proliferation of dialects is not only geographical, but also diachronic. There are generational dialects, which create peer-group solidarity among adolescents – for example, the emergence of the variant of English called Estuary English, because it emerged on the banks of the Thames, but which is spoken almost everywhere in England by that vague category the media call 'youth'. Finally, the standard dialect is subject to a process of 'becoming-minoritarian' by the return of dominated languages – in the United Kingdom, the Gaelic languages (Welsh, Scots and Irish). This involves the emergence of contact dialects (in the case of Wales, 'Wenglish'), but it also involves an inflection of the major language, of which literature becomes the privileged relay.

So there is indeed a linguistic imperialism, which is not merely uncontested domination, but a process of hybridisation, becoming-minoritarian, centralisation, and explosion all at the same time. One therefore has the impression that there is a struggle of dialects just as there is a class struggle and that its outcome is not predetermined. This is why English will end up like Latin: it will fall victim to its internal contradictions, just like the empire. Moreover, it is not certain that the political and economic situation of the empire is more secure than its linguistic situation – at least if Immanuel Wallerstein's analyses are to be believed.[7] The whole question is how long this situation will last.

---

[7] For a recent version of his famous analyses of the centre and the periphery, see Wallerstein 2003.

Readers can see that what interests me in the study of the English language is a much broader range of phenomena than the existence in its grammar of a gerundive or irregular verbs. The interface between the language and the world, the language and society, is what seems to me most important. But to focus on these phenomena, which are usually relegated to the margins of linguistics under the rubric of 'socio-linguistics', is to displace the object of linguistics. It is to indicate the concept of language that we need – which is not simply Saussure's *langue* or language-system.

The concept of language we need

The main characteristic of *langue*, according to Saussure, is that it is a system. Its study is then governed by a so-called principle of 'immanence': nothing external to the system of *langue* is relevant to its description. This defines a form of 'internal' linguistics, which constructs its object by firmly excluding a significant quantity of the phenomena that are usually classed under the concept of 'language'. It will be remembered that, for Saussure, the scientific study of *langue* stopped with morphology and excluded syntax, which was handed over to the arbitrary domain of *parole* – that is, the individual speaker's utilisation of the system of *langue*. The problem is that the phenomena that interest me here are excluded by the construction of the system, in that they are situated at the interface between language and society formed by its speakers. I therefore need an *external* linguistics – a term I borrow from Pierre Bourdieu, who found it (unless I am mistaken) in Marcel Cohen:[8] a linguistics interested in language as a social phenomenon. For it is clear that, for an Anglicist today, it is at least as important to be interested in the dispersion of the dialects that still make up what we call 'English', as with the exact value of the contrast between the deictics 'this' and 'that' within an 'English' which is simply an increasingly vague abstraction.

But the Saussurian system has another major characteristic, encapsulated in the concept of 'synchrony': it is stable – that is, temporally immobile. It is not denied that languages (e.g. the English language) have a history, but study of it is relegated to the margins of science under the agreeable rubric of 'diachrony'. But this 'point in time', as arrested as Zeno's arrow and recalling

---

[8] See Bourdieu 1982.

the Hegelian 'essential section' criticised by Althusser, ignores, in favour of the system whose construction it makes possible, the complex temporality of real languages (a differential temporality, which is not the same for the vocabulary, the syntax, or the phonemes); and the fact that languages are never immobile but constantly subject to historical change, rendering synchronic description somewhat arbitrary. The time of history is not to be stopped and languages evolve much more rapidly than linguists would like. We therefore need to conceive a language not as a stable, arrested system, but as a *system of variations*.

Finally, we need a conception of languages that does not ignore the proliferation of dialects, registers and levels of language; a conception which does not ignore the fact that, for reasons which are not unconnected with a *politics* of language, there is a major dialect, but that this *major* dialect is constantly subject to a process of *becoming-minoritarian*, which subverts it but also causes it to live. These terms are borrowed from the critique of linguistics by Deleuze and Guattari.[9]

Readers will understand that a linguistics, whichever one it might be, would be insufficient here, for both negative and positive reasons. For negative reasons: in taking as its object Saussure's *langue*, linguistics prevents itself from thinking the phenomena that interest us – the historicity of linguistic phenomena, the bond between a natural language and one or more cultures, and so on. This is, in a sense, its grandeur, but also its limitation. And for positive reasons: the controversy between Stalin and the supporters of Marr, whose aporiae I shall recall later, obliges us to let scientists work in peace. It is highly likely that Marxism as such has nothing to say about linguistics or any other scientific activity. On the other hand, it is indispensable when it comes to formulating a *philosophy* of language and criticising those adhered to by linguists, whether implicitly or explicitly. That is why I shall attempt to propose not a *theory*, but a Marxist *philosophy* of language: a theory of language would be nothing but a linguistics that dare not speak its name. And this philosophy will be understood in an Althusserian sense – as an instrument with which to draw lines of demarcation, as a political intervention in the field of language.[10]

---

[9] See Deleuze and Guattari 1986 and 1987.
[10] See Althusser 1990.

It will be understood why this philosophy must be a Marxist philosophy. Not only because its definition, as an instrument of class struggle in theory, is Althusserian – hence Marxist – in origin, but because what is involved is a struggle against the dominant philosophy in the domain of language: Anglo-American analytical philosophy. This philosophy is based on presuppositions which, if not directly utilitarian, are at least intentionalist and methodological-individualist: it articulates the liberal position as regards philosophy of language. To understand and criticise such a philosophy, we need the critical power that Marxism alone can still provide.

There is another reason. The most important contemporary philosophical work in this domain – that of Habermas – is explicitly derived from Marxism, which it aims to reconstruct on new bases (those supplied by the concept of communication, rather than that of labour). This philosophy merits criticism and the objective of this book is not to go back, but to enter, into the house of the bearded prophet. Hence some introductory theses.

Thesis no. 1. Despite a rich and varied tradition of thinking about language by authors identified with Marxism, there has never hitherto been a Marxist philosophy of language.

Thesis no. 2. This absence has deleterious consequences. The most important is the domination of the dominant ideology. What Marxist theory understands by ideology is, in reality, composed of language (and institutions, rituals and practices that furnish utterances and discourses with their pragmatic context). Not to produce a critique of language is to give free rein to the spontaneous philosophies that sustain the dominant ideology and reflect its practice.

Thesis no. 3. The class enemy has always understood the importance of linguistic issues. She has always employed armies of specialists charged with managing linguistic and cultural problems: teachers, jurists, journalists – i.e. the functionaries of the ideological state apparatuses, which do not function by duress *because they function by language*. It is not a question of practising an ingenuous ultra-leftism and condemning all journalist or teachers: being a functionary in an ideological state apparatus does not prevent one from criticising it (I am living proof of this); and if Marxism still survives today – especially in the anglophone countries – it is often thanks to academics. It is a question of weighing objective realities, the massive existence of discursive practices and theoretical reflections that furnish the bourgeoisie with the intellectual means for its domination. It can be said that the recent spectacular defeats of the workers' movement on a world scale have in no small measure been due to the fact that the class enemy has always won the battle of language and that the workers' movement has always neglected this terrain.

This indicates my line of march. So here is my route map. I shall begin with a critique of the philosophy of language that underlies the dominant version of global linguistics: the Chomskyan research programme. I shall also attempt a critique of Habermas's philosophy of language in as much as it does not reconstruct Marxism, but replaces it by a version of liberalism. I shall attempt to reassess the Marxist tradition of thinking about language, which is fragmentary and often sketchy. I shall make a certain number of positive proposals regarding a Marxist philosophy of language. A balance-sheet will be drawn up in the form of a box of conceptual tools that the Marxist tradition has bequeathed us, and which enable us to think the linguistic phenomena ignored by linguistics, but not by the dominant ideology.

Chapter Two
Critique of Linguistics

'Linguistics has done a lot of harm'

Abécédaire is a series of cassettes containing eight hours of filmed interviews between Gilles Deleuze and Claire Parnet.[1] Towards the end of his life (Deleuze had demanded that the cassettes should only be released after his death), the philosopher constructs a balance-sheet of his oeuvre, of which he presents the exoteric version, with all the clarity and enthusiasm of a great teacher. And as he speaks to us from beyond the grave, he can adopt a spiteful attitude, candidly say things that are usually precluded by courtesy. Thus, Wittgenstein is characterised as an assassin of philosophy, Umberto Eco is not spared, and linguistics 'has done a lot of harm'. Obviously, it is the last sentence that interests me.

The passage is to be found under the letter S: 'S is for Style'. Parnet asks Deleuze for a definition of style and he responds by making a detour via linguistics:

> To understand style, you don't need to know anything about linguistics. Linguistics has done a lot of harm. Why? There is an opposition between linguistics and literature: they are not attuned. For linguistics, language is a system in

[1] Deleuze and Parnet 1997.

equilibrium, of which one can construct the science. The remainder, the variations, are assigned not to *langue*, but to *parole*. When one writes, one is well aware that by its very nature language is far from being in a state of equilibrium, but is in permanent disequilibrium. There is no difference of level between *langue* and *parole*. *Langue* is composed of all sorts of heterogeneous currents, which are in disequilibrium with one another.[2]

Deleuze, then, defines style by two characteristics: style makes the language stammer, subjects it to an original syntactical treatment; and, by contorting syntax, takes all language to its limits, towards the border separating it from music.

These statements possess the advantages and disadvantages of exaggeration and hence injustice. They have the advantage of suggesting the framework of a philosophy of language that goes beyond the ordinary – that is, the dominant philosophy that informs and deforms most versions of linguistics. It can be expressed in typically Deleuzian fashion with the aid of a correlation: linguistics/literature; system/variation; homogeneity/heterogeneity; equilibrium/disequilibrium; *langue*/style; science/philosophy or art. We can see the extent of the shift. What is being challenged is the Saussurian concept of *langue*, in its opposition to *parole* in the technical sense – in other words, the foundation of all linguistic science. And it will have been noted that Deleuze refuses to construct an abstract object by reduction, and that he speaks in terms of 'language [*langage*]'.[3]

This position also has the disadvantage of being unjust. It is unjust in two ways. First of all, with respect to the science of language in general, whose undeniable advances it ignores (and which authorise it to assume the name of science: it will be recalled that, even if its star has dimmed, linguistics during the structuralist moment was regarded as a model of scientificity for all the other human sciences). All language teachers know full well that the grammatical description of the language they teach has made gigantic strides since Saussure. It also unjust in that it generalises and speaks of linguistics in the singular, whereas it should be referred to in the plural, so numerous and divergent are the theories. Deleuze was well aware of this since, under

---

[2] This is a rough transcription of what Deleuze says: there exists no printed edition of these interviews.

[3] For a more detailed analysis, readers are referred to Lecercle 2002, Chapter 2.

the influence of Guattari, he had read and used a number of linguists, from Hjelmslev to Benveniste and Gustave Guillaume.

But that is not the important thing. Behind these injustices and simplifications, there is a critique of the dominant philosophy in linguistic matters and hence, *a contrario*, proposals for a different philosophy of language. Deleuze had not waited until *Abécédaire* to formulate it: it is the subject of the fourth plateau in *A Thousand Plateaus*: 'November 20, 1923: Postulates of Linguistics'.[4] These postulates are four in number (and formulated in the conditional in the original French): (1) language is informational and communicational; (2) there is an abstract machine of language that does not appeal to any 'extrinsic' factor; (3) there are constants or universals in language that permit us to define it as a homogeneous system; and (4) language can only be scientifically studied when it takes the form of a standard or major language.

We can see what these counter-postulates are opposed to: to the construction of a linguistic science as proposed, for example, by Jean-Claude Milner in *L'amour de la langue*[5] – a text Deleuze and Guattari do not cite, but which they had possibly read (two years separate its publication from that of *Mille plateaux*). Rather than postulates, Milner proposes axioms (there is a difference). They are likewise four in number: (1) *langue* is to be constructed as its own cause (this is called the arbitrariness of the sign); (2) it will be constructed as formalisable, pertaining to a written form (this is inscribed in the Saussurian concept of the sign); (3) as regards the speaking being, only that which makes her the support of a calculation will be retained (in other words, the speaker, or subject of the enunciation, will have neither past nor future, possess neither an unconscious nor membership of a class, nation or race); and (4) as regards the community of speaking beings, only what is required for the calculation will be retained (this is called the schema of communication: sender/receiver).

There is no one-to-one correspondence between the four 'postulates' and the four 'axioms' (although the first postulate is the exact equivalent of the fourth axiom). But the overall opposition is clear. For Deleuze and Guattari, it is a question of refusing a conception of language that makes it an instrument of communication and information; of rejecting the 'principle of immanence', foundation of the structuralist conception of language, which does not want

---

[4] See Deleuze and Guattari 1988, pp. 75–110.
[5] See Milner 1978.

anything to intervene in the scientific study of *langue* that is not derived from *langue* itself (Milner's first, third and fourth axioms express this principle, which, for him, is key); of refusing to treat *langue* as a stable system (which does not mean that linguistic phenomena are sheer chaos: Deleuze and Guattari defend the idea that a language is a system of variations); and, finally, of rejecting the homogeneity of the object in another way, by taking account of the diversity of phenomena, the impossibility of defining an abstract, a-historical *langue*, at the expense of variations of register, dialect, and generations (as we have just seen in the case of English).

What Deleuze and Guattari bring out is the blind spot of most versions of linguistic science (in this respect, Milner is an exception): they presuppose a philosophy of language. Deleuze and Guattari at least possess the merit of suggesting one, even if it remains in outline state. In the remainder of this work, I shall attempt to develop it somewhat. This immediately poses a question: is the philosophy of language that can be developed starting out from Deleuze and Guattari a Marxist – or *marxisant* – philosophy?

Deleuze and Guattari's relations with Marxism are controversial and, at best, distant. Giving one's *magnum opus* the general title of 'Capitalism and Schizophrenia' is not innocent: it implies a certain relationship to Marxism, but also a deliberate shift, since Marxists are not in the habit of reflecting on madness and desire. However, there is one thing that Deleuze and Guattari did inherit from Marxism: critical vigour. It is insufficient to give us a Marxist philosophy of language, but it will enable us to sketch it out. This critique must be developed and its relevance established. To do this, I am going to consider the most solidly established research programme in linguistics worldwide, the one with which most mortals identify linguistics: Chomsky's.

The importance of the Chomskyan research programme in the history of linguistics, its dominant position (in a domain where theories proliferate: each linguist has her own grammar), are not the only reasons for my choice. First of all, there is its empirical importance – that is, its ability to account for linguistic phenomena. (In this respect, the history of the research programme, which is revolutionised by Chomsky every five years, is full of lessons: a sort of involution has seen the model take its distance from the explanation of grammatical phenomena, in order to concentrate on marginal phenomena and ever greater levels of abstraction.) But, above all, there is the explicit character of the model: Chomsky is one of the rare linguists who is fully aware that there is no good linguistics not only without a methodology of science, but without a philosophy of language. That his philosophical choice has fallen on Cartesian idealism obviously poses a problem, but this option at least possesses the advantage of being explicit, permitting critique. This is what I am now going to proceed to.

The conception of language in Chomsky

Chomsky has devoted numerous works to the philosophy of language – nearly as many as his political works or linguistic works in the strict sense. I shall base myself in the main on two texts: a collection of recent essays, *New Horizons in the Study of Mind*, and the entry on 'Language' written by Chomsky for *The Oxford Companion to the Mind*.[6]

The entry is modestly entitled 'Language: Chomsky's Theory' and involves presenting a theory that is seemingly one among others. The problem is that it is the sole entry for 'language' and so it is as if Chomsky's theory was the only one worth expounding. As usual, however, the entry has the advantage of explicitness and clarity: it presents the philosophical core of Chomsky's theory to us.

The conception of language that emerges from this text, as from the most recent articles (in this respect, Chomsky's thinking has not developed), is that language is a mental organ: a 'biological endowment' that is species-specific and innate. Chomsky clearly establishes an analogy between language – a mental organ – and the heart or eye – physical organs. We speak just as we breathe, possibly without thinking about it, but certainly without ever having learnt to. For, according to Chomsky, we no more learn to speak than we learn to grow arms or reach puberty: language develops in the same way that our body grows and this biological process has nothing to do with learning. Language is like a Leibnizian monad: an innate genetic programme unfolds. However, the analogy is not exact: whereas Leibniz's monad possesses neither doors nor windows, the human mind does. A certain amount of experience is required for the genetic programme of language to be 'triggered': without it, we would be in the position of wolf children who, not having been exposed

---

[6] See Chomsky 2000 and Chomsky 1987.

to a minimum of experience at the requisite age, do not speak at all. Accordingly, experience plays a necessary but limited role in language development.

What experience triggers is a series of 'parameters', which differentiate languages and explain why the same biological endowment does not lead Chinese children and English children to speak the same language (as regards the development of arms and sight, we can in fact consider that there is hardly any difference). However, it will be noted that this does not make the English language a specific object – at least not for the linguist: add or subtract a parameter or two, and we pass straight from German to Dutch and from Dutch to English.

Chomsky might be open to the accusation of physical reductionism – i.e. vulgar materialism. But he is careful. Certainly, the study of language is characterised by him as 'naturalist': he is concerned with a portion of nature like all scientists working in the hard sciences; and linguistics is a natural science. Its object is an aspect of what Chomsky calls 'the mind/brain'. The solidus is a sign of hope: it indicates that there certainly is a connection even if it remains obscure (but one day it will be established by science). Chomsky has an interesting position on what the Anglo-American philosophical tradition calls the 'mind-body problem': for him, the opposition is forced and the concept of 'body' is as problematic as that of 'mind' (this suffices to distinguish him from vulgar materialism). As we can see, Chomsky belongs to the Anglo-American tradition of Quine, Davidson and Putnam, who are his natural interlocutors and sometimes his opponents, and who continue to tackle the problems of materialism in a way which seems old-fashioned to those of us on this side of the Atlantic.

This position has a further consequence. Language is a faculty possessed by all members of the human species in the same way. This universalist position is to be welcomed: it rules out any form of linguistic paternalism and racism (a common position in nineteenth-century thinking about language). But this positive consequence itself has some negative consequences. I shall suggest three. Firstly, the differences between languages are purely superficial and, for the linguist, English and Japanese are practically (give or take the odd parameter) the same thing. The following quotation is typical:

> In the last twenty years or so, there has been a huge explosion of research which has dealt with typologically quite varied languages. We can suspect, and more or less know in advance, that they're all going to be more or less

alike. Otherwise you couldn't learn any of them. The basic structure of them, including the meaning of words and the nature of sentences, just has to come from inside. You don't have enough information to have all that richness of knowledge.[7]

Readers will no doubt have noted the exaggeratedly assertive, and hence imprudent, character of this position, which claims to know in advance what research will discover (and we can anticipate that research will discover what the researcher was determined to find at all costs), as well as the sole empirical argument, endlessly repeated by Chomsky. According to this argument, what he calls the 'explosion of competence' in a young child (who apparently learns the language more rapidly than the information she receives from the outside world can explain) can only be understood by postulating that the knowledge comes 'from inside' – in other words, is innate. The problem with this kind of argument ('there is no other explanation for these phenomena than . . .') is that it has a history: it is the argument that founds the physico-theological proof of the existence of God (the clock-world is too complex for there not to be a watch-maker). No wonder that Chomsky is sometimes called a linguist for creationists out of polemical spite.

If there is a single structure of language which is inscribed in our genetic inheritance; and if all social or cultural differences are, from standpoint of language, irrelevant, a second conclusion follows: each member of the human species is identical as regards the faculty of language, because language is inscribed in his or her brain. Language must therefore be studied in the individual: we are no longer dealing with a system that is external to individual speakers and independent of them (the central position of the linguistic tradition, from Saussure to structuralism), but with a set of individuals endowed with the same capacities; and language, at least as conceived by the science of language, has nothing to do with social existence. In other words, the logical consequence of Chomskyan naturalism is methodological individualism, which is characteristic of liberal thinking in economics and politics.

And there is a third consequence. It is clear that language, derived from a mutation that constituted the human species, has no history, or only the quasi-frozen history of the evolution of the species over the very long term and by leaps: human language has no history in the strict sense, since it cannot have

---

[7] Chomsky 2001, p. 207.

changed since its appearance at the dawn of humanity. Any historical phenomenon, any linguistic change is superficial, and irrelevant for the scientific study of the language faculty. Or, rather, there is linguistic change, but only at the level of the individual whose competence passes from an innate 'initial state' to a 'steady state', once parameters have been triggered by the linguistic environment.

The transition from infancy in the etymological sense to articulate language is therefore not effected by learning (or only at a superficial level); and the sole temporality of language is the retrospective time of recollection. The child who acquires (but does not learn) speech is like the slave in *Meno*: he remembers what he had always known, but did not yet know that he knew. Chomsky's position at least possesses the merit of coherence in its idealism. Later, we shall how or why it can combine a reductionist materialism and a fanatical idealism.

The object of linguistic science is obviously (and this is not a criticism) not language such as we use it, but an abstract construct, which Chomsky calls I-language. The letter I is the initial of the three adjectives that characterise language thus conceived: it is internal (there is at least one element that Chomsky takes over from structuralism – the principle of immanence); individual (language is not a social and cultural object); and intensional – a term taken from logic – by which Chomsky means that the language object he constructs is a generative grammar – that is, a limited number of principles capable of generating an infinity of utterances (this is what Chomsky calls the 'discrete infinity' characteristic of language).[8] The rest – i.e. language as we use it – is consigned to 'common sense', as the object of what Chomsky calls 'folk-linguistics' in all the senses of the term.

There is nothing objectionable about the idea that a science does not find its object ready-made in the world, but constructs it, by abstraction, against common-sense conceptions: the sun does not revolve around the earth and popular etymology is a symptom, not an explanation, of the origin of words. But on one condition: that the science thus deployed accounts for the phenomena. In the domain of language, this means: on condition that the

---

[8] An extensional definition enumerates the elements concerned; an intensional definition supplies the rule of their collection.

theory of language thus constructed enables us to explain, even if abstractly and indirectly, the grammatical phenomena of natural languages. And, in this respect, there is, as I have suggested, an involution in the Chomskyan research programme. In its initial versions, it offered rich perspectives for explaining grammatical phenomena, with significant paedagogical spin offs. In its latest version, it has completely abandoned these empirical ambitions (natural languages are no longer relevant objects) for increasingly abstract considerations, whose relation to linguistic phenomena is ever more uncertain.

Nor shall we be shocked by the idea that language is specific to the human species, that it assumes a 'biological endowment': chimpanzees do not speak (I am grossly over-simplifying: experts know that they possess forms of communication perfectly adapted to the needs of the species). But it is equally clear that there is no language without social practice, that language is imposed on its speaker in social interaction, and that, by this token, it must be learnt. We are therefore dealing with a gradient extending from the innate to the acquired.

Empiricists, for whom virtually everything is acquired, will concede that chimpanzees do not speak; and will also accept that, after a certain age, language-learning is no longer possible. (This is true of wolf children, which is less simple than it appears when considered in detail: if Victor of Aveyron was abandoned to the wilderness, it was possibly precisely because he was already displaying signs of mental handicap.) Chomskyan rationalists, for whom virtually everything is innate, will concede that Chinese babies do not speak English, but will argue that the rules of grammar, even the most detailed among them (e.g., as we shall see, the grammar of reciprocal pronouns), are innate and need only be triggered: they are always 'under-determined' by experience. Marxism, for which language is in the first instance a social phenomenon, and which does not believe in human nature, will tend to sympathise with the empiricist position: general learning capacities, bound up with the development of the human brain, which, like the hand, has a history, suffice to explain the apparent under-determination of linguistic competence by the experience of interlocution.

But sympathising with the empiricist position is not enough. The presuppositions involved in the innate/acquired opposition must also be criticised. It will be noted that both empiricists and rationalists adopt the standpoint of the individual, the individual speaker: whether the child is a *tabula rasa* or bearer of a programme that merely needs to be unfolded, social interaction plays only a secondary role (certainly more important in the case of empiricism: even Frankenstein's monster needs a family environment in order to learn to speak). In the case of political or economic science, this methodological individualism might have some justification (I am making a desperate attempt to be ecumenical here). But, in the case of language, it does not work: we enter into language, which pre-exists us and which we have hardly any purchase on. The English language is not the result of a composition of individual decisions or positions and, in the case of language, the metaphor of the invisible hand does not apply. This is what is expressed by the concept of system in Saussure and of structure among structuralists: they involve conceptualising a necessity (which is imposed on each speaker), but a *social* necessity, by position [*thesei*] – i.e. by a form of convention – and not a natural necessity [*phusei*].[9] In this respect, Chomsky, for whom language is unquestionably a natural organ and linguistics a natural science, is neither Saussurian nor structuralist.

If we abandon the standpoint of the individual and regard language as a social, collective phenomenon, the individual gradient becomes irrelevant. The individual speaker is interpellated by language (by which I mean the natural language that is her mother tongue). She therefore has the capacity to receive this interpellation in the mode of the always-already (just as she has the ability to learn to swim or ride a bicycle). These capacities are employed in collective human practices. The phrase 'innate ideas' in fact treats the brain as a mysterious entity: a materialist position will treat it as a material organ like the hand, whose development accompanies and induces the development of the human species. The same relationship obtains between the brain and language as between the hand and technique. Stone-cutting is not innate; neither is speech.

All this is highly abstract. The touchstone of Chomsky's theory is its ability to explain phenomena. My claim is that it does not. I shall mention two examples – one semantic, the other syntactical.

Chomsky suggests that in the following utterance we immediately understand that what is painted brown is the outside, not the inside, of the house:

---

[9] On this point, readers are referred to Milner 2002.

(1) *He painted the house brown.*

And he concludes his analysis as follows:

> The fact that a brown house has a brown exterior, not interior, appears to be a language universal, holding of 'container' words of a broad category, including ones we might invent: *box, airplane, igloo, lean-to,* etc. To paint a spherical cube brown is to give it a brown exterior.[10]

This is part of a more general claim that 'concepts are fixed'[11] – that is, they belong to the innate universal grammar of the I-language. The argument offered in support of this is the usual one: our rate of lexical acquisition is too rapid to be explained other than by the unfolding of innate capacities; we understand immediately and, in one go, nuances of meaning that are much more subtle than those registered by the most comprehensive dictionary.

Over and above the fact that I find this argument utterly unconvincing (it in no way corresponds to my experience of learning the vocabulary of a foreign language, or to that of my students: Chomsky will respond that we are too old and that, after the age of eight, the triggering does not occur), I find it difficult to accept that concepts – even the most simple among them, like 'house' (in contrast to theoretical concepts like 'surplus-value' or 'subject') – are 'fixed' in Chomsky's sense. Chomsky's claim is that what is fixed is not the concept 'house' itself, but a considerably more abstract concept of 'container', which serves as a superordinate for the names of all possible containers. And he will indicate the vagueness of this abstraction by specifying that the container is typically seen from the outside, as shown by the contrast between my initial utterance and the following one:

(2) *He painted his cave in red ochre.*

But this is a perceptual, not a linguistic, contrast: certain container objects are typically or primarily perceived from the outside, others from the inside. The house pertains to the former category, the grotto or flat to the latter. The choice is determined by the position of the speaker's body in relation to the object. What Chomsky describes is not a linguistic universal, but a feature of experience, as determined by the orientation of my body in space: this is what is inscribed and represented in language. Lakoff and Johnson's theory

---

[10] Chomsky 2000, p. 35.
[11] Chomsky 2000, p. 120.

of metaphor accounts for this phenomenon in a more simple and convincing fashion: it links perceptual schemata and metaphors of orientation.[12] Thus, the ball is 'behind' the rock (which, unlike a car, obviously has no front or back) because the rock is between my body and the ball. It is the outside of the house that is painted brown because I perceive the house from the outside, as a unified object, before entering it. The only universal feature we are dealing with here is the experience of bodily orientation.

We can take our critique further. For Chomsky's thesis is not even adapted to the detail of linguistic phenomena. Consider the following two sentences:

(3) *He painted the whole house brown.*

(4) *He painted the house off-white.*

In these two instances, it seems to me that it is not so clearly the case that we are dealing with the outside of the house. Another kind of reference to experience, in the form of an encyclopaedia (i.e. the whole set of beliefs and knowledge characteristic of a community of speakers in a given historical conjuncture) is required. Sentence (3) might of course refer to the exterior of the house. But, given that it is customary to paint the whole of the outside of a house in a single colour (people rarely paint a house in the colours of their favourite football team), unlike the inside, why does the sentence specify that the *whole* house has been painted brown? Consequently, I shall construe this sentence as referring to the interior of the house. The same is true of sentence (4): 'off-white' is a colour for interior, not exterior, decoration: the immediate interpretation of the sentence therefore concerns the rooms, not the external walls. Naturally, this does not preclude me painting the outside of my house mauve in order to upset the neighbours.

The conclusion is that the concept 'house' is definitely not 'fixed', but historically and culturally determined by an encyclopaedia and a historical conjuncture. Like all concepts, it bears within it the sedimented marks of a history and various types of social practice.

It might be thought that my critique involves a misunderstanding. Chomsky and I are not referring to the same thing. He is talking about an object constructed by science – the I-language – whereas I am referring to a social human practice. I am describing phenomena; he is furnishing their most abstract structures. I am writing an ode to the setting sun; he is an astronomer.

---

[12] See Lakoff and Johnson 1980.

However, this is not exactly true. For Chomsky naturally constructs his I-language on the basis of phenomena that interest me. So, at least in part, we are seeking to explain the same phenomena, even if we are not seeking the explanation in the same place or in the same theoretical language. My second example will bring this out clearly. It comes at the end of the entry on 'Language' in *The Oxford Companion to the Mind*, when Chomsky moves from the abstract description of his theory to its empirical justification by means of an example.

The example Chomsky takes is reciprocal pronouns ('each other', 'one another'). The rule of grammar governing the use of such pronouns is that they must have an antecedent in the plural. The problem is to find the antecedent. In most instances, it is present in the same clause (Chomsky gives his examples in English, which for him has no consequences because he is describing an aspect of universal grammar):

(5) *The men recognised each other*. (Note a difference between English and French here, since the latter does not normally employ an explicit reciprocal pronoun in this sentence: being highly intelligent, the French speaker immediately understands if I say to her *ils se sont reconnus* that the men recognised each other – not that they recognised themselves.)

But there are definitely complications, because the antecedent is not always in the same clause. We must therefore account for the fact that sentences (6) and (7) are grammatical, while (8) and (9) are not:

(6) *The candidates wanted each other to win*.

(7) *The candidates believed each other to be dishonest*.

(8) **The candidates believed each other were dishonest*.

(9) **The candidates wanted me to vote for each other*. (As is customary, the asterisk signals an ungrammatical sentence.)

In (8) 'each other' is the subject of the substantival clause '(that) X were dishonest'; and its antecedent is therefore not situated in the same clause, but in the main clause. In (9) the antecedent of 'each other' is the subject of the main clause. However, the explanation that I have just implicitly given (the relationship of antecedent does not hold across the clause boundary) is insufficient, for it should lead me to conclude that sentences (6) and (7) are equally ungrammatical, since in both cases the reciprocal pronoun is in the infinitive subordinate clause and the antecedent in the main clause. A complex grammatical rule appears to be at work here. Native English speakers apply it without ever making a mistake, even if they would be at a loss to formulate it. This state of affairs inspires the following conclusions in Chomsky:

> Such facts as these are known to all speakers of English, and analogues appear to hold in other languages. The facts are known without experience, let alone training. The child must learn that 'each other' is a reciprocal expression, but nothing more, so it seems. No pedagogic grammar would mention such facts are those described above; the student can be expected to know them without instruction. The principles that determine selection of an antecedent, it seems reasonable to assume, belong to 'universal grammar', that is, to the biological endowment that determines the general structure of the language faculty. From another point of view, these principles form part of a deductive, explanatory theory of human language.[13]

This text merits detailed analysis, for every sentence is problematic. The 'analogues' that 'appear to hold in other languages' are decidedly vague: how many other languages? Is the analogue sufficiently precise, and sufficiently extended, to allow us to speak of a linguistic universal? 'The facts are known without experience, let alone training': the elevated register and rarity of the construction ('the candidates believed each other to be successful' does not pertain to current popular English and presupposes speakers subjected to eight hours' education a day for years on end), render explanation by learning much more plausible. 'No pedagogic grammar would mention such facts as those described above': but these 'facts' are in reality conditioned by theory. Paedagogic grammars give a simpler rule ('a reciprocal pronoun has an antecedent in the plural that is usually the subject of the same clause'), which perfectly covers the great majority of cases and requires only some adaptation for complex cases, which (as we have just seen) do not presuppose a universal grammar, but a certain linguistic register in a certain language. 'The student can be expected to know them without instruction': as this construction is rare, and elevated in register, we are always dealing with a population of highly educated speakers. As for my francophone students, they commit every imaginable error in these constructions: the principles are not as universal as all that (and yet the French language also possesses reciprocal pronouns). Finally, 'the principles . . . belong to "universal grammar"': this fixity is doubtful, since the construction has a history and, given that the detail of the

---

[13] Chomsky 1987, p. 421.

phenomena is more complex than Chomsky allows, this universal grammar is threatened with assuming a Byzantine complexity and hence lacking credibility.

There are three troubling things about this text. It multiples the use of hedges ('appear to hold', 'so it seems'), which actually signal generalisations that are not justified by the facts. The vagueness of its formulations goes beyond what is justified by the nature of the text: Chomsky has a few pages in which to set out his theory and so we should not expect detailed analyses from him. To his credit, he seeks to conclude with a concrete example. However, his analysis is not only vague, but it sometimes ignores the facts and sometimes contradicts them. In so doing, it places the bar very high: innate grammar does not only concern very general and highly abstract phenomena, but extremely precise grammatical rules, like those governing reciprocal pronouns. If it can be shown that these rules do not really cover French – a language which is nevertheless typologically close to English – the Chomskyan monad will have the same complexity as its Leibnizian cousin and will require some transcendence to become philosophically credible. For, even if the detail of the linguistic phenomena – what differentiates French from English – is attributed to local parameters rather than universal principles, either these parameters are innate, and the human brain contains in its innermost recesses the totality of human languages, past, present and future; or they are not only triggered by experience, but determined by it – that is, acquired by the speaker. In the latter case, the imbalance between the acquired and the innate is reversed in favour of the acquired and, in order to explain the innate dimension of language, we only need some general human capacity for learning, which means that the offspring of human beings have more talent in this domain than those of chimpanzees (this, roughly speaking, was Piaget's position). I must therefore compare Chomsky's 'rules' with the facts, and not only those of the English language.

This is the sticking point, for the phenomena do not live up to Chomsky's expectations: the grammar of the reciprocal pronoun is not the same in French as in English. While Chomsky's native speakers observe these rules without ever erring (which seems to me a decidedly hazardous generalisation), my francophone students commit such 'errors' and find it difficult to distinguish between sentences (6) and (7) on the one hand and (8) and (9) on the other. Perhaps this is due to the fact that they have not been exposed to the English language before the age of eleven – too late for the parameters to be triggered.

But this takes us back to the monad and its complexity: the human brain is effectively too complex a watch to do without a watch-maker.

And, if we avoid these metaphysical complications, limit the innate to the universal principles of grammar, and thus leave the parameters that determine individual languages to experience and instruction, we shall end up by saying that almost all the rules governing reciprocal pronouns are defined language by language. Thus, my francophone students err as to the ungrammatical nature of sentences (8) and (9) because the rules governing the reciprocal pronoun are not the same in English and in French.

I begin with an actual error drawn from work by a student on an English degree:

(10) *In Gogol's 'The Picture', the character's dreams are embedded one within each other.*

The grammar that I try to teach my students stipulates that you should write: 'one within the other'. We can see the source of the error: the student is illicitly combining two reciprocal constructions – 'they looked at each other' and 'each looked at the other'. Chomsky only considers the latter and ignores the former. It is easy to see why: they do not have the same syntax. Thus, the first construction likewise obeys principles for selecting the antecedent (i.e. the innate component of language: Chomsky is not interested in reciprocal constructions as such, but in the more general principles governing them); and it should be the same principles, the difference being that the antecedent 'each' is always the same – which facilitates recognition of it. But the linguistic facts do not match this prediction, as the following sentences show:

(11) *Each candidate wanted the other to win.*

(12) *Each candidate wished that the other might win.*

According to Chomskyan principles, the first of these sentences is typically grammatical, but the second should not be.

And, if we turn to French, the difference is still greater, for French invariably neutralises the difference between reciprocal and reflexive, leaving it to the context to enable the listener to understand the sentence:

(13) *Ils se regardaient* [they looked at themselves/each other].

(14) *Je m'entends* [I understand myself].

(15) *Ils se sont compris* [They understood one another].

Sentence (13) is ambiguous (in order to disambiguate it, it is sufficient to add a clarification: 'they looked at themselves in the mirror' has a reflexive sense; 'they looked at each other' a reciprocal sense). Out of context, sentence (14) has a reflexive sense, while (15) has a reciprocal sense.

It is therefore clear that 'reciprocity' ('the child has to learn that "each other" is a reciprocal expression, nothing else'), if it is a 'universal', is not a syntactical universal. And it is not hard to envisage another level to which this universality can more credibly be attached: the reciprocal relationship is constitutive of the relationship of interlocution as a social activity. Or, in order to speak, there must be at least two people and the reflexive is a particular instance of the reciprocal (whence the fact that the sentence *ils se parlaient* first of all has a reciprocal interpretation [they were talking to each other], but can, if required by the context, assume a reflexive sense [they were talking to themselves]). Reciprocity is thus the expression in language of the otherness constitutively involved in the linguistic relationship. The syntactical constructions, in their variety, express this relationship. (French, like English, uses several: *ils se parlaient, ils se congratulaient mutuellement* [they were congratulating each other], *ils se moquaient l'un de l'autre* [they were mocking one another], *chacun était jaloux de l'autre* [each was jealous of the other].) It is the relationship which is universal, while the syntax varies from one language to the next and within each language.

In reality, the embodiment of this ('interlocutory') social linguistic relationship in an innate syntactical structure ('reciprocal expression' and the principles for selecting the antecedent that characterise it) is an example of a phenomenon with which Marxists are familiar: fetishism. A social relationship is reduced to the condition of a thing (to be specific, a genetic and/or neuronal inscription in the brain). Chomsky's false concretisation (which imparts a 'material' reality to reciprocal expression) is, in fact, a further degree of abstraction with respect to the scientific abstraction required to isolate and thus explain the phenomenon: linguistic science does indeed need to construct, starting out from the phenomena, a concept of the 'reciprocal'. Such abstraction squared is characteristic of fetishism.

We can even try to go further. Chomsky has chosen a good example. The reciprocal construction is rare (my English grammar informs me that there are fewer than 60 occurrences of the reciprocal pronoun per million words, as opposed to 25,000 for demonstrative pronouns);[14] and pertains more to

---

[14] Biber et al. 1999, p. 347.

written English and an elevated register than it does spoken English (the same grammar states that it is met with twice as often in academic texts and novels as in conversation and the news). It would appear to have the fixity sought by Chomsky. To see that this is an illusion, it suffices to compare it with a similar construction, but with far more occurrences (4,700 per million words) – the reflexive construction (in English, pronouns ending in '-self'; French uses the pronoun *se* – *il s'est regardé dans la glace* [he looked at himself in the mirror] – or pronouns composed with *même* – *il s'est blessé lui-même* [he wounded himself]).

The syntactical constraints on this construction likewise concern the determination of the pronoun's antecedent. Thus, sentence (16) is grammatical, while sentence (17) is not:

(16) *He wanted himself to win.*

(17) **He wished (that) himself wouldn't have to do it.*

The constraints are the same as for reciprocal pronouns (roughly, the antecedent must belong to the same clause as the reflexive pronoun); and it is sufficient to add that there must be agreement in person between antecedent and reflexive. But as the construction occurs frequently, it does not take long to come across counter-examples, which are perfectly intelligible and are not experienced by native speakers as solecisms. Here is one drawn from a detective novel. The station-master is trying to calm an irate customer who claims that the porter has insulted him and that this is bad for his heart:

(18) *If you've got a bad heart, I should calm yourself, Sir.*

This sentence seems to be the grammatically unwarranted combination of two sentences that conform to the rules:

(19) *If you've got a bad heart, you should calm yourself, Sir.*

(20) *If I had a bad heart, I should calm myself, Sir.*

In truth, the sentence pronounced by the station-master is not only intelligible, it is clever – perfectly adapted to the situation of interlocution. In one and the same sentence, he gives the customer some friendly advice, which is a disguised reprimand, and pretends to put himself in the customer's shoes, to adopt his viewpoint. The sentence is the happy result of a polyphony, a mixture of voices and viewpoints.

Chomsky would reply that this counter-example uses the rules more than it infringes them. Or, rather, at the very moment when it infringes them, it acknowledges them as rules. But rules that can be exploited for expressive purposes (as are all the rules of grammar) are not really the same thing as the linguistic translation of information inscribed in the genes or neuronal circuits: if the rule can be exploited, is made to be exploited, then it is a conventional rule [*thesei*], rather than a natural law [*phusei*], and it is difficult to conceive an innate property that anticipates the ways in which it will be exploited (which, by definition, are diverse and innumerable). In reality, the rules of grammar are pragmatic maxims of the sort 'say this and that' and, like all maxims, they are 'defeasible' (a term derived from English legal philosophy): 'say this rather than that if you need to do it in order to express what you want to say'. To describe the rules of grammar, I am in the process of passing from the domain of laws of nature to the domain of law and morality – i.e. social human practices.

We can go further in analysing the reflexive construction. Because the construction is frequent, and equally present in all the registers of language, it develops not in the quasi-immobile time of the evolution of the species, but in that of human practice – i.e. the time of history. We can therefore distinguish three synchronic uses of the construction, which are the sedimented image of three stages in its history.

First we have the *reflexive* construction proper (this is what Chomsky-type syntactic rules, attributed to universal grammar, capture – except that it is not innate or universal, but specific to the English language and subject to its history). It is found in sentences such as:

(21) *I said to myself* . . .

In such sentences, the syntax conforms to rules of reflexive antecedence and the meaning of the construction is homogeneous with its syntax: this reflexive construction has a reflexive meaning.

Next comes the *emphatic* use of the construction, where the syntactic constraints are roughly the same, yet the meaning is no longer reflexive but intensive: syntax and semantics are dissociated. We can see this in the contrast between (21) and the following two sentences:

(22) *I myself said it.*

(23) *Although I say it myself.*

Last comes the *honorific* use of the reflexive construction, where neither syntax nor semantics is reflexive, even though reflexive pronouns are still employed. Thus sentence (25) is a more polite, or more servile, version of (24):

(24) *Is it for you?*

(25) *Is it for yourself?*

We see how the syntax of the reflexive pronoun, supposedly inscribed in the genetic inheritance or the neuronal circuits, no longer applies: the 'yourself' has no antecedent. Its presence in fact obeys a pragmatic maxim of politeness, of the type: 'prioritise the conversational interests of your interlocutor'.

We can draw three conclusions from these examples and counter-examples: the rules of grammar are maxims, not laws of nature; they are specific to a language, not universal (French, for example, does not possess the honorific use of the reflexive); they are subject to historical evolution (according to a temporal layering: syntax develops more slowly than vocabulary), not fixed once and for all by an evolutionary leap.

We are therefore dealing not just with a linguistics but also with a philosophy of language. This philosophy is not confined to Chomsky, even if it is articulated with exemplary clarity and explicitness in his work. The moment has come to identify its main characteristics.

The four harmful characteristics of Chomsky's philosophy of language

The first characteristic is *methodological individualism* – that is, the idea that the language faculty is inscribed in the brain (the mind/brain) of each individual speaker. As we have seen, this is a major regression compared with the Saussurian conception of *langue*. (This is why Chomsky replaced Saussure's distinction between *langue* and *parole* by the individualist contrast between 'competence' and 'performance': it is individuals who are endowed with competence and realise performances.) This characteristic signals the introduction of liberalism into the philosophy of language: Chomsky does to Saussure what the analytical Marxists (Elster and others) have tried to do to Marx. Against this position, I shall try to defend a conception of language not as a biological endowment of the human species, but as a social practice, which produces effects of inter-subjectivity by means of interlocution, creating subjects/speakers through interpellation. Chomsky defends an a-social conception of language which goes to extremes, since it denies that communication is the function/origin of language (in this, of course, it is not wholly mistaken: communication is not the only function of language). A simple example will bring out the limitations of this a-social conception of language. If language is lodged in what Chomsky calls 'the mind/brain', economic production is lodged in what might be called 'the mind/hand'. Yet economics is not concerned exclusively with the study (which is fascinating and of vital importance) of the human hand or brain: economic structures (the productive forces) and economic relations (the relations of production) have their effective autonomy, which are attributable to their social nature. The same goes for language.

The second characteristic is *fetishism*. It reduces what is essentially a practice – human language – to a series of 'things' inscribed in the brain of the speaker or her genes: a Universal Grammar and a Language Acquisition Device (because the parameters have to be triggered). The reduction, by way of spatial metaphors (localisation, inscription), moves from practices to mechanisms, from human intelligence to artificial intelligence, to the calculating machine, which furnishes the constitutive metaphors: the human brain contains programs, and so on. Except that computers, however powerful and intelligent, do not have inter-personal – because interlocutory – relations and do not engage in class struggle. And this fetishism entails two consequences, which are the final two harmful characteristics of Chomsky's philosophy of language.

The third characteristic is the *refusal of history*. Clearly, Chomsky is aware of the existence of linguistic change. For him, however, such phenomena are irrelevant. Individual languages – their vocabularies, for example – can indeed change, but such alterations do not affect the language, which knows neither history nor development, other than phylogenetic development, which affects the entire species, and ontogenetic development, whereby the relevant parameters for her individual linguistic situation are triggered in each speaker. (Like the arm, the language organ grows.) This assumes that language is an individual phenomenon and not a property of *communities* of speakers. Chomsky's a-historicism is simply the flip side of his a-social conception of language.

But this refusal of history is consistent with the fourth characteristic: *naturalism*. This naturalism (the science of language is a natural science, the language organ is a natural phenomenon) involves a belief in human nature (the language faculty forms part of it) and its relative fixity (the biological endowment of the human species only changes at the pace of evolution and contains nothing from which to construct a history of it). The rules of grammar (since each Chomskyan monad foresees the organisation of languages even in detail) are therefore laws of nature, not defeasible conventions or pragmatic maxims. Being innate, the rules governing reciprocal and reflexive constructions are of the same type as the laws of physics. As we have just seen, the empirical phenomena do not justify these assertions: the rules in question are defeasible for expressive purposes; the constructions vary according to the natural languages; and they each have a history, which likewise varies according to the language. It will be noted that Chomsky's naturalism at least has the merit of coherence, since (as we have seen) it leads him to deny the existence of natural languages. From the standpoint of the science of language, 'English' does not exist: give or take a few parameters, and we move imperceptibly from one 'language' to another. For its part, the deep structure is universal and, from its standpoint, there is no difference between English and Quechua.

In a sense, Chomsky is not mistaken on this point – but for reasons that he would probably not accept. As we saw in the introduction, 'English' is a cultural and political construct embodied in institutions (schools, the media, international institutions). In reality, 'standard English' is a dialect (equipped with an army) and 'English' denotes a multiplicity of registers and dialects, which are possibly well on the way to diverging from one another, as attested by the great variety of 'New Englishes'. In the strict sense, it may therefore be argued that 'English' does not exist. But not in the sense that Chomsky understands this statement. It assumes an approach to language and natural languages as historical and social phenomena, capable of change, variation, and admixtures. Accordingly, we shall defend the paradoxical position that 'English' both does, and does not, exist.

For it exists. The ontological metaphor that leads me to transform the noun into an adjective by adding a definite article in French – *l'anglais* – cannot but designate a referent: to be specific, an ideological and political construct (there is a social history of 'English', its diffusion and teaching, of the constitution of a standard dialect and the canon of literary texts that illustrate it). In short, 'English' in this sense is a specific way of inhabiting language (to speak like Heidegger) or the vector of a conception of the world (to speak like Gramsci). But the other side of the paradox will also be defended: 'English' does not exist, since it is always-already dissolved in a variation of dialects, levels of language, and registers. Deleuze's concepts of continuous variation, minority, and collective assemblage of enunciation are of more use here than Chomsky's concepts. But to criticise these is not enough. We still have to explain their emergence and its necessity.

A spontaneous philosophy for scientists

There is an aspect of Chomsky's work that I have not yet broached. It is not the least important. As is well-known, Chomsky is an exemplary progressive thinker and activist. He is one of the most effective critics of the ravages of American imperialism. Certainly, he often says that he is not a Marxist; but then no one is perfect. So I am in the process of criticising the philosophy of language of someone whose political positions I fully endorse. It is also true that, when Chomsky descends onto the terrain of political theory or philosophy, the result is disappointing. The collective volume to which he contributed, *Liberating Theory*,[15] will hardly impress a Marxist: the ecumenicism that leads the text to treat all critical theories of society, whether based on economics, ecology, gender, race or culture, on the same plane cannot replace political analysis of the social totality (and, in passing, it reduces Marxism to its most vulgar variant: economism). But the linguistic phenomena that I accuse him of ignoring are not foreign to him. After all, he is the author of books with promising titles like *Propaganda and the Public Mind*, *Necessary Illusions*, and *Class Warfare*.[16] The following passage, taken from an interview with David Barsamian, his privileged interlocutor, is typical (the passage in italics is Barsamian's contribution to the discussion):

> *Talk about the power of language to shape and control political discussion. For example, the IMF's much criticized 'structural adjustment program' has now been renamed 'poverty reduction and growth facility'. The School of Americas, the notorious training facility for the Latin American military at Fort Benning, Georgia, is now called the Western Hemisphere Institute for Security Cooperation.*
>
> Let me just make clear, this has absolutely nothing to do with linguistics. There's no insight into this topic that comes from having studied language. This is all obvious on the face of it to anybody who looks. This is the topic that Orwell satirized, and of course it goes way back. If you have a war between two countries, they're both fighting in self-defense. Nobody is ever the aggressor. Furthermore, they're both fighting for exalted humanitarian objectives. To take some of Orwell's examples, if you're trying to control a population by violence and terror, it's 'pacification'.[17]

---

[15] See Albert et al. 1986.
[16] See Chomsky 1989, 1996 and 2001.
[17] Chomsky 2001, p. 210.

The situation is clear. On the one hand, there is the science of language, which is concerned with biological phenomena – language as mental organ and innate faculty; on the other, there is political critique, to which Chomsky gives a name and a literary referent – political satire as practised by Orwell. On the one hand, we have the I-language; on the other, what Chomsky sometimes calls (when he does not characterise it as literature or 'folk-linguistics') the E-language – i.e. external linguistics.

I could end the discussion here, express my agreement with Chomsky's critique of American imperialism, acknowledge that satire is not science, and that if there is a serious critical study of ideology (in the sense in which Marx engaged in a serious critical study of capital), it has nothing to do with the science of language. But serious problems remain that warrant critical examination.

The first is the division between internal and external linguistics. These two disciplines seem to share an object. English does not possess a word to contrast *langue* with *langage*; a single word is used which does not facilitate a distinction between the concepts. This would not matter if it did not induce confusion about the phenomena that fall under the jurisdiction of one or the other of the two disciplines. As we have seen, when he expounds his theory of the I-language, Chomsky talks not only about highly abstract universals, but also about semantic and syntactic phenomena that are likewise of great concern to external linguistics. A detour via the absurd will hammer the point home. Jack Goody[18] refers to anthropologists or mythologists inspired by Chomsky who maintain that mythical narratives form part of the innate genetic inheritance of the human monad, that they are therefore always – already contained in the recesses of the human mind – which explains the universal character of these narratives. It therefore seems to possess a tendency to expand that constantly extends the portion of the innate, in order to furnish a scientific explanation of as many phenomena as possible. The two disciplines – internal linguistics and external linguistics – therefore have border conflicts and obviously only confront another out of self-defence.

But the critique of Chomsky's position must go further. The ultimate justification of naturalist internal linguistics is that language is a specific property of the human species. For chimpanzees do not speak – not even bonobos, a species of dwarf chimpanzees who are the best equipped for

---

[18] See Goody 1997.

communication. To supporters of the primates, who laud the ability of bonobos to acquire vocabulary and use it in their interaction with human beings, Chomskyans can always reply that the specific characteristics of human language (in particular, the complexity of syntactic structures) are utterly alien to bonobos, which never go beyond the pre-linguistic competence of a two-year-old child (the age at which the innate programmes of the monad are not yet operative).

The fact is undeniable, but not the conclusions that Chomsky draws from it – i.e. naturalism, which makes language a mental organ, and innatism. What these two terms betray is a philosophical choice – a philosophy of language (rather than a self-evident scientific truth that is bound to strike 'anybody who looks'). Chomsky is betrayed by his metaphors, for the phrase 'mental organ' is of course metaphorical. I know what a physical organ – e.g. the organ of sight – is. It is called the eye and is the object of scientific study. This study does not simply explain the mechanism of visual sensations; it will also explain the role played by the brain in transforming these sensations into perceptions. And everyone will acknowledge that flies, moles, raptors, and human beings do not see in the same way. I note in passing that scientific studies of sight do not (or do not any longer) feel the need to resort to the philosophical concept of innatism. If Chomsky still has recourse to it, it is because language – unlike sight – possesses no single organ. It uses bodily organs like the ear and the larynx, but these are not specialist organs like the eye: the ear does not only detect articulate sounds and things other than words pass via the larynx.

What is more, the organs in question – the ear and the larynx – *do not belong to the same individual*: if language is an 'organ', it is not the same kind of organ as the eye or the arm – not because it is mental, but because it is social. In other words, language is not an organ at all; it is an activity, a *practice*. Adding the adjective 'mental' to the noun 'organ' only serves to render the noun metaphorical – that is, to strip it of any recognisable meaning. And this operation is neither innocent nor arbitrary; it is characteristic of ideology. Once again, Chomsky effects a dual abstraction. The first abstracts from linguistic activity, which is a relationship, an ontological metaphor – i.e. a concept. (Thus we refer to language, rather than saying 'linguistic practice' each time; we distinguish between *langue* and *langage*; and Chomsky speaks of 'I-language'.) The second is a false concretisation which, by metonymy, shifts responsibility from the metaphor (already on the road to fetishism, because not all metaphors are appropriate: that of 'organ' involves the second abstraction) to the individual who is the seat of the 'faculty' isolated by the concept. This false concretisation is, as we have seen, simply a further degree of abstraction: an example of fetishism.

Chomsky's science of language is thus heavily dependent on various philosophical theses, which explains why it combines, in a way that is hardly unexpected, materialism (of the mental organ) and idealism (of the monad). Behind Chomsky's science, and supporting it as the rope does the hanged man, lies what Althusser calls a 'spontaneous philosophy of scientists'.

In his philosophy course for scientists,[19] Althusser proposes a theory of philosophy, a theory of science, a theory of ideology in general, and a theory of what he calls the spontaneous philosophy of scientists (SPS). Philosophy is not science: it has no object, operates by means of categories rather than concepts, and its function is to intervene in a scientific conjuncture (a state of relations between science and ideology) to trace lines of demarcation. Its characteristic mode of expression is the formulation of theses, which compose a system. The most important aspect of this theory of philosophy is the distinction between the correct and the true. Contrary to tradition, Althusser maintains that the theses of philosophy aim not at the true but at the correct: a correct philosophical thesis is one that enables adjustment to the conjuncture, which, in the last instance, is always the conjuncture of the class struggle.

From this theory of philosophy we can draw, *a contrario*, a theory of science: a science has an object, concepts, and a method, but is exposed to ideology in the form of practical ideologies (formations of notions, representations and images in behaviour, conduct, attitudes, gestures: the set functions as a practical norm governing attitudes to real objects – I am paraphrasing Althusser's Thesis 19)[20] and SPS. Ideology, according to Thesis 9, is composed of propositions and '[a]n ideological proposition is a proposition that, while it is the symptom of a reality other than that of which it speaks, is a false proposition to the extent that it concerns the object of which it speaks'.[21] Readers will have recognised the celebrated Althusserian definition of ideology as a mixture of illusion and allusion. As for the SPS, the specific form of existence of ideology within science, it is the site of a contradiction between two elements:

---

[19] See Althusser 1990.
[20] See Althusser 1990, p. 83.
[21] Althusser 1990, p. 79.

a materialist and objective element, derived from scientific practice; and an idealist element, the reflection in science of philosophical theses elaborated outside it.

The typical example Althusser gives of a SPS is the case of Jacques Monod, Nobel Prize winner in biology and author of a book of scientific and philosophical popularisation that has been forgotten today, but which enjoyed some influence in the mid-1960s.[22] A scientist of great stature, Monod was also a man of the Left: he had been a member of the French Communist Party and it was whispered when he received the Nobel Prize that the party leadership, which was in a phase of popular union and cultural progress, suggested to him that he should rejoin, which he declined to do. What Althusser criticises is thus the thinking of a committed scientist with progressive leanings. He detects in Monod two contradictory impulses: a materialist tendency, which leads him to affirm the materiality of the object of biology against vitalists and to criticise finalism, counter-posing to it the concept of emergence; and a spiritualist tendency, centred on the notion of 'noosphere' taken from Teilhard de Chardin, and based on a thesis that is not irrelevant to us: 'language created man'. Althusser analyses this thesis as a philosophical thesis which, instead of separating mechanism and spiritualism, combines them:

> When he believes himself to be materialist, by giving as the biophysiological basis of what he calls the 'noosphere' – that is to say, the social and historical existence of the human species – the emergence of the *neurobiological support of language*, he is not a materialist, but . . . a 'mechanistic materialist' and in terms of a theory of human history, that now means that he is an *idealist*.[23]

Readers will have noted some superficial similarities between Monod and Chomsky: both are progressive in politics (a leaning much more strongly marked in Chomsky, who is a veritable anti-imperialist activist) and materialist in philosophy – but adherents of a mechanistic materialism which does not take account of the social and historical existence of humanity. Things are altogether clear in Chomsky, of whom one has the impression that, in philosophical terms, he left Europe before the end of the eighteenth century.

But we can go further – for example, by posing the preliminary question: is linguistics a science or merely one of the human sciences, that is, one of

---

[22] See Monod 1972.
[23] Althusser 1990, p. 151.

those non-sciences, characterised as 'literary' by Althusser, which, not really possessing an object in the scientific sense, have as their dominant function not knowledge, but the definition and instruction of practical norms? For it is not true that linguistics self-evidently has an object, the term 'language' being notoriously ambiguous and slippery. This is why I think that the external linguistics which I defend pertains to a philosophy of language: because its centre is constituted by a pragmatics – that is, the analysis of social relations, of a *praxis*. To situate Chomsky's position, we can compare his research programme with that developed by Milner, in the tradition which runs from Saussure to Jakobson and Benveniste via Meillet and the Paris school.[24] To get straight to the point, this is the structuralist tradition, which seeks to construct linguistics as a science by giving it a specific object, constructed by excluding the non-pertinent phenomena encompassed under the necessarily vague notion of 'language': *langue* in the technical Saussurian sense. Milner's axioms, referred to at the beginning of this chapter, are intended to constitute *langue* as an object of science, and to equip scientific linguistics with a method, not only a system of concepts. And it is clear that the Chomskyan research programme is constituted along parallel lines. But it is equally clear that the differences are considerable. The first, and by no means the least, is that, for the tradition running from Saussure to Milner, *langue* is a material object, a system – but a collective, public object, a conventional object [*thesei*], not a natural one [*phusei*]. This at least has the advantage of safeguarding this tradition from the form of materialism practised by Chomsky, which is a mechanistic reductionism. Chomsky would object that the term 'matter', when applied to a system, a collective, conventional object, has no definite meaning. But Marxists will not be troubled by this objection: the historical or dialectical materialism they practise has precisely such objects – party, class, state, capital, or language – for its field of application.

So, if it is agreed that Chomsky's aim is to constitute a science, we still need to ask what his linguistics aims to be the science of – that is, what its object is. For the I-language does indeed possess all the characteristics of a scientific object: it is presented as real – that is, as having a material existence in the brain of the speaker; it is specific, constructed by purging irrelevant phenomena; and it is abstract. But it is not obvious that this object is language, construed

---

[24] See Milner 1978, 1989, and 2002.

in the broadest or narrowest sense of the term. For Chomsky, in fact, linguistics can at best only be a provisional science; and, at worst, not a science at all – or, rather, not a specific science. At worst, the I-language is an object for scientific psychology, which will itself one day be reduced to biology. At best, it is currently the object of the science of language, pending the day when the advances in biology will render superfluous indirect description of the language faculty via grammatical structures which, whatever level they are envisaged at, can only be surface phenomena, effects of the material constitution of the mind/brain.

This position has consequences for explaining linguistic phenomena. As we have seen, the I-language excludes many of the phenomena that constitute language for common sense. This is regrettable for Marxists, who are precisely interested in the excluded phenomena, but it is perfectly licit: the linguistic science constructed by Saussure or Milner proceeds no differently. But we have also seen that Chomsky's position does not explain the phenomena that it seeks to explain. It will no doubt be objected here that the encyclopaedia article whose analysis of reciprocal pronouns I have criticised, being already rather old (it dates from 1987), cannot take account of the most recent state of the doctrine – the minimalist programme. However, in addition to the fact that the theory is revised from top to bottom every five years, and nevertheless claims at each step to state the truth of the non-temporal faculty of language – prompting me to take it with a pinch of salt – the evolution of the theory is proceeding towards an ever greater abstraction, rendering its capacity to explain grammatical constructions (which linguistic science must explain) highly uncertain.

To summarise. It seems to me that the reason for these uncertainties about the science of language is to be found in a decision that is not scientific, but philosophical, and which guides and constrains Chomsky's scientific practice: the philosophical thesis of the innate character of the biological structure of language. This thesis aims to account for an undeniable fact: chimpanzees do not speak; language is specific to *homo sapiens*. It is defended with an argument that is tirelessly repeated, but highly contestable, from the poverty of stimuli – the under-determination of linguistic competence by experience. This argument takes the form of a claim of impossibility: the linguistic clock is too complex, and so on. But there are other explanations: capacities for learning peculiar to the human species, but which do not concern the details of grammatical structure; generalisations from experience such as connectionism – that contemporary variant of behaviourism – envisages them; a parallel between the learning of language by infants and the construction of theories by the adult scientist (what is called the 'theory of theory'). In short, there is never only one possible explanation, any more than there is only one possible politics.

The result is that Chomsky's scientific practice is indeed governed by what Althusser calls a SPS, with two contradictory tendencies: a materialist aspect and an idealist aspect. And, as the idealist aspect is dominant and the materialist aspect, appearances to the contrary notwithstanding, dominated – that is, contaminated by idealism, of which it is only the flip side – we find ourselves faced, on the one hand, with an admixture of Platonic epistemology (the child speaker is like slave in *Meno* – his discovery is recollection) and Leibnizian monadology (the share of the innate in linguistic activity is unduly extended); and, on the other, a mechanistic materialism which reduces the phenomena of language to the physical, the individual, the a-historical. (Here, the contrast with Saussure, whose concept of *langue* avoids at least some of these defects, is glaring.)

Since there is philosophy of language, and it is inevitable (language is too serious a business to be left to the linguists), we shall look for it in a different form of materialism: historical and dialectical materialism. On condition, of course, that these entities exist: it is not enough to mouth old slogans. The rest of this book will be devoted to it, following a detour via another, more explicitly philosophical version of the dominant philosophy of language.

Chapter Three
Critique of the Philosophy of Language

Thinking with Habermas

To attempt to construct a Marxist philosophy of language is necessarily to encounter the thought of Habermas. For he has, in sense, already undertaken this endeavour and it may be that he has succeeded in it. Habermas's philosophy in fact possesses two characteristics that cannot leave me indifferent. The first is that it constitutes the philosophy of language as first philosophy. Habermas's declared goal is to effect a shift from the philosophy of consciousness, which in the European (especially German) tradition occupied a dominant position, to a philosophy of language. This is why my favourite object is not only admissible but central to the philosophical enterprise. The second is that this first shift involves another: an exit from historical materialism, which is one of the origins of Habermas's thinking, but one which is not so much a rejection as a reconstruction. And the reconstruction, which aims to preserve the emancipatory dimension of Marx's project, is effected by a move from the paradigm of labour to that of language. My favourite object is thus not only licit and central, but has already been dealt with.

Habermas's *œuvre* is sizeable and covers the domains of philosophy of language, sociology, political philosophy, and philosophy of law. But his central thesis, never abandoned and defended at length in his *magnum opus, The Theory of Communicative Action,* can be formulated in a few words: the very structure of language as interlocution presupposes agreement, or at least a striving for agreement. Philosophy will therefore start with an analysis of interlocution, which will take the form of a 'general pragmatics' – that is, a pragmatics which enables us to conceptualise the social, whereas Anglo-American pragmatics (that of Austin and Searle), which is Habermas's source of inspiration, is restricted to the linguistic activity of the individual. We can see the extent of the displacement with respect to traditional Marxism: the underlying tendency is to think the social in the mode of co-operation, not struggle. This does not mean that Habermas ignores the facts and that he is not aware of the concrete existence of class struggle, but that he theoretically reconstructs society on the basis of the co-operation implicit in the very constitution of language. This theoretical decision has at least one thing in common with Marxism: founding the social on interlocution, it avoids methodological individualism; it insists on the fact that language is a social phenomenon, that it can only be thought as an activity of interaction between human beings, and not as an individual faculty. Thus we are already far removed from Chomsky.

To base a philosophy of language on a universal pragmatics is thus to operate a dual shift in the direction of the social: it is to abandon Chomskyan naturalism for the scorned part of linguistic science called pragmatics; and it is to abandon a pragmatics that concerns the individual (her intended meanings, her speech acts) for one concerned with action that is not individual, but collective. Universal pragmatics is therefore organised around two concepts: inter-subjective understanding and the life-world.

The concept of *inter-subjective understanding* tells us that human activity, what characterises human beings in society – i.e. the whole of humanity, with the exception of Robinson Crusoe and Frankenstein's monster – is, first of all, a communicative activity. We can see how this decision turns Marx upside down. The infrastructure on the basis of which the whole of society is reconstructed is no longer labour – the activity of production and exchange – but what, for traditional Marxists, is at best an instrument of this productive activity – language – and, at worst, an element of the superstructure. We now understand the title of Habermas's work: what interests him is not language as a faculty and mental organ, but language as *action*. And communicative action is not based on struggle (linguistic struggle, class struggle), but on dialogue. Mutual understanding (like co-operation in Grice's theory of conversation, which is one of Habermas's sources of inspiration)[1] is the consensual negotiation of truth claims: Habermas's philosophy of language is an *ethics of discussion*, which generalises Grice's maxims of conversation to the social structure.

The second concept is that of *life-world*, whereby Habermas affirms his adherence to the European philosophical tradition (he is the only philosopher really to have attempted, and possibly succeeded in, a synthesis of the antagonistic European and Anglo-American philosophical traditions – what are sometimes called analytical and continental philosophies).[2] The concept is, of course, borrowed from Husserl. It aims to answer the question: why are speakers not a threat to one another? There are two answers: because the very structure of language obliges the speaker to co-operate with the other (this is the anthropological foundation of the possibility of a form of communism which is not exactly of the Marxian sort: but, of course, Habermas does not proclaim himself a communist); and because discussions always occur on the basis of background knowledge that is neither arbitrary nor separate, but which forms a life-world:

> Subjects acting communicatively always come to an understanding in the horizon of a lifeworld. Their lifeworld is formed from more or less diffuse, always unproblematic, background convictions. This lifeworld background serves as a source of situation definitions that are presupposed by participants as unproblematic. . . . The lifeworld also stores the interpretive work of preceding generations. It is the conservative counterweight to the risk of disagreement that arises with every actual process of reaching understanding. . . .[3]

This life-world, which involves recourse to the concepts of tradition and common sense, is at once a horizon and a limit to discussion and interpretation – that is, to what constitutes the very content of inter-subjective understanding.

The object of universal pragmatics is to study the presuppositions of communicative action. We are in what Habermas calls a 'weak transcendental',

---

[1] See Grice 1975.
[2] See Lecercle 1999.
[3] Habermas 1984, p. 70.

which takes interlocution to be a fact of experience, something ever pre-given, and seeks to describe the normative conditions of possibility of mutual understanding – in some sense, the forms of discursive intuition. The philosopher's task is therefore to establish the 'basis of validity of discourse', which for Habermas assumes the following structure: any speaker, simply by virtue of speaking, transmits four universal claims to validity. She must in fact (a) express herself intelligibly (intelligibility claim); (b) give it to be understood that something is the case (truth claim: we are only considering 'serious' locutions here – that is, those really directed at phenomena, and thus enjoined to truth, at least as a goal); (c) make herself understood by her interlocutor(s) (sincerity claim: making oneself understood in the framework of consensus is in fact to state the truth about oneself, to be sincere); and (d) agree with her interlocutor (accuracy claim, which is defined as a set of norms to which the interlocutors collectively subscribe). These four claims are the presupposed basis of inter-subjective understanding; they furnish language with its structure as interlocution; they are the basis of the agreement realised by each process of enunciation – that is, the basis of the fundamental consensus of which language is at once the source and the medium, and on which philosophy constructs its ethics of discussion. If, in fact, these claims are not honoured (for Habermas is not unaware that the facts do not correspond to the idyllic consensus he describes), it simply means that human beings quit the domain communicative action and embark on a different kind of action – strategic action – which does not presuppose the same validity claims.

We can see how this theory is situated in the framework of pragmatics. For the philosopher and linguist alike, it is a question of reconstructing the speaker's competence, but her communicative competence, not her phrasal competence – that is, her ability to produce grammatical sentences. The theory of sentences is in fact insufficient. There are specific presuppositions of discourse, due to the fact that (a) the sentence has a relationship with the external reality of what can be perceived (this is called reference); (b) it also has a relationship with the internal reality of the speaker's intended meanings; and (c) it has a relationship with the normative reality of what is socially and culturally recognised by the community of speakers (this is called a culture, an encyclopaedia, and serves as a foundation for the speaker's life-world). Readers will have recognised the source of the three claims to validity represented by truth (the discourse corresponds to external reality), sincerity (it corresponds to internal reality), and accuracy (it corresponds to social reality).

We see how Habermas takes up Anglo-American pragmatics – i.e. Austin and Searle's theory of speech acts – and Grice's theory of meaning as intended meaning, as well as his theory of conversation as obeying a co-operative principle. We can also see how he expands it, by introducing the normative – i.e. the social – with its historical sedimentation in the form of traditions, laws and norms. We can also see how this first philosophy of language is an ethics. At the centre of the adoption and extension of the concept of 'illocutionary force', which is itself at the heart of the theory of speech acts, is to be found the notion of 'commitment': the essential condition for an illocutionary act (promises are a good example) is that the speaker on each occasion makes a commitment which allows the interlocutor to trust her (as to the truth of the propositional content of the act, as to the sincerity with which the act is performed). For Habermas, this explains the illocutionary *force* of the act (which obviously does not correspond to physical violence or moral coercion): the fact that it leads the interlocutor to trust the commitment made. With Grice, who speaks in terms of the (co-operative) 'principle' and 'maxims' (of conversation), we were already in the universe of the second Kantian critique. With Habermas, we are explicitly, and not only allusively, in the universe of ethics: consensus, commitment, responsibility, trust. But, for him, it is not a question of a moral decision, of a constraint imposed on linguistic practice from without, but of the very structure of interlocution: mutual communicative obligations have a rational basis and to refuse them (e.g. to defend a theory of linguistic exchange as *agon* – that is, as a verbal contest) involves abandoning the framework of reason.

Thus we end up with a comprehensive theory of language – a truly universal pragmatics. Habermas distinguishes four sectors of reality (external nature, society, internal nature, and language), to which correspond four types of relationship to reality (objectivity, normativity, sincerity, and inter-subjectivity); our four validity claims (in order: truth, accuracy, sincerity, and intelligibility); and three functions of speech acts (the presentation of states of affairs, the establishment of inter-personal relations, and the expression of subjective experience). To readers who might protest that Habermas's obsession with making correlations (four elements per column) is not complete in the last column, it may be replied that the establishment of inter-personal relations is precisely what is common to the social and the linguistic, that inter-subjectivity is constructed on the basis of normativity, that intelligibility cannot be understood without accuracy.

To conclude on the philosophy of language proposed by Habermas. We have seen its advantages over Chomskyan naturalism, but also over Anglo-American pragmatics: it enables us to move from the individual to the collective – i.e. the social – and it locates communicative action in a general theory of action, counter-posing it not only to strategic action, but also to symbolic action (which is how Habermas describes such phenomena as art). We have also seen that this description of interlocution is almost obsessive in its coherence. In passing, it offers us non-trivial theories of truth (obtained by consensus on validity claims); of dialogue (based on *eirene* – co-operation – rather than *agon*, but, in any event, richer than the usual conception, which sees dialogue as a mere exchange of information); and even of reality (which, in Popperian fashion, combines an objective external nature, a subjective internal nature, and a third world – of tradition, sedimentation, the life-world shared by interlocutors).

This philosophy of language makes it possible to avoid three pitfalls. As it is situated immediately at the level of the social, or rather in that it seeks to found the social on the structure of interlocution (i.e. in that it is derived from Marx's emancipatory project), it avoids both Chomskyan naturalism and the methodological individualism characteristic of the dominant philosophy of language. And, as it takes into account the tradition and the encyclopaedia that inform the life-world of speakers, as it situates itself resolutely at the level of the normative – i.e. the collective – it also avoids, or at least it expands, the intentionalism that characterises the Gricean theory of meaning, and which feeds into his theory of conversation. So here we have a philosophy of language which involves a theory of subjectivation and individuation starting from the collective, where the *ego* is constituted through the intermediary of the *alter*, where the interior can be regarded as an internalisation of the exterior.

Yet, however effective, this philosophy poses problems and must be criticised. I must therefore think against Habermas.

Thinking against Habermas

I shall start from the basic thesis on the structure of interlocution, which presupposes agreement or strives for it. We are dealing here with a myth of origins and, in truth, a religious myth: it is enough to compare this presupposed agreement with the myth of the time before the tower of Babel. This structure of interlocution, being original and universal like Chomsky's grammar, ignores the diversity of natural languages, since it is always situated prior to that, pre-Babel. Although it appeals to the notion of life-world and tradition, it ignores the linguistic aspect of this tradition and this life-world: it ignores the fact that a natural language is also a cultural stock, a conception of the world, and thus it ignores the fact that the functioning of natural languages from the outset involves phenomena which are incompatible with rational agreement – for example, the constitutive existence of misunderstanding due to the diversity of languages, to the necessity of translation, to the proliferation of dialects, registers and levels of language. This conception thus implicitly postulates a single because universal language, in which understanding is a natural thing; and a standard language, which allows all speakers to speak the same dialect and thus understand one another: this object language. It ignores the fact that if there is a standard language, it is neither universal nor transcendental (even weakly), but historically, socially and culturally conditioned.

I shall run back over the argument, which is rather hasty and might seem unfair to Habermas. If the interlocutory structure of language *presupposes* agreement; if to understand a sentence is to *understand the reasons* that the speaker does or could adduce in support of what she says, in order to *validate* it with a view to agreement; if, moreover, the *illocutionary force* of a *speech act* aims to obtain a *rationally motivated* stance on the part of the addressee – then this description of the structure of language as defined by interlocution condemns Habermas to ignore a fair few phenomena and to lapse back into the philosophy of language which is dominant, from Stalin to Chomsky, and which makes it a neutral instrument (of information, communication, agreement).

What is it, then, that Habermas is condemned to ignore? First of all, explicitly agonistic linguistic phenomena – that is, all the situations where language itself is a vector of strategic action, where to speak is to seek to establish a hierarchy of places and a power relation. Let us take a fairly frequently speech act: uttering a threat. It is indeed a specific speech act, with its specific illocutionary force, forming part of a specific language game (one does not make threats willy-nilly, any more than one makes promises). Habermas broaches threats in a context where he is attempting to distinguish communicative action from strategic action. The framework of his thinking is familiar to us by now:

> Communicative action must satisfy certain conditions of cooperation and mutual understanding:
>
> The participatating actors must conduct themselves cooperatively and attempt to reach an agreement about their plans (in the horizon of a shared lifeworld) on the basis of common (or sufficiently overlapping) situation interpretations.
>
> The participating actors must be prepared to achieve the intermediate goals of a common situation definition and of action coordination in the roles of speakers and hearers by way of processes of reaching understanding, i.e. by means of the unreserved and sincere pursuit of illocutionary aims. . . .
>
> The manner in which mutual understanding in language functions as a mechanism for coordinating action is that the participants in an interaction agree about the validity claimed for the their speech acts, that is, they recognize criticisable validity claims intersubjectively.[4]

In Habermas's world, following the English expression 'let us agree to differ', the only possible expression of dissensus is another form of consensus. Since Habermas is a great philosopher, and does not deny the facts, he is aware that a certain number of linguistic phenomena offer counter-examples to his theory. The insult with which I started out in Chapter 1 is one of them. For his part, he opts to dispose of threats. This is what he has to say four pages later:

> Imperatives or threats that are deployed purely strategically and robbed of their normative validity claims are not illocutionary acts, or acts aimed toward reaching understanding, at all. They remain parasitic insofar as their comprehension must be derived from the employment conditions for illocutionary acts that are covered by norms.[5]

---

[4] Habermas 1992, pp. 79–80.
[5] Habermas 1992, p. 84.

The argument is manifestly circular. It sets out from the facts: threats are not obviously directed towards agreement, but pertain to the category of strategic acts. However, a threat is a speech act, governed by the interlocutory structure of language. A threat has a speaker, an addressee, a propositional content, and exercises illocutionary force over the addressee, producing a perlocutionary effect on her. It is therefore impossible to distinguish it at the level of the structure from the most common and consensual speech acts, except as regards the content of the illocutionary force, which is agonistic. Habermas thus finds himself confronting a manifest counter-example, which calls into question the universality of his consensual structure. And he gets out of it by a sleight of hand. He denies that threats possess an illocutionary force (they have 'lost' it) and postulates that they are a kind of indirect speech act, in which the agonistic character is the second product of an irenic illocutionary force exploited for the purposes of strategic action. But, in addition to the fact that it seems difficult, in any imaginable context, to attribute an irenic 'illocutionary meaning' to 'if you don't shut up, I'm going to smash your face in', there is clearly a slippage in Habermas as regards the concept of 'illocutionary force'. In Austin and Searle, the term refers to the force exercised by the speech act: it can just as easily be agonistic as irenic. And they distinguish illocutionary force from perlocutionary effect: the force exercised by my threat can produce various effects – fear, indignation, amusement – depending on the power relationship with my addressee. But Habermas reduces illocutionary force to perlocutionary effect: his 'force' is in fact nothing other than the goal of a consensual effect, it is determined by it, and is therefore consensual, since the intended effect is always to secure the listener's rationally motivated agreement. We can see why threats cannot be a speech act, but only the exploitation or travesty of a consensual speech act. The argument is manifestly circular: it claims to discover in speech acts a consensual interlocutory structure, but only counts as speech acts those of them that conform to this structure. This leads to counter-intuitive analyses: threats exercise no illocutionary force because, for Habermas, this 'force' is not a force exercised, but an attempt at agreement.

Habermas is therefore condemned to deny certain phenomena, since he excludes all agonistic speech acts – threats, insults, various forms of aggression. These are not the only ones. Habermas is an exception among his colleagues (from Derrida to Lyotard, from Heidegger to Gadamer) in that he very rarely talks about literature. This is because literary texts, envisaged as the product of specific speech acts, sit badly with his model of interlocution. In fact, almost the only way in which he can treat literature is in terms either of a contract of narration (between narrator and reader), or of generic constraints (agreement on the rules of a specific language game), which excludes playing games with contracts and constraints (everything that is called meta-fiction, characteristic of postmodern literature), texts that actively destroy generic constraints and refuse narrative contracts in favour of games with the signifier (the avant-garde position characteristic of modernist texts); but also *all* literary texts in that they are citatory and re-contextualisable – that is, in that they escape their initial context and live their textual life in a proliferation of interpretations. Here, Habermas is still dependent on Anglo-American pragmatics and vulnerable to the kind of critique that Derrida addresses to Austin in 'Signature Event Context'.[6] As regards literary criticism, this renders Habermas's thinking of little use. It condemns him to be almost as blind as Lukács to contemporary trends in literature or to slip into what Derrida calls phonocentrism. When Jonathan Culler criticises him for surreptitiously introducing understanding into all language games, and cites as a counter-example his computer manual (which is scarcely 'user-friendly'), Habermas replies in terms of legal contracts and 'face-to-face interaction'. It will be objected that not all philosophies are obliged to consider literary texts as objects of reflection, or even to appreciate them. But a philosopher whose first philosophy is a philosophy of language finds himself, in this respect, in a special situation: a theory of the structure of language, no matter what level it is situated at, which ignores the literary use of language or is incapable of accounting for it, is a problematic theory to say the least.

Finally, Habermas's model struggles to explain everything in language that is fixed, already thought or already expressed; everything imposed on speakers because language constrains their expression; everything, therefore, which cannot be described in the framework of a rational perlocutionary effect aimed at by the speaker: clichés, proverbs, stock phrases – everything pertaining to the ready-made thinking of the *doxa*, and which plays a very important role in the language of everyday life. As we have seen, Habermas is not unaware of these problems, which he explains by recourse to the Husserlian concept of the life-world shared by all speakers. Clichés and proverbs are then

---

[6] See Derrida 1982 and also the polemic with Searle in Derrida 1988.

interpreted as sedimentations of interlocutions that can be validated with a view to agreement, but which have been validated in the past. However, this validation that persists into the present poses a problem. There is nothing to stipulate that the conditions of validation are stable, unaffected by time and history, and that set phrases elicit a rational reaction from the addressee as they did (if they did) originally. Proverbs and clichés are not particularly rational ways of achieving agreement with interlocutors; they appeal to an uncritical respect for tradition and linguistic custom – its prejudices. Tradition does not equal reason. This explanation of linguistic ready-made thinking which bears within it dead, sedimented language (just as we speak of dead metaphors) is about as convincing as the explanation of the current social order by a social contract in a distant mythical past, to which I am assured that I am already committed, even though I never signed it. For my situation with respect to language pretty much resembles my situation with respect to the social contract: in acceding to speech, I enter into a world of significations and speech acts that are not all of them rational, which are imposed on speakers, and against which they must exercise their critical power (philosophy is the name for this critique).

It therefore emerges that, in Habermas, agreement is a myth, that his philosophy of language is first philosophy in that it is the expression of a myth of origins, a mythical starting-point from which he reconstructs not only language as a human practice but the whole of society (in this, Habermas is indeed the inheritor of the Frankfurt school and, through it, of Marx and Weber). We shall not criticise him for having a mythical starting-point; all philosophers need one. But *this* starting-point has unfortunate consequences. It has the disadvantage of naturalising a myth. What Habermas claims to describe is the structure of interlocution. Even if his recourse to the transcendental is said to be 'weak', since interlocution is a given of phenomena, the very fact of such recourse imparts to his description of phenomena the form of a description of inescapable conditions of possibility – a *structure* of interlocution. This explains Habermas's central argument, which is as terroristic as Chomsky's (the impossibility of any explanation other than innatism): that the priority of agreement cannot be challenged, for the very fact of challenging it presupposes at least the possibility of agreement and aims at it in reality. Any attempt to make *agon* the foundation of interlocution therefore ends up in irrationalism. This argument must be considered calmly: it naturalises a myth of origins which, on the contrary, is in need of historicisation, and is doubtless not a good myth. (The Marxian myth of the constitution of the social around the labour relationship has considerable advantages over it, to which I shall return.) All the more so in that this myth of origins, while it has the advantage over Chomsky's philosophy of language of trying to think language as a social phenomenon and therefore of attempting to think society, paradoxically does not avoid a form of individualism, which it always risks lapsing back into. Recourse to the phenomenological notion of the life-world is typical. This life-world is certainly *shared*, but it nevertheless assumes an individual subject as its starting-point: it is me whose experience this is, who lives this world, and the community is built on the intersection of individual life-worlds. This individualises and, if readers will allow me the expression, biographises that which is of the order of language and the encyclopaedia, and represents a regression by comparison with Popper's 'third world', which is constitutively situated at the level of the collective, like the system Saussure calls *langue*. The problem is that Habermas conceives linguistic interaction on the model of the legal contract – a marginal, complex language game that belongs to the exclusive domain of the legal superstructure, and hence is not conducive to explaining linguistic activity in general, of which it is a product or effect at the end of the chain, rather than a constitutive relation. In order to think language as a social phenomenon, we need to start from a much more fundamental social relationship: what makes human groups societies is not the formalisation of their relations by means of contracts, but the common activity that unites and divides them, of which language is simultaneously the product, the expression and the instrument. Readers will have recognised labour as the Marxian myth of origins. And they will have understood how, in order to reconstruct historical materialism, Habermas abandons any form of Marxism: to found society on a contract (legal-linguistic) is to regress from the collective to the individual (an individual multiplied by two does not compose a collective); appearances to the contrary notwithstanding, it is to practise a form of methodological individualism. This individualism leads Habermas to re-state the old myth, originally formulated by Haeckel, that ontogenesis recapitulates phylogenesis, and to set great store by Piaget's theory of learning, from which he extrapolates in order to explain social evolution. For him, society evolves not by the accumulation of contradictions and revolutionary upheaval, but by the teaching and accumulation of knowledge (this point is, to say the least, open to challenge). We can see why he inverts the Marxian myth of origins, why language becomes the condition of emergence of labour and hence society: language as understood by Habermas is not strictly individual, but inter-individual (in this respect, his theory of interlocution is derived from Anglo-American pragmatics, which is resolutely individualist), and the social is an effect of this divided individual.

The Habermas conjuncture

Thinking with Habermas and, at the same time, thinking against him – i.e. regarding him as a major philosopher – subjects him to the same fate as Marx inflicted on Hegel or as he himself inflicts on Marx: standing him back on his feet. And to do this is literally to operate an inversion on his philosophy: to consider it not as a first philosophy, bearer of a myth of origins, but as a last philosophy, expression of an eschatological hope. For Habermas's ethics of discussion can be criticised for betraying the facts, but the eminently desirable character of its realisation cannot be denied. Construed not as an origin but as a programme, it elicits our enthusiasm, not only because we are people of good will and prefer agreement to squabbling, but because we are communists and our objective is a classless society – that is, the end of exploitation and the class struggle it incites. In short, what Habermas proposes to us is linguistic communism: not the fundamental structure of interlocution, but an idea of reason (this was how the late Lyotard characterised communism), necessary for our survival even if its realisation is uncertain and endlessly deferred. Doing a pastiche of Marx, I shall reformulate Habermas's basic thesis in eschatological terms: 'from each according to her reasons discursively expounded via validity claims, to each according to her rational discursive reactions embodying her disposition to understand the other and reach an agreement with him'. To transform a myth of origins into eschatology in this way has the advantage that we are no longer obliged to exclude or ignore a large number of real phenomena (the idea of reason is maintained even if it is contradicted by the facts, which obviously presents a considerable philosophical advantage); and it avoids transforming a human aspiration (which, it might be claimed, helps to make us human beings) into a natural phenomenon. Linguistic activity can now include phenomena of *agon* as well as those of agreement. They can even be regarded as dominant in the conjuncture or primary, like man's exploitation of man (and for the same reasons): it is our duty to strive with all our might for their disappearance, their withering away. To make agreement an eschatological hope has an additional advantage: it enables us to avoid teleology – the form of naturalism which the Marxist tradition has lapsed into, through the medium of the succession of modes of production. Therein history is progress as well as progression and advanced communism is the inevitable goal of human history. In this respect, Habermas is situated in the tradition of continuators of Marx's emancipatory project, who reject the teleological vulgate. It runs from Walter Benjamin, and his critique of the ideology of progress in the 'Theses on the Philosophy of History' and the *Arcades Project*, to Daniel Bensaïd, who absolves Marx of the sin of teleology.[7] And, of course, it includes Jacques Derrida, who in large part bases his reading of Marx and his concept of the messianic without Messianism on a distinction between eschatology and teleology.[8] We can appreciate how Habermas, in an important sense, does not simply abandon the Marxist tradition, but continues and develops Marx's emancipatory project. But he does nevertheless abandon it and putting him back on his feet will consist in returning to the first philosophy of Marx, from which Habermas separated himself by inverting it, and which makes labour – not language – the founding social relation. Labour is not reducible to an inter-subjective relation, but is immediately social, in that it assumes a practice which, even if it is solitary, assumes meaning only within a collective – that is, neither within individual subjectivity nor within the dual individuality of dialogue. Man, like the ape and the ant, and unlike the cat or duck-billed platypus, belongs to a social species – a sociality imposed by his constitution and way of life (size, eating habits, means of defence, etc.): man's humanity is the result of an evolution in which language has played a role and which has brought it about that human sociality, fruit of labour, produces individual subjectivity at the end of the chain, as an effect. On this point we can re-read the work of the Vietnamese Marxist Tran Duc Thao.[9] Habermas's myth of origins inverts this evolution. Hence his stress, so as not to go too far in denying the facts, on the difference between hominids (who work but who do not speak) and human beings (who speak). Language can then be treated

---

[7] See Benjamin 1999 and 1973; Bensaïd 1992.
[8] See Derrida 1994.
[9] See Thao 1973.

as the defining characteristic of human beings and the qualitative leap from hominids to human beings, which recalls Chomsky's thinking on the genetic endowment of the human species, makes it possible to forget a causal link between labour and language: that the objectivity of labour in common produces in human beings the subjectivity of which language is the symptom, the vector and the instrument. Putting Habermas back on his feet, understanding that his first philosophy is, in reality, an eschatological hope, is a better way of understanding the emergence of language (a notoriously obscure phenomenon that can only be approached by the most speculative of philosophical speculation – i.e. a myth of origins: like Habermas's or like the one I attribute to Marx), and its character as a social practice, to which I shall return. Incidentally, it is also a way of providing ourselves with resources for understanding the nature of art, which (according to Lukács's aesthetics at least) re-runs the process of subjectivation that led humanity to make the transition from industrious objectivity to linguistic subjectivity.[10]

Nevertheless, it is not enough to put Habermas back on his feet. We must also explain why he is standing on his head. The thesis that I wish to defend here is that there is a Habermasian conjuncture, a historical moment when Habermas is a major philosopher; when his philosophy of language, law and politics is, as they say, key; when his exit from Marxism is justified and perhaps even inevitable; and when his ethics of discussion seems to be the most adequate framework in which to think about society. Today, this conjuncture has passed.

Roughly speaking, the Habermasian conjuncture corresponds to the years 1975–95. And it is explained by the combination of two politico-cultural factors. The first is post-Nazism. Habermas, who was fifteen in 1945, was formed in a society and culture haunted by the need to rid itself of the authoritarianism and totalitarianism of Nazism. In this sense, his philosophical antonym and sometimes his explicit antagonist is Carl Schmitt. This negative requirement was accompanied by a positive requirement: that of thinking through what has been called the *trente glorieuses*, the post-war economic and social conjuncture in Western industrialised societies, marked by the triumph of parliamentary democracy, the integration of the working class into the welfare state, the end of imperialism – at least in its most brutal and brazen

---

[10] See Lukács 1981.

form: colonialism – and the establishment of a semblance of international legal order by means of international organisations like the UN. In this conjuncture, it seemed that human societies could stabilise themselves and develop through compromise, discussion and consensus fixed in legal contracts; and thus that the ethics of discussion supplied these dominant social practices with the requisite philosophical substratum.

The second factor can be called post-communism: this is the high point of the Habermasian conjuncture, heralding its disappearance. The key moment here, of course, was the fall of the Berlin Wall. The type of society that Habermas seeks to found philosophically, or rather its partial embodiment, had won the Cold War. This society no longer appeared to be the least bad, but the best – that is, the only possible one. As a theory of society, Marxism was now disqualified not only because of its association with the Evil Empire, but – even more radically – because its concepts no longer explained real phenomena. One of the results of this collapse was that in philosophy political thinking was infected, if not replaced, by ethics. Habermas is the exemplary embodiment of this historical development.

The decade that began in 1995 reversed the trends on which Habermas based his consensual theory of society, his philosophy of communicative action, and his ethics of discussion. What economists call neoliberalism had certainly begun much earlier (readers are referred to the works of Gérard Duménil and Dominique Lévy: they date its growth from the end of the 1970s and the Thatcher-Reagan period).[11] But only after 1991 was its full social impact felt across Europe. To go quickly, we shall note the imperial position of the United States, sole superpower, exercising its power without any restraint; the imperialist wars of expansion that ensued (in Iraq, Kosovo, etc.); the globalisation of exploitation and class struggle, and accelerated immiseration in the Third World, a category in which some of former socialist countries must be included today (readers will remember the collapse of Argentina, indicating the extremes to which imperialist domination leads).

In Europe, this change in conjuncture issued in the dismantling of the welfare state and hence abandoning the policy of working-class integration of which it was the vector. In particular, following pressure on direct wages by the recreation of a reserve army of labour (the choice lying between a very high

---

[11] See Duménil and Lévy 1998 and 2003.

rate of unemployment or very low wages), the whole indirect wage, which the welfare state had the role of administering, was under challenge: pensions, public transport, health, education, when not already privatised and subject to the laws of the market, were threatened with so being in the short term.

These developments were accompanied by a loss of confidence in parliamentary democracy, which seemed like the mask for a power relation, and in international institutions, whose 'democratic' resolutions applied to Serbs and Iraqis, but not Israelis or Turks. The imperialist war in Iraq, conducted in total contempt for UN resolutions, as well as the discussions in the UN preceding the war, which had nothing to do with an ethics of discussion and everything to do with the imposition of their imperial will by the dominant Anglo-American imperialist countries via threats and corruption, are striking examples of the inability of Habermas's irenic philosophy to account for the most commonplace facts.

The consequence of the change in conjuncture is that Marxist concepts are once again relevant and their eclipse seems to have been temporary. Ten years ago, the old concept of imperialism was outmoded; today, it serves directly to account for US policy. Ten years ago, any critique of bourgeois democracy was a capitulation to totalitarianism; today, the limits of representative democracy are daily plainly apparent (massive expression of the popular will did nothing to prevent the British government from embarking on the imperialist adventure: the lies of the 'dossiers' presented to parliament in order to secure a majority do not help to enhance popular confidence in the democratic character of representative democracy). Ten years ago, it seemed that the urgent thing was to develop a moral theory to replace the cynicism of the power relations analysed by Marxists; today, the ethical pronouncements of Bush and Blair seem like the height of hypocrisy, a trompe-l'oeil, an ideological weapon to camouflage the most violent and least consensual of practices. Ten years ago, the Western democracies had won the Cold War because they defended human rights by equipping themselves with an effective system of legal protection; today, American treatment of prisoners of war from Afghanistan in Guantanamo and the extension of the state of exception force us to ask if Carl Schmitt's decisionism (sovereign is he who decides the state of exception) is not a more useful instrument for describing the policy of the US administration than Habermas's ethical universalism.

The conjuncture of Habermas has therefore been superseded. Today, Habermas finds himself in a position of weakness with respect to the Marxism that he abandoned, just as it was in a weak position vis-à-vis him in the previous conjuncture. We must therefore reconstruct Habermas just as Habermas sought to reconstruct historical materialism. We must change myths of origin and first philosophies, without abandoning Habermas's essential intuition: that the philosophy of language is of crucial importance for understanding society as a whole and getting some purchase on events.

Because Habermas is a major philosopher, he is conscious of the changed conjuncture. In a text published in *Le Monde* in May 2003, he referred to the Bush administration, or rather its ideologues, as 'revolutionaries', in that they had revolutionised the conjunctural political set-up which his philosophy naturalised by basing it on the structure of interlocution. He could only note, and deplore, the destruction of the international order based on renunciation of the 'right to war' embodied by the UN, as he observed that the 'negotiations' conducted by the US administrations (Clinton and Bush equally) before both the Kosovo war and the second war against Iraq had nothing to do with a search for consensus and everything to do with the brutal imposition of a balance of military might. They bore a strange resemblance to the discussions between the wolf and the lamb in the fable (asymmetric war makes it possible to impose disarmament on opponents prior to the aggression to which they will inevitably be subject). What the 'revolutionaries' around George W. Bush had revolutionised was precisely the universalism that founds the ethics of discussion and the politics of contractual negotiation. While this observation did not impart the form of a jeremiad in the etymological sense to Habermas's text, it did give it a nostalgic, disillusioned tone, with a mixture of lucidity (on the current conjuncture, which is one of resurgent imperialism) and hope in the face of the facts (this is not a critique: Marxists adopt precisely the same position):

> In the United States itself, the administration of a perpetual 'wartime president' is already undermining the foundations of the rule of law. Quite apart from the methods of torture that are practiced or tolerated outside nation's borders, the wartime regime has not only robbed the prisoners in Guantanamo of the rights they are entitled to expect according to the Geneva Convention; it has expanded the powers of law enforcement and security officials to the point of infringing the constitutional rights of America's own citizens. . . .
>
> The universal validity claim that commits the West to its 'basic political values', that is, to the procedure of democratic self-determination and the

vocabulary of human rights, must not be confused with the imperialist claim
that the political form of life and the culture of a particular democracy –
even the oldest one – is exemplary for all societies.[12]

The language here – 'universal validity claim', 'must not be confused' – cannot
disguise a stumbling block in this line of thought: for the 'basic political
values' in question are closely bound up with the 'imperialism' whose
expansion they scarcely inhibit. If by 'oldest democracy' is meant American
democracy (unless it refers to British democracy), then given their history
over two centuries, from the Opium War in the mid-nineteenth century right
up to the active complicity in the massacre of a million Indonesians in the
1960s (and the unfailing support given for forty years to the bloody, corrupt
dictatorship that followed it), it will be difficult to persuade us that these
basic political values are anything but an ideological screen for the imperialists.
And it will be remembered that what Habermas rejects with typical casualness
('conventional explanations . . . in terms of ideology . . . trivialise [the situation]')[13]
precisely, albeit traditionally, makes it possible to think the relation between
values and acts: Habermas lacks a theory of ideology. His consensual
philosophy of language is what prevents him from constructing one.

To summarise: Habermas's philosophy of language, first philosophy, is
worth retaining, but only as a last philosophy – that is, a philosophy of
messianic hope for communism in language. If we stick with this first
philosophy, we are as it were condemned to an agreement that is always in
the process of being achieved (even if it is difficult to demonstrate that it
already has been). Here we might detect a form of the determinism characteristic
of the vulgar Marxism sometimes associated with its social-democratic version:
the economic structure of society dictates the advent of socialism; there is a
tendency to socialism at the very heart of capitalism, as its mandatory
supersession. Similarly, the interlocutory structure of language dictates a
striving for consensus, if not its realisation in the short term. The problem is
that this produces a politics of dishonest compromise and impotence and a
philosophy of language which blithely ignores a fair proportion of the facts.

If, alternatively, we adopt this philosophy as last philosophy, if we declare
ourselves communists in linguistic matters, then we accept the reality and

---

[12] Habermas 2003, pp. 706–7.
[13] Habermas 2003, p. 704.

actuality of *agon* in the name of messianic values of linguistic irenism, just as we concede the existence of exploitation and struggle against it in the name of values that demand its disappearance. In so doing, we become conscious of the linguistic form taken by exploitation. This is called the dominant ideology, whose vector and privileged instrument is language. This leads us to realise that, when it comes to philosophy of language as well, there is also a dominant ideology. It is time to say a little more on this subject.

The philosophy of language and the dominant ideology

It might be feared that the expression 'dominant philosophy of language' is one of those phrases-slogans to which the Marxist tradition is partial and which can be summarised in the circular definition according to which 'the dominant ideology is the ideology that dominates'. The drawbacks of this tautology are clear: it amalgamates very different ways of thinking about language (Chomsky, Habermas, Saussure, one struggle, one fight!) and permits a cheap victory over them. We must therefore try to impart a more precise content to the phrase. I shall do so in three stages. I am going to indicate the structure of a dominant ideology; I shall enumerate six characteristics of the dominant philosophy in linguistic matters; and I shall suggest the converse characteristics, foreshadowing the reconstructive phase of my enterprise.

A dominant philosophy dominates in three ways. First of all, in the form of a *doxa*. When it comes to language, this *doxa* is usually called 'ideology of communication', where the term 'ideology' must be understood in Barthes's sense – that is, as a purely negative term (there is no question here of an allusion inseparable from illusion).[14] This ideology is embodied in a simple formula: 'language is an instrument of communication'.

What is striking about this formula is its irrefutable character. For it is clear that I speak in order to communicate with another person – that is, in order to exchange information with her. 'Can you tell me what the time is?' is the canonical utterance: this is what language is for, that is why it is at my disposal. Linguistic particles flow from a mouth to an ear and this flow is then recip-

---

[14] See Barthes 2002.

rocated, as in the famous diagram in Saussure's *Course in General Linguistics*. A singularly paradoxical mentality is required to deny that this diagram corresponds to a daily – and essential – experience of linguistic activity.

It is only when we replace this formula by others, which are logically possible and/or historically attested – for example, 'language is an instrument for expressing ideas', 'language is a weapon that enables us to convince and persuade', 'language makes it possible to master the world by naming it', or 'language is derived from action in common, which it facilitates and develops' – that we realise what is partial (in both senses of the word) about this formula. For it now appears that language is also something other than an instrument of communication and that it is possibly not always even an 'instrument'.

This *doxa* has three main characteristics: (i) it does not need to be explicitly formulated, because it is lodged in the mind of each and every one of us; (ii) when it is formulated, it is in the mode of a self-evident fact: it does not need to be argued for, because it tells things as they are and there is nothing to repeat or add; (iii) it is all the more effective in that it does not need to be defended.

Its effectiveness, its power can be gauged by the extent of its investment of society. It in fact possesses its sector of the economy (the public relations industry, in which all forms of advertising can be included), its institutions, and their countless agents (every kind of media, for whose existence it supplies an intellectual and ethical justification). Today, communication is a key sector of advanced capitalism.

We can note, in particular, two symptoms of this investment of the whole of the social structure. The ideology of communication is the ideological foundation of educational policies of language teaching: it therefore invests the central ideological state apparatus of capitalism – schools. For to learn a foreign language is to learn to communicate in this language. We shall therefore not trouble ourselves with culture and literature and will develop the general *doxa* with the following particular formula: 'If you don't know English, then go to Berlitz rather than school or university'.

The second symptom is the increasing importance assumed by the *doxa* of communication in the field of capitalist politics. Imperialist aggression is always preceded by a communications campaign. It will be noted that here we are no longer dealing with propaganda, which aims to persuade and convince, even when it is not particular about the methods employed. What is involved is communication, which 'informs' populations about 'how things stand', which in turn determines – 'beyond political and ideological divisions' – 'the only possible policy'. Thus we see ministers communicating to those for whom they are responsible their latest opuscule, prime ministers 'writing' to the French, and 'dossiers' being presented to the public on the existence of weapons of mass destruction. That these dossiers are total fabrications, that the 'sources' of this 'information' are kept secret and, when disclosed, prove to be completely unreliable, is of no importance. The object of 'political communications' is not to establish the truth, to convince people of the justice of the actions envisaged, or of their appropriateness in the political conjuncture. It is to interpellate each citizen to a position of recipient of information, and to bring them into a process of communication rather than of common action or decision-making. Hence the importance of 'spin' and the political figure of the 'communications director', which tends to occupy the centre of political life. It is through her that the government comes to power (she formulates the most 'communicative' – i.e. the most irresponsible – electoral promises); it is through her that it enters into crisis (as happened in Britain the summer of 2003).

Obviously, this *doxa* is not a natural object but a historical construct. A Marxist will have no difficulty demonstrating that the ideology of communication is the one that suits capitalism; that it represents liberalism in linguistic matters, in that it fetishises and relates two ideal speakers – a Sender and a Receiver – whose position is, in principle, reversible. This is where the ideology of communication cannot help revealing its ideological nature. For, in reality (in the field of public relations or political communication), *the Receiver never becomes the Sender in turn*. If she tries to, the rules of the game suddenly change and the Sender, who is responsible for the country's destiny, *does not understand what the citizens are saying to her*. Thus, the massive popular demonstrations organised against the war in Spain, Italy and Great Britain hardly succeeded in communicating (in any sense of the term) their conviction to the governments of those countries.

We can now understand Deleuze's hostility to communication (by it he also understood what French academics call *communications* [papers] – i.e. participation in conferences). A philosopher who, with Félix Guattari, engaged in joint composition more than any other, did not believe in the virtues of dialogue as a philosophical form of communication and preferred writing – that is, the fashioning of concepts.

The second form of domination of the dominant philosophy is what, following Althusser, I have analysed in connection with Chomsky: the spontaneous philosophy of scientists (SPS), which informs most contemporary linguistics. In general, we find it in the opening pages of linguistics treatises, where the author feels obliged to run through some generalities on language before proceeding to serious matters. Its most frequent form hesitates between Chomskyan naturalism and the intentionalism of the Anglo-American pragmatists, methodological individualism being what unites them. These SPS are more diverse, less brutal, but also less powerful than the ideology of communication, from which they are nevertheless derived. They represent one of the explicit faces of the dominant philosophy of language.

This takes a third, wholly explicit form: that of a consciously formulated philosophy of language, which, by that token, is more complex and more interesting than the two preceding forms. In the current conjuncture, this philosophy of language has two main forms, one of which derived from the development of the other: the Anglo-American speech-act theory of Austin, Searle and Grice; and Habermas's theory of communicative action. As we have just seen, this philosophy must be criticised but also reinvested: we must think against – but also with – Habermas.

It is the articulated set of these three forms which composes the dominant philosophy of language (and, here, the term ideology can no longer have purely negative connotations: the illusion is also allusion). When explicit, it is presented to us in countless variants, varieties and variations. But it always imposes a choice on us, political as well as philosophical: abandon it or, in a spirit of compromise, patch it up. If (and readers will not be surprised to learn that the Marxist position inclines me to make this choice) we opt to abandon it, we must formulate the principles of a different philosophy of language. I shall do so straight away.

The dominant philosophy of language is articulated around six principles. Not all its variants accepts all six principles; and perhaps none does. But they all acknowledge a sufficient number of them to possess what Wittgenstein calls a 'family resemblance'.

The first principle is the *principle of immanence*. We recall that it characterises structural linguistics and distinguishes between internal and external linguistics. This principle tells us that the functioning of language can be understood – i.e. offers purchase to a scientific study – only if language (or rather Saussure's *langue*) is considered in itself – that is, separated from all other phenomena, abstracting from any contact between language and the world. Internal linguistics does not ignore the mundane context: it deliberately excludes it. Hence its angelic subjects and a language possessing only its standard form, relegating anything pertaining to intercourse between language and the world to the dubious realm of socio-linguistics.

The second principle is the *principle of functionality*. Language performs functions (we remember the six functions of language in Roman Jakobson, deduced from his diagram of communication: referential, phatic, conative, emotive, metalinguistic, poetic).[15] Of course, there is a hierarchy among these functions: while all of them are necessary, or represented in linguistic phenomena, the function of exchanging information (the referential function) is presented as essential or primary. This is because language is, in the first instance, a means of communication, an instrument at the speaker's disposal: I speak my language, which means that I make it function as I intend. By means of it – through it – I say what I mean. Any linguistic phenomenon which does not boil down to this instrumentality or intentionalism (what I say is what I mean to say, the meaning of the utterance is a function of the speaker's intended meaning) will be disregarded as noise, in the literal sense of the term – a contingent and (it is to be hoped) temporary communication difficulty.

The third principle is the *principle of transparency*. It follows from the preceding principle. If language is an instrument of communication, its foremost characteristic is its capacity to make itself invisible. What interests me is to bang in the nail: the shape of the hammer's handle and its colour are of little importance to me. It follows that everything in language must be adapted to the easy and efficient transmission of information. To take an obvious example, when we speak our mother tongue, we employ a complex set of grammatical rules, of which we are generally not aware. But when they are explained to us, we become aware (like Monsieur Jourdain) that we knew them without knowing them. It is that here language renders itself transparent and knows how to make itself invisible. The moments when it is recalled to our attention, as in a poetic text, must remain strictly limited to specialist, marginal language games.

---

[15] See Jakobson 1963, pp. 214–21.

The fourth principle is the *principle of ideality*. *Langue* is an abstract, ideal system, realised in *parole,* or a biological competence realised in performance. Even if competence is materially inscribed in the body, the genes, and the neuronal circuits, it stands in the same relation to concrete acts of *parole* as the sonata does to its interpretations. Its existence is ideal; it is a (re)construction of the mind.

The fifth principle is the *principle of systematicity*. This is the principle which states that language is a fixed code, that a language is a set of rules, that what is relevant for the study of language is not *parole* – endlessly variable and chaotic – but *langue,* in that it is systematic. (Various systems of rules will be distinguished, at various hierarchical levels of the system: phonological, morphological, syntactic, semantic rules – *langue* is a stack of levels.) This reinforces the principle of immanence: it is because *langue* is systematic that it is self-sufficient, at least for the purposes of scientific study.

The sixth principle is the *principle of synchrony*. The system is immune, if not to change, then at least to history. This means that linguistic change does indeed occur, but it is not constituted in history: we pass in one bound from one system to the next. The system is studied in the a-historical present of the essential section. And since it has to be conceded that there is change in language, a couple of concepts are fashioned: synchrony – the ideal, abstract moment of the analysis of the system – and diachrony – the transition from one synchronic moment to another. Obviously, as is always the case with philosophical dichotomies (mind/body, etc.), one of the terms is hierarchically superior to the other: diachrony is relegated by systematic linguistics to its margins. And, yet, we can ask in the case of a given language – English, for example – what this a-temporal moment of synchrony is. If it is comparatively easy to decide that the texts of Old or Middle English belong to different synchronic moments (and thus to other languages – even though they are always named as variants of 'English'), we can ponder what should be done with seventeenth- or eighteenth-century English, which presents considerable differences from contemporary English (it is hard to read Shakespeare unless the text is heavily annotated).

These six principles constitute the skeletal structure of the dominant philosophy of language: they underpin the ideology of communication, form the substratum of the spontaneous philosophy of scientists, and are developed, refined, and sometimes contradicted in explicit philosophies of language. We have seen that they lead to excluding a fair few linguistic phenomena from the field of study (everything that comes under 'external linguistics' – language as a social, historical, political and material phenomenon); and to relegating language games that are essential for an understanding of language – e.g. literary language games – to the margins. To reconstruct the philosophy of language that has just been criticised is, first of all, to formulate the converse principles of what might be *a different philosophy of language*. Obviously, this inversion is insufficient: to invert is to remain in the universe of what is inverted and under the domination of what is inverted. But it is a start: there is no deconstruction without destruction. I am therefore going to state the six converse principles.

The first principle is the *principle of non-immanence*. Naturally, in this context the converse of immanence cannot be transcendence: despite my admiration for Walter Benjamin, I am not seeking to defend a mystical conception of language. This principle affirms that it is impossible to separate language from the world in which it emerges and of which it is an integral part. Hence the need for an external linguistics, which studies language as it is *in* and *of* the world: there is no radical separation between language, the society of speakers, the bodies of individual speakers, and the institutions that interpellate them as subjects. There is, therefore, no separation between language and the rest of human action.

The second principle is the *principle of dysfunctionality*. Language is not an instrument at the speaker's disposal. It is an experience and an activity; it is not an object distinct from speakers and manipulated by them. One enters into language, one slips into language, one inhabits language (to use the old Heideggerian metaphor). As a result, sometimes I speak the language (which gives me the impression of using it like a tool); and sometimes it is the language that speaks through my mouth and guides my statement or imposes it on me. We have this experience on a daily basis: it is called lapsus, cliché, echo or quotation. Consequently, communication cannot be the sole function of language (independently of the fact that the term 'function' proves inadequate, in that it slices up the totality of experience into tranches and thereby transforms it into an object); and Jakobson was right to distinguish between several functions. It is arguably not even the most important of them: language is also the site of the expression of affect, a terrain of play and learning about the world, and so on.

The third principle is the *principle of opacity*. The transparency of language, or of meaning, is an illusion. Language never makes itself invisible (a lapsus is an example of this refusal of transparency). The speaker negotiates her expression with her language: we say what our language allows us to say; we speak with – but also against – our language; and the meaning of our utterance is always a compromise between what we would like to have said and what we discover (sometimes to our horror) that we actually did say. This experience is likewise an everyday occurrence: it affects poets and English students alike.

The fourth principle is the *principle of materiality*. Language is not separable from its realisation in the form of speech or performance, in that an utterance is always a vector of *power* – what Anglo-American pragmatists call 'illocutionary force', which they tend to understand in idealist fashion as a mere indicator for classifying speech acts. Language is therefore never a mere vector of information, the currency of the mind; and a language is not an ideal system but (if it is a system) an embodied one, a material body acting on other bodies and producing affects. Elsewhere, I have tried to describe this situation under the generic title of 'the violence of language'.[16] Readers will understand why a Marxist is interested in this concept of power lodged at the heart of language, why she recognises it as a concept with which she is familiar – that of power relations – and will also understand why this principle leads us, *contra* Habermas, to stress the agonistic aspect of linguistic exchange rather than its irenic aspect.

The fifth principle is the *principle of partial systematicity*. A language is not a system, except in the fetishistic abstraction imposed on it by the linguist, but a set of sub-systems or partial systems in constant variation. This has two consequences. The first is that language is not utterly chaotic, but not wholly systematic either. Hence the countless examples of exceptions, of exploitation in Grice's sense (when the speaker infringes a 'rule' for expressive purposes – such rules are thus eminently 'defeasible' and closer to moral maxims than natural laws), of playful, deliberate non-grammaticality. (This experience is not confined to poets, but is at the heart of our everyday lives.) The second consequence is that language is not stable and that it cannot be fixed in the frozen time of synchrony. The rules of grammar, even those most firmly

---

[16] See Lecercle 1991.

established and strictly imposed for paedagogical purposes, only last for a period of time and the language is constantly changing. And French readers will understand here why I cheerfully pass from *langue* to *langage* and seem to confuse the two notions: *la langue*, embodied in the form of a 'natural language' like English, is only the temporary, variable materialisation, in an ideological and cultural conjuncture, of the activity of *langage*. It is not an ideal system, an independent and stable object. Hence my final principle.

The sixth principle is the *principle of historicity*. Partially systematic, language is also partially chaotic – not because it is naturally disorganised or partially organised, but because it is the trace of a process of historical sedimentation of rules, conventions, maxims, and meanings. The synchronic value of a grammatical marker (e.g. a modal auxiliary in English or French) is never independent of its history, any more than the meaning of the utterance 'she painted the house brown' is independent of its cultural context and the history of the culture in question.

As the names of my six counter-principles indicate (they are designated negatively for the most part), they are still dependent on the dominant philosophy of language with which they seek to break. The enterprise of reconstruction has only just begun. It involves exploring a different tradition of thinking about language: an explicitly Marxist tradition.

Chapter Four
The Marxist Tradition

Two Marxists converse with us about language

'There is no Marxist philosophy of language' is a paradoxical thing to say. It is clear that, within Marxism or Marxisms, there is no body of constituted doctrine in linguistic matters in the same way that there is for other fields, like political economy or even (to a certain extent) aesthetics. This has at least one advantage: we are not labouring under the weight of a dogma when it comes to language. And it is also a disadvantage: there is no tradition of debate on the issue between Marxists. This has deleterious political consequences. It leads to abandoning the field of language to our opponents, who have occupied it to their satisfaction: the ideology of communication has thus duly invaded politics, where it constitutes an essential weapon; it has informed the spontaneous philosophies of scientists in the field; and it has infected existing philosophies of language.

But there is another aspect to the paradox. For it is wrong to say that there has never been a book or opuscule devoted by Marxists to the philosophy of language. The book by Voloshinov-Bakhtin, which I shall deal with in the next chapter, carries precisely such a title, as does Stalin's pamphlet.[1] And a

---

[1] See Voloshinov 1973 and Stalin 1973.

multitude of Marxist authors have discussed language. I have already
mentioned the Vietnamese Marxist Tran Duc Thao. But we can add the names
of Henri Lefebvre, Alfred Sohn-Rethel, Ferrucio Rossi-Landi, Jean-Joseph
Goux and his numismatics, Robert Lafont and praxematics, Renée Balibar on
educational language and the constitution of the French national language,
Michel Pêcheux, and Bourdieu (assuming we disregard his proclamations of
non-Marxism).[2] Not to mention bits and pieces in the founding fathers: Engels
is the author of a pamphlet on German dialects.[3] Gramsci frequently tackled
linguistic issues in his *Prison Notebooks*.[4] Lenin is the author of a text on
slogans.[5] And, although Althusser seemingly scarcely interested himself in
linguistic questions (a note in his text on the 'Ideological State Apparatuses'
refers to the errant ways of linguists), I have sought to show elsewhere that
some instruction on the functioning of language can be drawn from his theory
of ideology.[6] To this long and already distinguished list, I shall add Pasolini
and (as I have already suggested) Deleuze and Guattari.

This paradoxical situation has a historical origin. For a spectre haunts
Marxist thinking on language: the spectre of Stalin and his pamphlet *Marxism
and Linguistics*. This text merits a serious Marxist analysis of the sort that
Dominique Lecourt once devoted to the analogous case of Lysenko.[7] Such a
study, which is not my intention here, would examine the political meaning
of this weighty intervention by the great leader in a *scientific* domain that
politicians are not usually interested in, even if they are active agents of the
ideology of communication. (It is difficult to imagine George W. Bush
polemicising directly with Chomsky.) It would take account of the development
of Soviet nationalities policy and the linguistic policy that flowed from it in
the post-war USSR, as well as the struggles for influence of various schools
in the Soviet ideological and educational apparatus. What I am interested in
here is the effects of Stalin's intervention on the Marxist tradition of thinking
about language generally. They seem to me to have been two-fold. The first

---

[2] See Duc Thao 1973; Lefebvre 1966; Sohn-Rethel 1978; Rossi-Landi 1983; Goux 1973
and 1984; Lafont 1978; Balibar 1974 and Balibar and Laporte 1974; Pêcheux 1982;
Bourdieu 1982.
[3] See Engels 1991.
[4] See Gramsci 1971.
[5] See Lenin 1964.
[6] See Lecercle 1999b.
[7] See Lecourt 1977.

was one of relief. After the damage done by the Lysenko affair and the doctrine counter-posing proletarian science to bourgeois science, Stalin's intervention seemed full of good sense and his dead opponent, Nicholai Marr, appeared to be one of those 'literary madmen' who claim to demonstrate the squaring of the circle or maintain that the earth is flat. The reaction of Marcel Cohen, member of the Paris School and a follower of Meillet, who at the time performed the function of official linguist of the French Communist Party, is typical of this mind-set: in linguistics at least, one could once again be both a loyal activist and a scientist respected by one's peers.[8] This relief still finds orthodox expression in a passage in *For Marx* where, at one point in his analysis, Althusser evokes the 'madness' of Marr, which Stalin had reduced to 'a little more reason'.[9] This *doxa* was widely shared by the academic linguists of the time and their successors.

Fifty years on, readers will not be surprised to learn, this relief cannot as readily be shared. In the first place, it simplified for Western purposes a discussion in Soviet linguistics where it is not obvious that the contrast between the good and the bad, the sane and the mad, was so clear cut. In particular, the condemnation of Marr's theoretical eccentricities (his theory of the four elements, his theory of stages) eclipsed the positive impact of the New Theory of Language – for example, as regards the description of the languages of the countless Soviet nationalities.[10] And, by declaring it closed, it buried the issue of the relations between language and the social totality, between language and the superstructure – that is, the question of what constitutes the specificity of Marxism when it comes to thinking about language. We must therefore induce a dialogue, from beyond the grave, between two Marxists: Stalin, whose intervention is all too famous, and Pasolini, author of a little-known text with the revealing title of 'Dal laboratorio (appunti *en poète* per una linguistica marxista)'.[11]

For obvious reasons, Stalin's text has not been reprinted in France for a long time. Short extracts appeared in 1966 in *Cahiers marxistes-léninistes*, when the Althusserians were (briefly) interested in Stalin as a possible antidote to

---

[8] See Cohen 1950 and 1971.
[9] See Althusser 1969, p. 22.
[10] On these discussions, see Marcellesi and Gardin 1974; L'Hermitte 1987; and *Langages* 1969 and 1977. [Editorial note: also see Brandist].
[11] See Pasolini 1972.

the prevailing revisionism, and in Marcellesi and Gardin's manual, where they are submitted to a critical discussion. In this manual, the extracts are preceded by sub-titles, which state the main theses of Stalin's text. I shall adopt them. There is a main thesis and various secondary theses that follow from it.

The *main thesis* is formulated at the beginning of the text. It stipulates that *language is not a superstructure*. The following quotation gives an idea of the thesis, obviously, but also of the tone and style of the Great Leader's intervention:

QUESTION: *Is it true that language is a superstructure on the base?*
ANSWER: No, it is not true.

The base is the economic structure of society at a given stage of its development. The superstructure consists of the political, legal, religious, artistic, and philosophical views of society and the political, legal, and other institutions corresponding to them.

Every base has its own superstructure corresponding to it. The base of the feudal system has its superstructure – its political, legal, and other views and the corresponding institutions; the capitalist base has its own superstructure, and so has the socialist base. If the base changes or is eliminated, then following this its superstructure changes or is eliminated; if a new base arises, then following this a new superstructure arises corresponding to it.

In this respect language radically differs from superstructure. Take, for example, Russian society and the Russian language. During the past thirty years the old, capitalist base was eliminated and a new, socialist base was built. Correspondingly, the superstructure on the capitalist base was eliminated and a new superstructure created corresponding to the socialist base. The old political, legal, and other institutions were consequently supplanted by new, socialist institutions. But in spite of this the Russian language has remained essentially what it was before the October Revolution.

... As to the basic vocabulary and grammatical structure of the Russian language ... far from having been eliminated and supplanted ... [they] have been preserved in their entirety and have not undergone any serious change – [they] have been preserved precisely as the foundation of modern Russia.[12]

---

[12] Stalin 1973, pp. 407–8.

The paedagogical clarity of these remarks cannot be denied. But readers will doubtless have noted the dark irony of the use on four occasions of the verb 'eliminate': in this domain, at any rate, Stalin knew what he was talking about. The intention is not only paedagogical; it bears the stamp of plain good sense. For it is true that the October Revolution did not revolutionise the Russian language. The implicit adversary here is not only Marr, whose Marxism was belated and naïve, but Paul Lafargue (who is explicitly criticised at another point in the text), whose text on the language of the French Revolution was one of the first (and not the least) attempts to think about language in the light of Marxism.[13] In the context of post-war Stalinist repression, and the wave of nationalist delirium that had gripped certain sectors of Soviet science (and which was formulated in the ultra-leftist concept of 'proletarian science'), we can understand why Western linguists of all kinds breathed a sigh of relief: better good sense, even if a bit dull, than pseudo-scientific elucubrations. But it is sufficient to shift the focus of attention slightly to appreciate the extent to which Stalin's text is problematic, for two reasons. In fact, Stalin adopts as a self-evident truth the architectural metaphor of base and superstructure, which derives from Marx's overly famous text in the Preface to *A Contribution to the Critique of Political Economy*.[14] This metaphor poses countless problems, not the least of them being the determinist conception of the superstructure which it seems to propose. Stalin's good sense therefore naturalises (which is generally the function of good sense) a complex, debatable philosophical construct. All the more so in that Stalin's addition to it, which represents his theoretical contribution – the existence of a 'socialist mode of production' distinct from the communist mode of production and preceding it – is even more problematic. Today, we regard it as an unhappy attempt to theorise and naturalise a particular historical situation: socialism in one country. And, if it is accepted that Soviet 'socialism' is not a mode of production, the argument about the continuity of the Russian language falls: there is no reason for it to be profoundly revolutionised if the mode of production has not radically changed, but only begun to change – that is, if socialism is conceived as a transition period. Obviously, this does not mean that the October Revolution did not affect the capitalist bases of Russian society. It

---

[13] See Lafargue 1936.
[14] See Marx 1975, pp. 425–6.

means that, despite Stalin's best efforts, it did not 'eliminate' them. We shall therefore inspect the Russian language not for an abrupt change, a linguistic leap, but for the effects of political and social changes. For, as we have seen, languages are not subject to historical change as single, solid objects, but are layered like the social structure in Althusser's description of it; and its different strata develop at different speeds. Accordingly, more rapid changes will occur at the lexical level than at the syntactical level, and so on. And it is precisely these changes that the Marrists, over and above their master's elucubrations, sought to bring out. And this is precisely what Stalin wanted to put a stop to, as the secondary theses defended in the rest of the text indicate. It therefore emerges that Stalin's 'good sense' is not only the naturalisation of a historical and theoretical construct, but an instrument for defending a politics.

We are familiar with the second thesis, albeit not in a Marxist context. For Stalin, *a language is an instrument of communication serving all the people*: 'the role of language as an auxiliary, as a means of intercourse between people, consists not in serving one class to the detriment of other classes, but in equally serving all society, all classes of society'.[15] Here, we have the expression of what, by way of a pastiche of Althusser, I propose to call a SPL, a Spontaneous Philosophy of Leaders. And we must grant Stalin one merit: the desire to theorise his linguistic policy, which is closely bound up with his nationalities policy. It is sometimes suggested that Stalin was not the author of this text, any more than he was the author of the history of the Bolshevik Party that he signed; and that the real author was the anti-Marrist academician Vinogradov. But there is no need to go to such extremes: Stalin's theoretical interest in the nationalities question is indisputable, as was his ability to write his own texts on the subject. (The comparison is interesting: one can scarcely imagine Tony Blair or Jacques Chirac publishing theoretical interventions, let alone George W. Bush.) In truth, the real author of the text is of little moment: what matters, beyond the authority of the signature, is the collective voice that makes itself heard in it – the *Marxist version of the ideology of communication*. The 'Marxist' supplement to the rawest formulation of this ideology consists in the mention of 'all society' – an ecumenicism that owes nothing to the Marxist conception of the class struggle and everything to the idea that, under the 'socialist mode of production', it was in the process of withering away.

---

[15] Stalin 1973, p. 409.

In order to measure the distance between Stalin and Marxist orthodoxy on this point, it is sufficient to reread Bukharin's manual of Marxist sociology, whose rigidity and dogmatism were criticised by Gramsci. The following two passages situate Bukharin vis-à-vis the two theses of Stalin to which we have thus far referred:

> *Language* and *thought*, the most abstract ideological categories of the superstructure, are also functions of social evolution. It has sometimes been fashionable among Marxists or pseudo-Marxists to declare that the origin of these phenomena has nothing to do with historical materialism. Kautsky, for example, went so far as to claim that the powers of human thought are almost unchanging. Such is not the case, however; these ideological forms, so extraordinarily important in the life of society, constitute no exception to the other ideological forms of the superstructure in their origin and evolution. . . . It would lead us too far a-field to point out in detail that the character, the *style* of a language also changes with the conditions of social life; but it is worthwhile to mention that the division of society into classes, groups, and occupations also impresses its mark on a language; the city-dweller has not the same language as the villager, the 'literary language' is different from 'common' speech. This difference may become so great as to prevent men from understanding each other; in many countries there are popular 'dialects' that can hardly be understood by the cultured and wealthy classes; this is a striking example of the class cleavage in language.[16]

These analyses are not strikingly original, but they indicate that the author is conscious that a 'national language' is a historical and political construct, and that the 'language of the whole people' is a myth which Marxists should examine to see what politics it expresses.

The third thesis identified by Marcellesi and Gardin seems to effect a return to a form of Marxism. It suggests that if language is not a superstructure, it is because *it is directly connected with production*:

> Language . . . is connected with man's productive activity directly, and not only with man's productive activity, but with all his other activities in all spheres of work, from production to the base and from the base to the superstructure. That is why language reflects changes in production

---

[16] Bukharin 1925, pp. 214–15, 217.

immediately and directly, without waiting for changes in the base. That is why the sphere of action of language, which embraces all spheres of man's activity, is far broader and more varied than the sphere of action of the superstructure. More, it is practically unlimited.[17]

The aim of this thesis is once again to distinguish language from the superstructure. And it might be thought that, since Stalin erects the architectural metaphor into a dogma of Marxism, if language is not an integral part of the superstructure, it is because it forms part of the base, which is why it is directly linked to production. Here, Stalin would be anticipating certain developments in post-Marxism, in Negri and Hardt or Marazzi, for whom communication has become a productive force, so that language is directly involved in production – i.e. in the base (to the extent that post-Marxism retains the old contrast).[18] But Stalin's aim is different: it is to situate language somewhere else – an elsewhere that is not the social structure of a class-divided society, but a direct anthropological relationship between humanity and nature in the form of production. Hence the apparent contradiction which leads Stalin to say that language is not affected by a change in the mode of production and that it 'immediate and directly' reflects changes in production: we pass from a historically imperturbable language to one that is hysterically affected by technological change. Obviously, the problem posed by this vulgar technologism lies in the concept of 'reflection' ('language reflects changes in production'), which avoids Marr's sociological determinism only immediately to succumb to a form of determinism that is probably worse.

The fourth thesis asserts that *language has no class character*. What is interesting here is the reason adduced in defence of the thesis:

> The second mistake of these comrades is that they conceive the opposing interests of the bourgeoisie and the proletariat, the fierce class struggles between them, as meaning the disintegration of society, as a break of all ties between the hostile classes. They believe that, since society has split and there is no longer a single society, but only classes, a common language of society, an national language, is unnecessary. If society is split and there is no longer a common national language, what remains? There remain classes

---

[17] Stalin 1973, pp. 411–12.
[18] See Michael Hardt and Antonio Negri 2000 and Marazzi 1997.

and 'class languages'. Naturally, every 'class language' will have its 'class' grammar – a 'proletarian' grammar or a 'bourgeois' grammar. True, such grammars do not exist in nature. But this does not worry these comrades; they believe that such grammars will appear in due course.[19]

Here, we see the function of good sense and its limits. In attributing to the supporters of a relationship between language and class a counter-intuitive absurdity – the existence of a 'class grammar' (one can then imagine linguistic forms of the proletarian passive as opposed to the bourgeois passive) – Stalin effects two politico-linguistic operations. He implicitly criticises the ultra-leftist position that counter-poses proletarian to bourgeois science (hence the relief of Western Communist scientists); and he focuses the issue of language on that of the national language, common to all the people. The price to be paid for an operation manifestly bound up with nationalities policy in the post-war USSR is the fetishisation of language, which escapes its social and political determinations to become a neutral object, independent of the struggles of the human beings who use it as a tool of communication. In this respect, Stalin's position is situated four-square within the ideology of communication.

The fifth thesis anticipates a possible objection, since Marxists maintain that the division of society into classes involves cultural differences. It therefore applies itself to the task of dissociating language and culture, postulating that 'culture and language are two different things. Culture may be either bourgeois or socialist, but language, as a means of intercourse, is always a common national language'.[20] The argument is that, in the socialist USSR, the Russian, Ukrainian, Uzbek, etc. languages serve the common socialist culture as they served the bourgeois or feudal cultures that preceded it. We therefore have two or more cultures, probably coexisting, since superseded cultures leave behind survivals, but only one language. The effect of this thesis is to fetishise language in another way: it is not only in some sense released from the struggles and contradictions that constitute the social formation, but is also released from history, which alone can explain the present state of the social formation. For cultures develop, succeed one another, and divide up the field, but not language, which is therefore a stable object unaffected by cultural change – i.e. history.

---

[19] Stalin 1973, pp. 417–18.
[20] Stalin 1973, p. 419.

So we see that even the great Marxist leader does not avoid contradictions – which is only natural. On the one hand, he seems to locate himself without qualms in the dominant philosophy of language, whose watchword is the instrumentalisation of language, neutral tool of communication, and whose effect is its fetishisation, since language is thereby released from the class struggle and from history. In Stalin's text, readers will have recognised a 'Marxist' – i.e. slightly left-wing – version of the principles of immanence (language is an object independent of classes engaged in struggle, its speakers are angelic); functionality (language performs its function of communication in the service of the whole society); transparency (language is a tool and hence we are not going to examine it for the opacity entailed by its anchorage in social contradictions); ideality (language is fetishised as an object independent of the human beings who speak it: this is the Marxist equivalent of the linguists' ideal abstract system); systematicity (in truth, Stalin expresses no opinion on this point, his grammatical references being elementary); and synchrony (language is not affected by historical developments). The most astonishing thing about all this is that such a set of opinions did not give Marxists pause. But who was in a position to say that the emperor had no clothes? On the other hand, Stalin's text possesses an undeniably Marxist style in that it manifestly constitutes a political intervention, connected to a linguistic and nationalities policy, whose complexity could only be unravelled by a historical analysis of the ideological conjuncture of the USSR in the 1950s. In his practice, the political leader therefore contradicts the principle of immanence or neutrality proclaimed in his theory: this clearly resembles a SPL.

It is not therefore not surprising if a change of historical conjuncture should have produced effects. In 1960s Italy, the Marxist response to questions of language was formulated differently.

As is well known, Pier Paolo Pasolini was a scandalous film-maker, a novelist of the slums of inner-city Rome, a poet, and a homosexual activist. Less well-known is the fact that he was a communist. A collection of his essays, *Empirismo eretico*, brought together texts published in the weekly paper of the Italian Communist Party, *Rinascita*. One of them, written in 1965, provoked a polemic in the Italian press. It was entitled 'News from the Laboratory: Poetic Notes for a Marxist Linguistics'. Pasolini's desire to take up the issue of Marxist thinking about language from a completely different perspective is clear. And readers will appreciate the irony of scientific appearances (the linguist in a white coat in his laboratory) combined with literary and poetic reality: our linguist is, first and foremost, a poet.

The Marxist tradition within which Pasolini writes is very different from that of Stalinist 'diamat'. It is dominated by the thought of Gramsci, who was interested in language in a quasi-professional way, having been trained as a philologist at university, and who had very different positions on the relations between language and culture from those of Stalin. The following two quotations will suffice to make it clear that we are in a different mental universe:

> If it is true that every language contains the elements of a conception of the world and of a culture, it could also be true that from anyone's language one can assess the greater or lesser complexity of his conception of the world. Someone who only speaks dialect, or understands the standard language incompletely, necessarily has an intuition of the world which is more or less limited and provincial, which is fossilised and anachronistic in relation to the major currents of thought which dominate world history. . . .
> A great culture can be translated into the language of another great culture, that is to say a great national language with historic richness and complexity, and it can translate any other great culture and can be a world-wide means of expression. But a dialect cannot do this.
> It seems that one can say that 'language' is essentially a collective term which does not presuppose any single thing existing in time and space. Language also means culture and philosophy (if only at the level of common sense) and therefore the fact of 'language' is in reality a multiplicity of facts more or less organically coherent and co-ordinated. At the limit it could be said that every speaking being has a personal language of his own, that is his own way of thinking and feeling.[21]

We can see the difference of historical and political conjuncture: the question which, for Stalin, is posed in terms of national language(s) is posed, for Gramsci, in terms of dialects. And Gramsci, who was Sardinian and knew what a dialect was, is hard on them: we find in him a form of linguistic Jacobinism. But we can also see what this difference implies in terms of philosophy of language: here there is no longer a distinction between language and culture,

---

[21] Gramsci 1971, pp. 325, 349.

language and superstructure. If a language is the vector of a conception of the world ('even in the slightest manifestation of any intellectual activity whatever, in "language", there is contained a specific conception of the world'),[22] it cannot be in the service of the 'whole nation', unless we conceive a totally homogeneous society – that is, one not shot through with class struggle and divided into the classes issued from it. Similarly, we cannot conceive a language that is not subject to historical change – that is, not only to the slow evolution of the structure. A different philosophy of language emerges in outline here, at the antipodes of Chomskyan naturalism ('the nature of the human species is not given by the "biological nature" of man . . . One could also say that the nature of man is "history"');[23] but also of structuralist *langue* understood as a system. In Gramsci, language – a word often used between quotation marks – splits up, is transformed into a partially organised multiplicity, in the dialectic of the collective (the linguistic-cultural community) and the individual ('every speaking being has a personal language of his own'). And, of course, the boundaries between language and the world, which are posited by linguists to make their lives simpler, become blurred.

It is precisely with the young Gramsci that Pasolini begins his notes. He ponders the dreadfully pompous style of the early texts of Gramsci, a Sardinian in whom schooling has inculcated a grandiloquent standard Italian; and he tries to reconstruct Gramsci's accent in the Turin years – probably a mixture of a Sardinian accent and a Piedmontese petit-bourgeois accent. A polyphony can be heard: the grandiloquence of a humanist literary education, the scientific style inspired by French culture and by reading Hegel and Marx, the mixed accents of two provinces. The speaking being does indeed have his own language in the most literal sense: he is spoken by a Babel of languages. The implicit philosophical point of this initial analysis is Gramscian and at the antipodes of Stalin: Pasolini does not describe language as a neutral structure, but as a structure in constant variation – historical and social variations which interpellate the speaker to a place in the social totality.

Whence Pasolini's main thesis: as speakers, we do not use a linguistic system (language, the language that we speak) as an instrument of communication, any more than we are determined – spoken – by it. We concretely live the

---

[22] Gramsci 1971, p. 323.
[23] Gramsci 1971, p. 355.

tendency possessed by this distortable structure to alter, to become a different structure. Language is, therefore, less a structure than a process – which rules out any Saussurian synchrony. In the case of Pasolini himself, 'Italian' is composed of a northern dialect – the dialect of Frioul – adapted to the Roman dialect and to the institutional Koine – i.e. the Tuscan dialect transmitted by schools. Language is not a stable structure, but a process in constant variation, a disequilibrium, an anxiety.

That is why, for Pasolini, the dichotomy that enables us to grasp linguistic phenomena is not the Saussurian or Chomskyan dichotomy (*langue/parole* or competence/performance), but the opposition between spoken language and written language, or rather between a purely spoken language and a spoken-written language.

This involves a poetic dichotomy, whose metaphysical character will not escape us. Spoken language is (i) pre-historic, (ii) the product of physical need, (iii) continuous, (iv) located outside the opposition between base and superstructure, (v) concrete, and (vi) motivated. Spoken-written language possesses the converse characteristics. It is (i) historical, (ii) the product of a cultural practice, (iii) subject to change, (iv) caught up in the base/superstructure opposition, (v) abstract, and (vi) arbitrary. This is a primitivist, and hence highly mythical, conception of spoken language as the language of origins, born out of the cry, the needs of personal expression and communal existence, and surviving within the language captured by culture. Pasolini's reference here is not so much Marx or Gramsci as Rousseau, thinker of the origin of languages. But this yields an interesting concept of language as *langue*: for Pasolini, it is the point of contact between spoken language and spoken-written language, the point where culture is substituted for nature.

The illustrations provided by Pasolini of 'purely spoken language' are drawn from personal memories and experiences. A single one will suffice. He evokes the character of Ninetto, a young Calabrian of sixteen, who finds himself in the company of Pasolini in northern Italy and sees snow for the first time. His exclamation, his cry of delight 'Hè-eh, hè-eh!',[24] reminds Pasolini of the Greek and pre-Greek interjections (he claims to have heard a similar exclamation among the Denka shepherds in the Sudan) of ancient Calabria – something that illustrates the continuity and persistence of spoken language,

---

[24] Pasolini 1976, p. 69.

its anchorage in the bodies of speakers, its expressiveness. We are clearly dealing with a primitivist myth.

But this myth allows Pasolini to offer a highly pertinent analysis of the state of the French language just before the Revolution and during it. He asks what the French language was composed of at the point that it became the national language, in opposition to dialects – i.e. at the end of the *ancien régime* – in a process which was to be significantly accelerated by the Revolution and Napoleonic centralism. This situation could not but fascinate an Italian, for whom the question of the relations between dialects and the national language remained a topical one. French at the end of the *ancien régime* was the product of the addition of three components: a spoken component, a spoken-written component, and 'the language' produced by their intersection. The spoken component was the result of a continuum – i.e. of a historical sedimentation: the historical continuity that runs from Latin to old French and modern French – but also a cultural sedimentation, of superstructures that have become antiquated – such as the culture of the burgher communes of the Middle Ages or that of the Roman period. A kind of gravitation caused the spoken-written culture to subside into the oral state once it was no longer living: here we have a possible theory of cultural survivals. The spoken-written component was composed of the various languages of superstructures that were still active, which gave 'the language' its content in a concrete historical conjuncture. The language lay at the intersection of these two components: it inscribed royal power throughout the whole territory, which thereby became national territory, and gave the French nation its identity. This 'language' is not construed as a Saussurian system, but as a point of contact between spoken language and the spoken-written language of the superstructures (military, literary, scientific, religious).

What happened with the Revolution? Here, Pasolini distinguishes himself from Stalin, for whom revolutionary change also affects the language and, in advance, from Bourdieu, who analyses this conjuncture in terms of the triumph of the national language over dialects. For Pasolini, the spoken language did not change: speakers continued to speak the same language, enriched by sedimentation from the ruins of superstructures that were no longer contemporary (snatches of courtly language even percolated into popular language). Here is something to gratify the good sense of Marr's opponents. But the language changed; the 'social language' characterised by the domination of the feudal model adapted to the new conjuncture. Pasolini's example is a classic one: the extension of the 'vulgar' pronunciation of *roi*, which we have conserved, at the expense of its socially valorised pronunciation, *rouais*. And this change in the language, which was determined by the change in historical conjuncture (here Pasolini approximates to Marr, or, rather, to Paul Lafargue), was due to a more fundamental change in the oral-written languages of the superstructures. The new élites spoke the technical, philosophical and industrial languages of the ascendant bourgeoisie – that is, adds Pasolini, 'the language of the infrastructure'. The economic and political triumph of capitalism over feudalism was accompanied by a linguistic revolution, which had direct effects on one of the levels of language – the 'national language' – in that it substituted the language of the infrastructure for that of the superstructure. *Pace* Stalin, the bourgeois revolution is clearly inscribed in the language.

Even if the conclusions are sometimes strange (one would like to know more about this 'language of the infrastructure': does it simply involve technical terminology adopted as a stylistic model or the does the infrastructure 'speak'?), we can see that we have left behind the dominant philosophy of language in at least two respects. There is no longer any question of naturalism here: human nature is simply the name given to the set of social relations – that is, to a cultural and historical conjuncture. With naturalism disappears methodological individualism. The linguistic experience is obviously individual (it is I who speak), but, in linguistic matters, this individuality is always-already collective, in the sense that my statements, my language(s), are the historical products of a collective conjuncture. At the moment when the speaker opts, as the most profound expression of her personality, to say *roi* and not *rouais*, she enters into a historical process of which she is not necessarily conscious: she is spoken by the language she is convinced she speaks.

Perhaps the most interesting thing is the dissolution of the object *langue* – that is, of the Saussurian system or Chomskyan universal grammar. For it appears that, under the names of *langue* or *langage*, we fetishistically transform a complex linguistic situation into a single object. The Pasolinian model of three types of language, in the form of a hourglass or X, has the advantage of not denying or excluding the majority of linguistic phenomena. The bottom half of the X corresponds to spoken language, stable and sedimented, subject to historical change through the accumulation of the ruins or monuments of past conjunctures and experience (and sources of experience that are present for the poet, who brings them back to life in his texts). The cross of the X corresponds to the language, understood as the national language: a partial system, since subject to constant variation according to historical conjunctures, and site of communication. Here, Stalin's language as instrument of communication for the whole society finds its embodiment, with the help of ideological state apparatuses: for language in the sense of *langage* also serves the purposes of communication with one's fellow citizens within a national language. Finally, the upper part of the X corresponds to the different superstructures, each of which has its own language (jargons, technical languages, etc.), subject to historical change, and percolating, like coffee into its filter, down to the two lower levels. (We shall avoid – something this model seems to prompt – interpreting the X as a hierarchy – i.e. making spoken language a linguistic 'base'.)

Thus we observe that, while Stalin's intervention is located at the heart of the dominant philosophy in linguistic matters, in that it exemplifies most of its six characteristics, Pasolini's is located outside it and exemplifies the converse six principles. For it is clear that, for Pasolini, language does not obey the principle of immanence: in order to talk about *langage* or *langue*, we must speak of the whole of the society or culture. And his conception of language corresponds to the principles of dysfunctionality (it is the language that speaks Ninetto, a language as old as the world that he speaks unawares); opacity (the speaker says what the historical conjuncture in the language permits her to say: there is therefore a *linguistic conjuncture*); materiality (for Pasolini, the language is the site of a power relation and its materiality is as much corporeal as social); partial systematicity (the X schema provides us with a remarkable illustration of this seemingly bizarre concept); and, obviously, historicity: Pasolini is the direct inheritor of the Italian philosophical tradition, Marxist or non-Marxist, of historicism.

The opposition between two philosophies of language – the dominant one and the one aspiring to replace it – therefore runs through Marxism. The dialogue beyond the grave between my two Marxists reproduces this opposition. Appearances to the contrary notwithstanding, however, it is not obvious that the political leader is more faithful to the Marxist tradition, as embodied in the founding fathers, than the marginalised poet and communist. Let us examine this more closely.

2. The founding fathers: Marx and Engels

The harvest is sparse, but not non-existent: a few digressions on language by Marx, mainly in the early works; a rather more assertive discussion in *The German Ideology*; the pamphlet by Engels referred to above, which is somewhat disappointing; a marginal note by Lenin in his *Philosophical Notebooks* – 'the history of thought = the history of language??' – enclosed in a square surrounded by a circle.[25] Nothing particularly striking, except perhaps for Marx's early texts. The most famous and most precise text is a passage from *Dialectics of Nature*, where the elderly Engels is gripped by dogmatism and offers us the Marxist myth of the origin of language in labour:

> Much more important is the direct, demonstrable influence of the development of the hand on the rest of the organism. It has already been noted that our simian ancestors were gregarious; it is obviously impossible to seek the derivation of man, the most social of all animals, from non-gregarious immediate ancestors. Mastery over nature began with the development of the hand, with labour, and widened man's horizon at every new advance. He was continually discovering new, hitherto unknown properties in natural objects. On the other hand, the development of labour necessarily helped to bring the members of society closer together by increasing cases of mutual support and joint activity, and by making clear the advantage of this joint activity to each individual. In short, men in the making arrived at the point where *they had something to say* to each other. Necessity created the organ; the undeveloped larynx of the ape was slowly but surely transformed by modulation to produce constantly more developed modulation, and the organs of the mouth gradually learned to pronounce one articulate sound after another.
>
> Comparison with animals proves that this explanation of the origin of language from and in the process of labour is the only correct one.[26]

By now, we are familiar with this language, which combines scientistic dogmatism ('this explanation . . . is the only correct one') and unbridled imagination, and which does not hesitate to lapse into cliché ('necessity created the organ'): it is the language of the spontaneous philosophy of the scientist.

---

[25] Lenin 1961, p. 89.
[26] Engels 1976, pp. 172–3.

It is clear that scientific assertion is the language in which the most mythical of myths comes to be formulated. The paragraph that follows is touching and indicates that the old Engels shared the love of domestic animals for which the natives of his adopted country are renowned: he refers to the dogs and cats who ended up realising through their contact with human beings that they would very much like to talk, but are prevented from so doing by their undeveloped vocal organs. He also evokes the parrot, as skilful when it comes to insults as a Berlin vegetable seller.

What we have here is a myth of the origins of language. But it is, ultimately, more credible than Chomsky's, in that it does not require any transcendence (the evolutionary leap needed to explain Chomskyan innatism bears an amazing resemblance to a creation); or Habermas's, in that it does not lead denying a fair proportion of linguistic phenomena and does not rest upon a specious distinction between hominids, who work but do not speak, and human beings, who do both. Among theories of the origin of language (the 'bow-wow' theory, which has language engendered by imitation of animal cries; or the 'ding-dong' theory, which attributes a musical origin to language), Engels's so-called 'yo-he-ho!' theory ('heave ho!' in English), is not the most fantastic. Nevertheless, we would hope to find something other than myth in the founding fathers.

Looking through Marx's early texts, we come across a series of notes or digressions in the course of an argument, where language is summoned either as a privileged example or as a subject. A series of theses emerges, which recur even if they are not systemically (and not always explicitly) formulated. I shall suggest some of them; and they will not surprise us. The first concerns the *social* – i.e. non-individual – nature of language. As one might expect, Marx does not engage in methodological individualism. The following passage is typical:

> But even if I am active in the field of science, etc. – an activity which I am seldom able to perform in direct association with other men – I am still *socially* active because I am active as a *man*. It is not only the material of my activity – including even the language in which the thinker is active – which I receive as a social product. My *own* existence *is* social activity. Therefore what I create from myself I create for society, conscious of myself as a social being.[27]

---

[27] Marx 1975, p. 351.

The second thesis concerns the *material* nature of language:

> Man's first object – man – is nature, sense perception; and the particular
> sensuous human powers, since they can find their objective realization only
> in *natural* objects, can find self-knowledge only in the science of nature in
> general. The element of thought itself, the element of the vital expression
> of thought – *language* – is sensuous nature. The *social* reality of nature and
> *human* natural science or the *natural science of man* are identical expressions.[28]

These two passages are still formulated in the language of the young Marx –
the language of an abstract, grandiloquent humanism. That these theses
survived when Marx became Marxist emerges from the following passage,
which is drawn from the *Grundrisse*, in a chapter of the 'Principles of a Critique
of Political Economy' devoted to precapitalist forms of production and the
types of property they involve:

> As regards the individual, it is clear e.g. that he relates even to language
> itself *as his own* only as the natural member of a human community. Language
> as the product of an individual is an impossibility. But the same holds for
> property.
>
> Language itself is the product of a community, just as it is in another
> respect itself the presence ... of the community, a presence which goes
> without saying.[29]

A note clarifies this passage: 'The abstraction of a community, in which the
members have nothing in common but language etc., and barely that much,
is obviously the product of much later historical conditions.'[30] Language is
therefore described as a form of *praxis* – that is, as a social phenomenon (here,
we encounter the Marxian version of Wittgenstein's argument for the
impossibility of a private language), finding its materiality in social relations,
which are material relations, and in the institutions to which they give rise
(the comparison with property is illuminating). It is also, inextricably, a
historical phenomenon, in as much as it is the mode of expression of a
community that is not a simple community of speakers defined by its
competence in an abstract system, but a national, historical community of
which it is simultaneously the 'mode of expression' and the 'presence': this

---

[28] Marx 1975, pp. 355–6.
[29] Marx 1973, p. 490.
[30] Ibid.

double determination precludes any conception of language as an instrument of communication, in the service of an already constituted community. We must conceive of language as constituting the community (the speaker is spoken by her language and her *subjective* existence is a product of this language, through interpellation) and constituted by it, in that it sediments its history and expresses it.

We must nevertheless acknowledge that the mature Marx is only rarely concerned with questions of language – a subject that is evidently too philosophical and too fuzzy to retain the attention of the scientific economist. The main sites of Marx's thinking about language are therefore to be found in the 1844 *Manuscripts* and *The German Ideology*. I propose two illustrations.

In the *Manuscripts*, we find the following text, devoted to 'mutual theft' drawn from Marx's reading notes on James Mill and his theory of property:

> The only comprehensible language we have is the language our possessions use together. We would not understand a human language and it would remain ineffectual. From the one side, such a language would be felt to be begging, imploring and hence *humiliating*. It could be used only with feelings of shame or debasement. From the other side, it would be received as *impertinence* or *insanity* and so rejected. We are so estranged from our human essence that the direct language of man strikes us as an *offence against the dignity of man*, whereas the estranged language of objective values appears as the justified, self-confidence and self-acknowledged dignity of man incarnate.[31]

This text is astonishing: Marx has an inexhaustible capacity to surprise his followers and to rouse them from their dogmatic slumber. For two inversions of the utmost importance are effected here. The first is that the language we use every day is not directed to communicating our thoughts to others, for those thoughts, irredeemably contaminated by our emotions, can only provoke negative reactions in others: the nature of human language is to be agonistic; we do not speak in order to co-operate by means of a peaceful exchange of information, but in order to fight, to dominate the opponent, to claim a place in the field, which is evidently a battlefield. Rather than a co-operative ethics of discussion, we have here a primitive situation in which speakers represent

---

[31] Marx 1975, pp. 276–7.

a threat to one another. This situation is due to a phenomenon of alienation ('We are so estranged from our human essence . . .'), of which everyday language is the product and the expression: the only language that could serve as a social bond is the alienated language of objects, of 'material values'. Alternatively put, we become speakers, and hence subjects, only in so far we accept to alienate ourselves in a language of objects, which the language-system – an external entity that imposes its constraints of meaning on us – embodies. There is a second inversion here: the interiority of human beings – subjective consciousness – is the product of an externality, the alienated language that interpellates human subjects to their places. Obviously, I am translating this old text into a subsequent language, that of a theory of ideology (whose Althusserian origin will not have escaped readers). But, for me, this text is of the utmost importance for what appears in it by way of anticipation: the possibility of radical break with what I have called the dominant philosophy of language.

The second illustration is drawn from *The German Ideology*. The texts are well known and have often been commented on. In them language is described as 'the immediate actuality of thought',[32] 'practical, real consciousness':

> The 'mind' is from the outset afflicted with the curse of being 'burdened' with matter, which here makes its appearance in the form of agitated layers of air, sounds, in short, of language. Language is as old as consciousness, language *is* practical, real consciousness that exists for other men as well, and only therefore does it also exist for me; language, like consciousness, only arises from the need, the necessity, of intercourse with other men. Where there exists a relationship, it exists for me: the animal does not '*relate*' itself to anything, it does not '*relate*' itself at all. For the animal its relation to others does not exist as a relation. Consciousness is, therefore, from the very beginning a social product, and remains so as long as men exist at all.[33]

In this famous passage, we find the totality of what now feature as Marx's 'theses' on language: the stress on the materiality of language; the stress on language's character as a social practice (the text seems to be unjust on the subject of my cat, with whom I have the most affectionate relations and who,

---

[32] Marx and Engels 1976, p. 446.
[33] Marx and Engels 1976, pp. 43–4.

as we have seen with Engels, is not bereft of speech: but Marx is in the process of defining the concept of 'social relation'); and the inversion that makes subjectivity an effect of social objectivity. The speaker is interpellated by the linguistic relation she has with others; she does not use an instrument, does not employ a faculty. The consequence of this position is an open anti-intentionalism: language is not the translation and transmission of a thought that pre-exists it (what some English linguists today call the myth of 'telementation'[34] is rejected in advance).

I shall end with a short text, which occurs a few pages before the one quoted above. This passage is equally celebrated, for it defines ideology as a *camera obscura*. Here, I am interested in the beginning of the paragraph and the curious expression: 'The production of ideas, of conceptions, of consciousness, is at first directly interwoven with the material activity and the material intercourse of men – the language of real life.'[35] I wonder whether the expression 'the language of real life' is a simple metaphor, since 'real life' is no more liable to possess its language than flowers. And I would like to think that Marx's formula goes further. At first sight, this text repeats the materialist thesis that ideas have a material origin, in 'real life' understood as a material activity – i.e. labour and production – and material relations – i.e. social relations: language is the product of social relations which it helps to fix and develop. But why characterise this real life as 'language' or attribute a 'language' to it? Because the materialist thesis is, in fact, two-fold: it affirms not only that ideas have a material *origin*, but also that they have a material *existence*. And the material existence of ideas precisely takes the form of language and of the institutions constructed around it. Here, language plays a similar role to the imagination in Kant, which, as is well known, serves as an intermediary, by means of its schemata, between intuition and understanding: language serves as an intermediary between real life and the ideas that derive from it. Because it has a material aspect, because it has a 'sensory nature', language does not merely represent or express material existence (i.e. is not merely a tool of reference), but participates in this material existence. But it is also what enables human society to achieve self-consciousness, to abstract from relations with nature and social relations, and

---

[34] See Harris 1998.
[35] Marx and Engels 1976, p. 36.

to conceptualise them in the form of ideas which are only the immaterial, abstract aspect of language.

This is where a concept that Marx and Engels had still not formulated at the time of *The German Ideology* – fetishism – comes in. Readers will remember the analysis of fetishism offered in the chapter of *Capital* devoted to the commodity: 'the definite social relation between men themselves . . . assumes . . . for them the fantastic form of a relation between things'.[36] This false concretisation is, in fact, a second-degree abstraction – i.e. a bad abstraction. By naming them, language abstracts social relations from the concrete reality of the phenomena that constitute them – linguists call this an ontological metaphor[37] – and fetishism abstracts from these conceptualised relations a false concrete reality, which takes the form of a second degree of ontological metaphor. This is how transcendence is generated, for, at the top of this conceptual pyramid, we will find the grand abstraction: God. As *commodity* fetishism, fetishism is associated with the capitalist mode of production. But it is not unconnected with language, as is indicated by the continuation of the text I have just quoted, which is one of the few passages in *Capital* where reference is made to language:

> The private producer's brain reflects this twofold social character of his labour only in the forms which appear in practical intercourse, in the exchange of products. . . . Men do not therefore bring the products of their labour into relation with each other as values because they see these objects merely as the material integuments of homogeneous human labour. The reverse is true: by equating their different products to each other in exchange as values, they equate their different kinds of labour as human labour. They do this without being aware of it. Value, therefore, does not have its description branded on its forehead; it rather transforms every product of labour into a social hieroglyphic. Later on, men try to decipher the hieroglyphic, to get behind the secret of their own social product: for the characteristic which objects of utility have of being values is as much men's social product as is their language.[38]

---

[36] Marx 1976, p. 165.
[37] See Lakoff and Johnson 1980.
[38] Marx 1976, pp. 166–7.

Language features twice in this text. In its own right, first of all, as a term of comparison: like value, it is a 'social product', created by productive activity and social relations. But it also figures, in duly encrypted form, in the shape of a 'hieroglyph', which is the effect that value has on each product and which, as it were, transforms the product into a text that needs to be deciphered – i.e. interpreted. Here, language is the channel through which fetishism produces its effect. Language therefore has a dual character: it is the means of abstraction that makes it possible to think real life and become conscious of it (it is this very consciousness: the consciousness of social relations); and it is also what freezes and veils this same consciousness, in the form of the bad abstraction of fetishism. This dual character enables us to understand why we spontaneously tend to conceive interlocution in terms of exchange and words in terms of coins; and why the dominant philosophy of language makes this 'structural metaphor' (as Lakoff and Johnson call it) its basic thesis.

On this point we might reread the work of Sohn-Rethel,[39] for whom language is generated out of labour in common and not exchange, which presupposes private property and what he calls its 'practical solipsism': in fact, exchange has no need of articulated language, for an indicative gesture will suffice and a minimal semantics containing signs for 'yes' and 'no' and indications of quantity. Commodity exchange is not a co-operative exchange of information conducive to an ethics of discussion: it is based upon exclusion (from property: I seek to acquire what I am deprived of) and separation (of the agents of exchange, with their divergent interests), which are not apt to produce a linguistic community.

We can, therefore, draw from the fragments of the founding fathers of Marxism both a myth of origin of language that is more satisfying than its competitors and an anticipatory inversion of the dominant philosophy of language, which insists on the social and material nature of language, and poses the question of the relations between abstraction and fetishism. For fragmentary notations, that is not bad.

---

[39] See Sohn-Rethel 1978.

3. Lenin

Lenin's contribution to thinking about language is not limited to the marginal note that we have already cited. In truth, it has a paradoxical character. In July 1917, declared an outlaw by the provisional government and having taken refuge in the area around Lake Razliv, Lenin took the time at a moment of acute political crisis to write a text on the nature and selection of slogans.[40] Obviously, it does not set out a general theory of slogans, but rather consists in a concrete analysis of the political conjuncture, from the standpoint of formulating correct slogans. But it seems to me that this short text is fundamental for the formulation of a Marxist philosophy of language.

The principal thesis defended by Lenin is that slogans are, to put it anachronistically, performatives, that they exercise power. There is nothing surprising about this: it is what slogans are for – a watchword, a slogan, was originally a war cry. Lenin's original contribution is situated in the analysis of this 'power', which has nothing to do with the vague notion of force – 'illocutionary force' – among Anglo-American pragmatists (where it simply has a role in classifying speech acts). The text indicates three aspects of the power exercised by a good slogan. (i) It serves to *identify* the moment of the conjuncture – in the particular case to hand, this means: on 4 July 1917, the first, virtually peaceful phase of the revolution is over and the slogan that encapsulated it – 'All power to the soviets!' – is outmoded. (ii) Consequently, a correct slogan *names the political task* corresponding to the moment of the conjuncture: the task of this moment is to prepare for the 'decisive battle' – that is, the overthrow by force of a government that has become counter-revolutionary. A correct slogan makes its possible to name the *decisive* moment. (iii) In as much as it does this, a correct slogan exercises a power because it *condenses* and *embodies* the concrete analysis of the concrete situation. The implicit Leninist slogan here is: 'without correct slogans, no successful revolution'.

The central place accorded to a concrete power has consequences for what a Marxist philosophy of language should be. Naturally, Lenin's text does not explicitly set them out, but gives them to be understood. I shall suggest five. (i) We have here a concept of *meaning* (of an utterance) that is bound up with

---

[40] See Lenin 1964.

the conjuncture in which the utterance is produced: the meaning is the result of a *power relationship*: not of a co-operative language game, but of a political struggle (which has no hard and fast rules, but rather rules that are in a state of constant variation, which need to be reformulated with each variation of the conjuncture). (ii) As a result, an utterance is not the description of a state of affairs within a conjuncture, but an *intervention* in the conjuncture: it reflects, but also helps to alter, the balance of forces that gives it its meaning. We now understand the importance of slogans or order-words: they – and not descriptive or constative utterances – are the primary utterances on which discourses are constructed. (iii) A good slogan is a *correct* slogan, one which corresponds to the conjuncture in that it is adapted or relevant to it There is a reflexive circularity between the slogan which names the moment of the conjuncture and the conjuncture that allows it to make sense. The conjunctural character of meaning is the content of the concept of correctness (an appropriate slogan is not true but correct), whose utilisation by Althusser we have noted. (iv) The word 'truth' is nevertheless used by Lenin: one 'tells the truth' to the people. The people must know who really holds state power in the conjuncture and that means the representatives of which class or class fraction. But this 'truth' is strictly dependent on the correctness of slogans; it is an effect, if not an affect, of this correctness. To speak like the theoreticians of speech acts, illocutionary correctness exercises a perlocutionary truth effect. It is this hierarchical combination of correctness and truth that guarantees the effectiveness of the meaning that is brought out in the conjuncture. (v) Finally, the concept of discourse outlined here is *political* in kind: a discourse is an intervention. Lenin's text denounces the illusions of petty-bourgeois morality – the blurring of the 'essence of the situation', which is political, by moral questions. The problem is not to be kind to the Mensheviks and Socialist Revolutionaries, to bring them to see the errors of their ways and reform themselves, but to say to the masses that they have betrayed the revolution. And this opposition between politics and morality is an opposition between the concrete and the abstract. Hence another Leninist principle: in revolutionary periods, the main danger facing the revolution is to prefer the abstract to the concrete.

My rapid reading of this text, which provides me with the elements of a Marxist philosophy of language, is not situated in a vacuum. It was preceded by two readings, the first of which is famous, while the second has been completely forgotten.

As is well known, Deleuze and Guattari read Lenin on slogans in one of the chapters of *A Thousand Plateaus*.[41] They are fascinated by the date of 4 July 1917, turning-point in the revolution. Prior to this date, a peaceful outcome was possible and the slogan 'All power to the soviets!' was correct; thereafter, only the violent overthrow of the Provisional Government could save the revolution and the slogan had to be revised. In this they see an 'incorporeal transformation', an effect of language, but a language endowed with a singular performative power, which operates this turn. And their analysis goes much further: the power of the slogan is not only performative, it is constitutive of the class that it summons into existence. The First International's stroke of genius had been to extract a class from the masses by means of the slogan, 'Workers of the world unite!'. Similarly, Lenin's slogan extracts a vanguard, a Party, from the totality of the proletariat. The slogan anticipates the political body that it organises. And Deleuze and Guattari suggest that this analysis concerns not only political language, but language in general, in that it is always shot through with politics. The 'regime of signs' or 'semiotic machine' that they describe is a mixture of utterances (in this instance, order-words), presuppositions (the actions that follow from order-words), and incorporeal transformations (effected by the performative power, the power of nomination, of order-words). These are the internal variables of the collective assemblage of enunciation of which the order-word forms an essential part.

The context of their reading of Lenin is the critique of the dominant linguistics and its postulates in the fourth plateau of *A Thousand Plateaus* and, in particular, of the first of these postulates, according to which language is informative and communicative. This critique produces a series of concepts (force, machine, minority, style, stammering), which I consider to furnish the outline of a different philosophy of language, close to Marxism. We may therefore take the reference to Lenin as a symptom (I shall return to this point).

The second reading of Lenin's text, today totally forgotten, is to be found in numbers 9–10 of an old publication, whose title at best causes a nostalgic frisson, *Cahiers marxistes-léninistes*. The text, which takes up the whole of the issue, is entitled 'Vive le léninisme!'.[42] It is unsigned, but rumour at the time attributed it to Althusser. We are evidently dealing with some lecture notes. Whether they are from the hand of the master or dutifully collected by a

---

[41] See Deleuze and Guattari 1988, p. 83.
[42] See *Cahiers marxistes-léninistes* 1966.

follower, like Saussure's *Course*, is of little importance: 'Althusser' is here the name of a collective assemblage of enunciation. The journal was the organ of the Communist Students Union society at the École normale supérieure, which shortly afterwards gave rise to the Maoist sect called the UJC (M-L). The text therefore pertains to a period prior to the rupture between Althusser (who always refused to leave the French Communist Party) and his Maoist followers. It reflects the climate of the time in that the object of analysis is what the text calls Leninist 'sciences'.

Althusser identifies the heart of Leninist science in the concept of conjuncture: the sole objective of Lenin's thinking is the correct description of the conjuncture, its class determinations, the balance of forces operative in it, and the precise moment in which the analyst finds himself. The concept is only another name for the dialectic of general scientific principles and the analysis of concrete situations, which is Lenin's specific contribution to Marxist theory. Hence the structure of the three 'sciences' of Leninism.

First of all, there is the main science – the science of concrete analysis, which proceeds in five stages: (i) description of the elements of the conjuncture, furnished by class analysis; (ii) determination of the limits of the conjuncture, of what dictates its violent transformation; (iii) acknowledgement of the impossibility of certain combinations of these elements (some alliances are unnatural, which *a contrario* establishes the possibility of other alliances); (iv) determination of the variations of the conjuncture, which supplies a guide to political action; and (v) consideration of the constraints imposed by the strategic perspective of the proletariat. Analysis of the conjuncture therefore operates a dual constraint: that of the limits of the conjuncture itself and that which a strategic perspective imposes on it.

The principal science is insufficient: it is complemented by two secondary sciences, which govern its application to political practice: the science of slogans (or, rather, of their articulated system through which the conjuncture is named) and the science of political leadership (or how to bring the masses to understand that the slogans are correct). Leninist science is therefore an articulated hierarchy of disciplines or fields, which enable the revolutionary successfully to implement the party programme according to its three levels: the general level of the theory of revolution (i.e. the principles on which the communist programme is based: the theory of modes of production, the laws of tendency of capitalist development, stage of development of society); the level of the concrete analysis of the social formation; and the level of the tactical and strategic analysis that determines the tasks of revolutionaries on a day-to-day basis. Lenin's contribution to Marxism consists in displacing the centre of the structure from the first level – that of the general theory (the Marxian or Menshevik theory of the strongest link) – to the dialectical relationship between the second and third levels – that of the concrete analysis of the social formation and the determination of the tasks tabled by the moment of the conjuncture. In other words, he replaces the Marxian theory of the strongest link by that of the weakest link and of the complexity of the structure of the social formation, implying that the road leading to revolution is not the Nevsky Prospekt.

The scientistic language of Althusser's reading has passed out of fashion or conjuncture: to treat Lenin as a scientist, even as a scientist of politics, hardly helps. And, compared with Deleuze and Guattari's reading, we note that the issue of language has passed to a secondary level – the 'secondary science' of slogans. First comes the science of concrete analysis and next that of its adaptation to political practice; first comes the theory of the conjuncture and of the balance of forces between the classes in struggle, and then its translation into a series of correct slogans. The production of the class by means of the slogan that anticipates its constitution, which summons it into being, has disappeared; and language is characterised by the representation of a situation prior to discourse and not by the performative character of the intervention. Nevertheless, I believe that the three levels on which theory and practice are articulated provides us with the framework for a Marxist philosophy of language.

Let us metaphorically take the three levels of the communist programme for the levels of a research programme into the functioning of language, which I scarcely dare characterise as scientific.

We start from the level of the general theory, that of principles. At this level, in order to be faithful to Lenin, we need to ask what a *materialist* philosophy of language might be: is not the task of the Marxist philosopher – a task eminently performed by Lenin himself – to intervene in the philosophical struggle to defend materialism? As we have seen, such a materialism cannot be Chomskyan naturalism. But Lenin precisely enables us to conceive a form of materialism that is not a physical reductionism or a naturalism: the materialism of *power relations*, by which the vague concepts of illocutionary force and the performative character of language assume a new meaning. We are dealing with a power that is collectively exercised, in political action, in the establishment of power relations. Language is material not only in the sense that it exercises a material power on bodies (this might be called the Castafiore principle, after the character in *Tintin*), but because it has something of the nature of the materiality of institutions. There exists a causal chain, which I propose to call the Althusserian chain of interpellation, which runs from institutions to rituals, from rituals to practices, from practices to linguistic acts: each link has its own materiality and has something of the materiality of the whole chain. We understand why, for Deleuze and Guattari, the basic utterance is not a judgement, which contains and transmits a proposition, but an order-word, which intervenes in the conjuncture. Lenin is indeed the source of a different philosophy of language – an agonistic, as opposed to an irenic or co-operative, one: neither Habermas nor Chomsky.

The second level of the communist programme is the concrete analysis of social formations. In the field of language, this involves the analysis of natural languages in as much as they are national languages. Here, again, we encounter Chomsky and his negation of the pertinent existence of national languages: give or take a few parameters, and we pass from German to English; the universal grammar remains the same. As against this denial of history, what Lenin enables us to conceive is the importance of natural-national languages as objects of linguistics. If language is structured by power relations, *as* power relations, the site of those relations is a national language; and the concepts of major language (Deleuze and Guattari), glottophagy (Calvet), and external linguistics (Bourdieu) become essential.

The third level of the communist programme is the level of strategic and tactical analysis. This is the level that supplies the analyses which directly guide day-to-day political action. If, as Althusser maintains, Lenin puts Marx back on his feet by privileging the second and third levels of the communist programme (concrete analysis of the social formation and political analysis in terms of strategy and tactics), at the expense of the first (the general principles of the theory), it follows that there is no possible analysis of the moment of the conjuncture which is sufficiently stable, embodying verifiable predictions and derived from general principles, to be characterised as *true*. What we are dealing with is a series of political proposals, embodied in *correct* slogans – in other words, an interpretation. Lenin is the master of the correct interpretation of the text of the situation: this interpretation is correct because it is adequate to the moment of the conjuncture that it succeeds in naming in one or more slogans – an essentially fleeting moment. The essence of a concrete analysis of a concrete situation consists in deciding that yesterday's slogan is no longer valid today. This does not mean, since it appears that the main political task of the moment is to produce an interpretation, that there are as many interpretations as there are interpreters; or that there is a choice to be had between several, equally correct interpretations. We are not in the aesthetic domain and each moment demands its correct analysis. This must be imposed in political struggle, embodied in a slogan, in order to generate an effective intervention which will produce truth-effects in the masses. In matters of interpretation, what is correct logically and chronologically precedes what is true. This insistence on the correctness of the naming of the moment of the conjuncture by the slogan is what distinguishes good old 'propaganda', in the Leninist sense of the term, from the 'political communication' that the imperialists are so fond of, which aims to sell a policy in the same way that an advertising slogan sells a product. The pathetic failure of the advertising campaigns designed to restore America's image among the Muslim masses in the run-up to the imperialist war in Iraq is not attributable to the backwardness of those masses, but to the fact that a 'branding strategy' is incapable of producing a correct slogan in the conjuncture, because it does not see its task as a political and historical analysis. It therefore ignores everything that might produce a truth effect among these masses – to be specific, analysis of American policy in the Middle East and its complex history. Here, we reach the limits of the form of linguistic politics which Anglo-Americans call 'spin': the facts, Lenin used to say, are stubborn and no advertising slogan can make the American intervention in Iraq anything other than an imperialist aggression. This is why the Americans fairly rapidly abandoned their ambitions in the sphere of public relations and let the tanks do the talking.

From all this we can draw two conclusions for constructing a Marxist philosophy of language. The first is that the meaning of an utterance is given in its interpretation – that is, in the struggle required to impose this interpretation, in the power relationship that it establishes. The second is that we need a concept of *linguistic conjuncture* which combines the state of the encyclopaedia (the compendium of knowledge and beliefs of the community of speakers); the state of the language (sedimentation of the history of the community of speakers: taken together, the language and the encyclopaedia form what Gramsci calls a 'conception of the world'); and the potentialities of interpellation and counter-interpellation that exist in the situation. An interpretation is an intervention in the linguistic conjuncture: it is constrained by it and transforms it, so that the ultimate meaning of the utterance is a function of the interpretation that it embodies in the form of an order-word and its intervention in the conjuncture which it transforms.

It seems clear that on the banks of Lake Razliv, a political leader who had many other things to do with his time laid the bases for a philosophy of language which avoids both Chomskyan naturalism and Habermasian irenism: this is because the question of language, as the class enemy has always known (but with varying degrees of success, as we have just seen), is a political issue of the first importance.

Obviously, the tradition does not stop there. Contrary to what its detractors would like to think, Marxism is a living tradition and the founding fathers have had some successors.

Chapter Five
Continuations

We have arrived at the point where the tradition becomes a diaspora. Henceforth, Marxism is declined in the plural and the vicissitudes of history mean that we must refer to post-Marxism as much as to Marxism. This involves the whole range of topics covered by the Marxist tradition, but is particularly glaring in the case of language on account of Stalin's suffocation of debate. That is why, rather than offering a catalogue of insights into language by authors identified with Marxism (a list has been suggested in the previous chapter and I am bound to have forgotten some names), I am going to focus my efforts on two conceptualisations of language, one of which – Voloshinov's – explicitly identified itself as Marxist, while the other – Deleuze and Guattari's – has a complicated relationship with Marxism which for the most part remains implicit.

1. Voloshinov

Marxism and the Philosophy of Language, the only work that explicitly seeks to elaborate a Marxist philosophy of language, has a complicated history. The text was published in French in 1977 under the name of Bakhtin, in a collection directed by Bourdieu.[1]

---

[1] See Bakhtin 1977.

Published in the USSR in 1930 under the name of Voloshinov, it has been known in the West since 1973 in an English translation that likewise attributed it to Voloshinov.[2] The origin of the text is therefore a matter of controversy. It is universally agreed that it emerged from the work of what is called the 'Bakhtin circle'. At the time of its publication by Bourdieu, various testimonies affirmed that it was the work of Bakhtin, who had had it published under the name of one of his followers (which he is also thought to have done with Medvedev's book),[3] for reasons that are not altogether clear. More recent research indicates that Voloshinov is not simply a borrowed name, that he had written a thesis in which the book's main themes are already present,[4] and that there is therefore no reason to deprive him of his work in favour of his more famous friend. Not having access to the primary sources, I cannot form a definite opinion on the subject. I use the name 'Voloshinov' to indicate a collective assemblage of enunciation: the Marxist dimension of the works of the Bakhtin circle. For, as his title claims, Voloshinov's work does indeed contain the outline of an explicitly Marxist philosophy of language. And this Marxist dimension is not limited to a single work: various of Voloshinov's essays should be added to it, as well as his book *Freudianism*.[5]

Readers will recall the founding concepts of structural linguistics as set out by Milner in the form of axioms:[6] the arbitrariness of the sign, the sign as defined by Saussure, the angelic speaker, and the schema of communication – or the principles of immanence, calculation (writing), and exchange. Voloshinov too has his axioms or his inaugural concepts. They are not the same, but they likewise number four.

The first is the concept of *sign*. But this is not the Saussurian sign, which, for Voloshinov, is not a sign but a signal. In effect, the signal is stable, arbitrary, and lends itself to calculation. The sign, of which natural languages are composed, is very different: it is the site of a process of signification – a term that is to be understood, etymologically, as an active production and not merely a passive reflection; it emerges in the course of social interaction; it

---

[2] See Voloshinov 1973.
[3] See Medvedev 1978.
[4] See Brandist 2002.
[5] See Shukman 1983 and Voloshinov 1976.
[6] See Chapter 2.

embodies the social *agon*, for words are traces of the ideological struggles that have been conducted by them and for them; it is therefore 'multi-accentuated', for the sign, which does not exist prior to social interaction, always bears the trace of the past discourses in which it was inserted; and finally, it does not reflect the world of referents, but refracts it – meaning that it intervenes in the situation in which it emerges and of which it is one of the elements, and does not simply represent it. In short, the sign according to Voloshinov is an element not of an abstract system, but of a social practice. We can see how it differs from Saussure's sign.

The second concept is *ideology*. This term is to be understood in the sense it possessed in Russian at the time. *Ideologiya* referred not to a system of ideas, but to a human socio-cultural activity, construed in a very broad sense: for Voloshinov, the arts, sciences, philosophy form part of the domain of ideology. And ideology is what is conveyed by the linguistic sign: it does not exist outside of its expression in the material signs of language. We can see how this differs from the usual concept, including in its Marxist forms: an ideology is not a set of ideas, not the mark of an illusion, or even of a necessary illusion – i.e. an allusion. And we can also see what the concept offers: the idea that language and ideology are inseparable, because, in Voloshinov, ideology is signification in as much as it is collective, or rather social: it is a set not of ideas but of signs, which form the content of consciousness.

The third concept is *word*. This term, more or less abandoned by structural linguistics on account of its vagueness (the concepts of 'morpheme' or 'moneme' constructed by science are preferred) occupies a central place in Voloshinov. For him, the word is the unit of analysis of discourse, it is the sign in that it is a component part of a process of signification, in that it takes concrete shape in social practice, in so far as it is the bearer of an ideological content: it is the embodied, practical sign. Making the word, rather the sign, the basic unit of discourse has at least one advantage: it underscores the crucial importance of semantics in the analysis of language. And it will be recalled that a striking feature of structuralist linguistics, and even of the original Chomsky, is the exclusion of semantics from the field of the science of language, as too vague to be formalised satisfactorily (only with the linguistics of enunciation was semantics restored to its rightful place). Similarly, making the word, rather than the sentence, the basic unit of linguistic analysis underlines the fact that pragmatics cannot be excluded from the field of science (words assume their meaning in the use made of them; they carry with them a history; they have an ideological and political content). The essential task of the study of language is not, as the dominant linguistic tradition from Chomsky to enunciation analysts would have it, to study grammatical structures or grammatical markers, but to account for the life of language – that is, language as a human practice. We shall, therefore, find in Voloshinov a critique of formalism in linguistics. It will be noted that, according to Voloshinov, the word possesses a set of characteristics which make it a collective entity, not an individual one. Words do no possess the meaning I wish to impart to them; even if I have the impression of inventing them, they are always-already collective; they are endowed with 'semiotic purity' (a word is an independent element, separable from the discourse into which it is inserted); words are 'ideologically neutral' (in the sense that more than one content can lay hold of them in the course of ideological struggles); they are involved in the everyday use of language (here, we once again encounter the metaphor of the coin, but this means that a word has a history, that it is engaged in the history of its speakers); they can be internalised (and we shall soon importance that internal discourse has in Voloshinov's thinking). Finally, words are necessarily present in every form of consciousness, and in any conscious activity, for the psyche is composed of words. We can draw the conclusion that the study of ideology is the same thing as the study of words.

The fourth concept is *consciousness*. In my view, this is Voloshinov's most interesting contribution: in him we find not only a critique of Saussure, but also a critique of Freud (made explicit in his book on Freudianism). He stresses the importance of conscious practice and takes seriously Marx and Engels's formula in *The German Ideology* according to which 'language is practical consciousness'. Consciousness is thus defined as the effect of social practice: it does not exist outside of its objectification in gestures, cries, words. But it is a structured practice – structured by the word as a social entity. In other words, consciousness is always-already interlocution. Here, we are definitely in the ambiance of the Bakhtin circle, for we detect an echo of the Bakhtinian concepts of dialogism and polyphony. What is derived from them is a philosophical inversion of the utmost importance: ideology is not the product of consciousness (it cannot therefore be a set of 'ideas'), because consciousness is the product of ideology. Consciousness is ideology made concrete and individual. Whence three characteristics of consciousness, which render the concept of consciousness thus defined, if not a complete philosophical novelty, then at least highly original: (i) consciousness is not interiority but the internalisation of an exteriority; (ii) consciousness is not irreducible individuality but an in-between, an effect of the sociality of interlocution; (iii) psychic individuation cannot therefore simply be the result of an interpellation (the Althusserian term is anachronistic here, but the idea that consciousness derives from a social role, just as, in Mauss, the person is derived from a mask – *persona* – is already unquestionably present in Voloshinov).[7]

From these four founding concepts, Voloshinov draws three methodological rules for studying language. The first enjoins us to never sever ideology from the material reality of signs. Ideology is not abstract and ethereal; there is no transcendent realm of ideas: it is always embodied – in gestures, intonations, expressions. The second recommends that we never sever the sign from the concrete forms of social communication – hence both the central importance of a form of pragmatics and the rejection of any form of methodological individualism. The speaker is always-already collective. The third encourages us not to sever social communication from its base in the material infrastructure. External linguistics takes priority; and language is to be analysed as social and historical practice. The issue is not who speaks, and if she clearly expresses what she means to say; it is to determine the place in the overall social structure from which a voice – *this* voice – is raised.

This methodological starting-point has at least three significant consequences, expressed by three original concepts, to which I have already alluded in passing. The first is the concept of the *multi-accentuation* of the sign. We recall the test that Stanislavsky imposed on trainee actors: pronounce a simple word – e.g. the exclamation 'Good!' – in sixty different ways, in order to give the utterance thus produced sixty different meanings. Voloshinov makes this exercise not a curiosity or an exception, but the starting-point of analysis. Every sign is multi-accentuated not only because it contains a multiplicity of possible meanings, realised by the use of the sign in concrete interlocution, but in that it is history-laden, in that it sediments the meanings which these realisations have imparted to it. To emit a linguistic sign is to take one's place in a chain of voices, which constrain – albeit never completely – the meaning

---

[7] See Mauss 1990.

that it can take on in my utterance. Things are clear when it is a question of ideologically charged signs; and everyone knows that the word 'freedom' does not have the same meaning in Eluard's poem and Berlusconi's mouth. But everyone also knows that each occurrence of this word summons up its whole history, even if only to deny it. Hence the importance in the Marxist tradition of thinking about language of the outline of a historical semantics proposed by Raymond Williams in *Keywords*.[8]

The second concept is *refraction* – the refraction of social being in language. The term is obviously intended to avoid and replace the traditional Marxist concept of 'reflection' (notoriously, this concept has poisoned Marxist aesthetics and its concept of realism). For Voloshinov, language does not 'reflect' social being; it 'refracts' it. The obvious difference between the two terms is that refraction implies distortion, meaning that language cannot be a mere representation of a reality external to it. We must therefore think outside of any separation between language and the world. And, manifestly, if there is no divide, language can scarcely be an instrument at everyone's disposal, given that it is caught up in the social interaction – i.e. the class struggle – in which it intervenes. Voloshinov thus demarcates himself in advance from Stalin's good sense. Moreover, in his work there are some positive references to Marr, in which we should not simply read a declaration of allegiance to the then dominant linguistics in the Soviet Union, but a form of convergence. For Voloshinov actually does what Marr only claimed to do: he elaborates a Marxist theory of language. Refraction is not a simple image, mere representation; and the action of language is a mixture of representation and intervention: the image of the world conveyed by language is not only deformed, it is transformed and, in return, transformative. And this applies not only to slogans, but to all utterances in that, according to Deleuze and Guattari (as we shall see shortly), they are always also order-words. The innocent question 'What time is it?' clearly has the aim of obtaining information about the world and I would like the response to reflect the state of affairs accurately (if not, I risk missing my train). But it can also express an affect (if I pose the question twelve times in five minutes, my interlocutor will be justified in regarding this as a symptom); or convey an indirect request, if the slowness of my interlocutor in finishing her preparations risks making

---

[8] See Williams 1976.

us miss the train. And we can finish by observing, with Canetti,[9] that questions are never innocent: in as much as they demand a response, they are markers of power; they display the right of the speaker to pose a question and expect a response. A power relation takes shape in the most innocuous of questions, which finds its culmination in the police interlocution: 'We ask the questions here!'.

The third concept is *internal monologue*. This is a phenomenon which fascinated the ancients, but which the moderns have almost completely neglected – at least, the linguists and philosophers (as is well known, the question has greatly preoccupied writers and literary critics). The question is simple: what happens in my head when I 'speak' to myself? Is what expresses me to myself formulated in a natural language or a mental language – what the Anglo-Americans calls 'mentalese', which is only metaphorically a language? This question of the *logos endiathetos*, with its two contrasting solutions, has a long tradition in ancient and scholastic philosophy behind it.[10] Among contemporary thinkers, it has been tackled virtually only by Voloshinov, Vygotsky, George Steiner in *After Babel*,[11] and a few cognitivists who firmly opt for 'mentalese'.[12] Like Vygotsky, Voloshinov is in the other camp: for him, internal discourse is the internalisation of external discourse – that is, social public discourse. As it were, he stands the definition of *The German Ideology* back on its feet: language is practical consciousness because consciousness is internalised, subjectified, and subjectifying discourse. For what is called consciousness is nothing other than internal discourse.

On these bases, Voloshinov engages in an uncompromising critique of the dominant way of thinking about language in his time. It has two aspects. The first is what he calls *subjective idealism*. We find it in romantic philosophies of language, in German thinkers like Herder and Humboldt. But we might anachronistically bring the critique to bear on contemporary linguists of enunciation. This linguistics is characterised by a set of positions: it conceives language as *energeia* – that is, as an uninterrupted creative process, which is materialised in the discourse of each individual speaker. It therefore conceives the laws of linguistic creation as psychological laws, in that the site of linguistic

---

[9] See Canetti 1960.
[10] See Panaccio 1999.
[11] See Steiner 1976.
[12] See Fodor 1975 and 1994.

creation is the psyche of the speaking individual. It thereby makes linguistic creation an analogue of aesthetic creation. The result of this creation – language as *ergon*, product and not creative process – is an inert sediment, captured by the image of congealed lava. It is in this unhappy state that language becomes a simple instrument of communication. Thus the opposition between these two aspects of language – *energeia* and *ergon* – is conceived like the contrast between living metaphor and fixed or dead metaphor. This position with respect to language has obvious advantages. It does not ignore the most complex forms of language – encountered, above all, in literary texts – and even makes them its starting-point. It enables us to understand why language is so often conceived instrumentally and why this way of thinking soon encounters its limits. But it is also open to criticism, in that it involves a form of methodological individualism and makes the human psyche the source of linguistic creation, taking us back to romantic conceptions of the speaker as author-creator which are very dated. Finally, the Aristotelian concept of *energeia* always ends up being conceived in biological terms, the central metaphor enabling us to think language being that of the organism (in a sense, this is the converse of the computer metaphor dear to cognitivists, which is also mythical). In both cases – creationism and biologism – what disappears is language as a social and historical phenomenon. Hence the inability of this philosophy to account for the process of communication other than in terms of dereliction.

The second aspect is *abstract objectivism*, which is mainly associated with the name of Saussure (but, with a few modifications, Chomsky might be included in this current). This philosophy possesses the converse characteristics from the preceding one. It envisages language as a fixed system of linguistic forms, which are supplied, in some sense with immediate effect, to the individual consciousness of the speaker. It treats the rules of language as objective laws and its ego ideal is the positive sciences – hence the principle of immanence and the stress on internal linguistics. It has recourse to a concept of 'value' (in Saussure, the linguistic unity has no intrinsic 'meaning', but assumes a 'value' in opposition to all the other units with which it forms a system), which has nothing to do with ideological value – that is, the active creation of meaning. *Parole* is nothing but individual variation on the norm represented by *langue*, with the result that the ensemble evolves according to its own tendencies and the system consequently ignores human history – that of the community of its speakers. For Voloshinov, beyond the attempt to objectify language in order to make it an object of science (which is a way of refusing to make language an individual creation: in Saussure, at least, the object of science is a system and hence a collective object), this position has nothing but drawbacks, because the theses it defends are largely false. Language in fact is not an abstract system but a human practice, which emerges in social interaction, is transformed by it, and transforms it in turn. Accordingly, it is not possible to study language as an immanent phenomenon: it is *in* the world and *of* the world. Pragmatic maxims are to be preferred to the 'laws' of language (I am translating Voloshinov's critique into anachronistic terms here, but I do think that I am betraying it), which have the advantage of being useable and defeasible for the purposes of social interaction (during the establishment of a power relation). The 'value' of a linguistic unit is not oppositional, but evaluative: it consists in the ideological content with which social interaction invests the particular unit. Finally, there is no opposition between *parole* and *langue* (I would like to add between *langue* and *langage*), but only a process of historical action in and through language.

This critique enables Voloshinov to propose a Marxist philosophy of language in the form of positive theses. The aim is to abandon Saussure's formalism, which fetishises linguistic practice into an abstract system. We should, therefore, stop treating linguistic material as a series of dead texts in the manner of philologists (of whom Saussure is the direct inheritor) and take concrete interlocution as the starting-point. In other words, and here we are also referring to Bakhtin, the materials of language will be approached not in a monological optic but a dialogical one – a 'dialogue' whose horizon is resolutely social.

I propose to summarise this philosophy of language in the form of five theses.

The *first thesis* is negative: it maintains that language conceived as a system is a mere scientific abstraction that does not make it possible to account for concrete phenomena. In other words, *langue* is a bad abstraction, an example of fetishism. This thesis rejects the construction of a scientific object through separation and exclusion – which is precisely what the object of Saussurian linguistics is.

The *second thesis* is the positive converse of the first. If language is not an abstract system, it is because it is a human practice – that is, a continuous process realised in verbal interaction, which is a social interaction. We have here an example of the post-Cartesian inversion which makes subjectivity a result of inter-subjectivity, not vice-versa. The result is that the language in question, which one will no longer seek to distinguish from *langage*, is not a fixed code of rules, which are sometimes conventions and sometimes laws of nature (depending on whether one adopts Saussure's position or Chomsky's), but regularities identified in usage. This position is not specific to Marxist thinking about language: it is formulated in Roy Harris's research programme, which he calls integrational linguistics.[13]

The *third thesis* maintains that the laws of linguistic evolution are sociological, not psychological. It follows from the previous thesis. If language is a process in a state of constant variation, and if this process is social, then any form of psychologism – i.e. any form of methodological individualism – is excluded. In the same way, any form of intentionalism is excluded: the meaning of the utterance does not depend on the speaker's intended meanings; or, rather, the speaker negotiates the meaning of her utterance with her interlocutors, who are present in the dialogue, or who are in the past and represented by the sedimentation of meanings in the language which constrains the present utterance. An utterance never emerges in a vacuum, is never an origin, but a link in a chain of utterances.

The *fourth thesis* is a consequence of the third. Linguistic creativity, which has always fascinated linguistics (every sentence I pronounce is virtually completely new – except, of course, for this one, which I have pronounced annually in front of cohorts of students), is usually explained by the utilisation and/or exploitation of a set of rules. Thus, Chomsky speaks of 'rule-governed creativity'. Voloshinov attributes linguistic creativity – and this is his *fourth thesis* – not to the utilisation of rules, but to the ideological content of the speech acts emitted in interlocution. It is ideological constraints – those of the sedimentation of meanings and the interpellation of speakers as sub-jects – that are subject to creative exploitation. For any interpellation summons a counter-interpellation. The insult that wounds me and seeks to fix me in

---

[13] See Harris 1998 and Harris and Wolf 1988.

an interlocutory, subjective position which I do not want to occupy can not only be returned, but taken up, taken on, and revalued.

The *fifth thesis* summarises the positions formulated in the first four. It maintains that the structure of utterances is social and is only realised in the interaction of concrete speakers. Unlike in most research programmes in linguistics, it is no longer a question of making phonology, morphology or syntax the heart of the study of language. The heart of linguistics is pragmatics – a pragmatics which, unlike Anglo-American pragmatics, is not individualist, but socialised – that is, conscious of the historical and political nature of language. The following chapter will be devoted to the systematic development of this thesis.

Turning from these general theses to the concrete study of language, Voloshinov has recourse to two new concepts: the concept of *theme*, by which he refers to the global meaning of the utterance – that is, a singularity bound up with the concrete situation of enunciation; and the concept of *signification*, by which he means repeated elements of meaning, which are transmitted from one situation to the next. Here, we once again encounter the difference between pragmatic meaning and semantic meaning – the difference between the multiplicity of meanings of the exclamation 'Good!' in concrete situations and its sedimented meaning in a dictionary. But this conceptual distinction goes a little further: the transition from signification to the theme involves an active process of meaning (we return here to the previous meaning of 'signification' as the active forging of meaning), an active understanding which takes not only the words, but also the *intonation*, of the utterance, into account. Voloshinov is, in fact, one of the few linguists or philosophers to take an interest in the phenomenon of intonation, which is largely neglected and yet whose contribution to the meaning of an utterance is of the first importance. The same utterance can assume totally different – even opposed – meanings when the intonation changes (irony, irritation, seductiveness, weariness: all these emotions can be sensed by means of the intonation of the utterance as much as by the actual words employed – and sometimes rather more so than by the latter).[14] And this concept of language leads Voloshinov to interest himself in another linguistic phenomenon in a

[14] See Voloshinov 1983.

spectacularly fruitful way: we do not expect a work devoted to the Marxist philosophy of language to contain a chapter, which is still read and commented on by specialists, on indirect free speech – a concept more common among literary critics than political activists. But the dialogical conception of language, the fact that any utterance is not only caught up in a current dialogue, but contains the sedimentation of past dialogues as well as the anticipation of future dialogues (the chain of utterances has no beginning and no end), renders the study of reported speech crucial for understanding the functioning of language. For, in an important sense, *there is only reported speech*: every text is a tissue, according to etymology, but a tissue of voices and not only of words. This theme is taken up by Deleuze and Guattari.

I shall end with a few words on Voloshinov's second book, devoted to a critique of Freudianism. For conjunctural reasons, this book has been completely ignored in France (despite a translation published in Switzerland). It was difficult to criticise psychoanalysis without lapsing into a reactionary position; and it will be remembered that Althusser witheld the text in which he criticised Lacan and that it was only belatedly published and against his will.

The interesting thing about Voloshinov's critique of Freudianism is that it is utterly consistent with his philosophy of language. Thus, he approves of the notion of the 'talking cure', in that Freud deals with a material which is always verbal – the utterances produced by the analysand speaker being the only mode of access to the unconscious. Contrariwise, he criticises what he calls Freud's 'subjectivism' – that is, his version of methodological individualism (to each subject his individual consciousness) – and his biological reductionism. The unconscious conceived in terms of metaphors of depth and surface – what was formerly called 'depth psychology' – is incompatible with subjectivation through language, in the practice of interlocution. And he likewise criticises – and here he is not alone – psychoanalysts' belief in a form of human nature (in the shape of libidinal energy, drives, universal Oedipal structures, etc.).

Against what he perceives as the essential positions of psychoanalysis, Voloshinov posits two theses. The first is that the unconscious is not located in the depths of the psyche but on the outside, in interlocution. We therefore have an unconscious which is external, public, collective and social (meaning that this 'unconscious' is not one: it is – or aspires to become – conscious). What Freudians call 'unconscious' is nothing but the internalisation of public dialogue. In other words, the concept of unconscious, like the Saussurian concept of *langue*, is the result of a process of fetishism.

The second thesis is that the operation of transference is a social operation, involving linguistic *agon* and the establishment of a power relation. Voloshinov is interested in the psychoanalytic relationship between analysand and analyst as a speech genre (and we recall Bakhtin's interest in this concept, to which he devoted one of his best-known essays).[15] This social relation is once again subject to a process of fetishism: it then becomes the Freudian topic, individualised and internalised, of ego, super ego, and id. The well-known kinship between the super ego and God is explained by the fact that they are both products of fetishism. The following quotation at least has the advantage of offering us an original analysis of the relations between the psychiatrist and his patient:

> I refer to the complex relations that are formed between the psychiatric doctor and his neurotic patient – a social microcosm marked by a particular kind of struggle, in which the patient seeks to hide certain aspects of her life from her doctor, to mislead him, to become fixated on her symptoms, and so on and so forth. This is a highly complex social microcosm, in which the economic base, physiological factors, and the weight (aesthetic as well as moral) of bourgeois ideology combine to define a set of concrete relations. The doctor responds to this situation as a practitioner, seeking to divine the real forces that condition it and learning to control them, but without being able to integrate them in all their complexity into a (materialist) scientific theory – which is not surprising, given that study of the physiology of neuroses has as yet scarcely started. . . . And onto this ignorance of the theory *metaphor*, or a *dramatic personification of the practitioner's orientation*, is grafted, which (like every personification) is subjective and relative – something that in no way detracts from its utility.[16]

The scientistic language of psychologism, to which Voloshinov is committed as the only possible form of materialism, reflects the climate of the time. But it will be agreed that the Freudian metaphor of the unconscious as another scene receives an explanation here that is worthy of interest. For the relationship

---

[15] See Bakhtin 1986.
[16] Bakhtin 1980, p. 65.

between analyst and analysand is indeed a power relation, as is any relationship between doctor and patient. To approach these relations through the interlocutory exchanges between the two parties and the power relations that are operative in them is a good way of accounting for them, going beyond the image which the participants – especially the analysts – seek to project. And it has the advantage of involving a philosophy of language that places the concept of power relations at the centre of its reflection. On this point, as on so many others, Voloshinov has had at least two successors: Deleuze and Guattari.

2. Deleuze and Guattari and Marxism

I have already referred to the work of Deleuze and Guattari on two occasions. I used their critique of linguistics at the beginning of Chapter 2 and I cited their reading of Lenin's text on slogans in the final section of Chapter 4. This is because I believe that we can find in their work – especially in *A Thousand Plateaus* – the outline of a Marxist philosophy of language. This poses two questions: are my authors in fact Marxists (or am I in the process of press-ganging them)? And how exactly does the philosophy of language implicitly, and sometimes explicitly, to be found in their work help me to construct a Marxist philosophy of language? I am going to deal with these two questions in order.

A Marxist opens *Anti-Oedipus* at page one. She is immediately plunged into an exotic universe, totally foreign to her. Certainly, it functions, but it eats, it shits, it fucks, and so on. These activities are not alien to Marxists, but they are not in the habit of theorising them. However, if Marxists persevere in their reading, they will discover familiar aspects to this universe. The 'it' which shits and fucks, but which also produces, is a machine, a set of machines. And our Marxist has crossed at least two thresholds, the title of the first part – 'Desiring Production' – and the title of the whole work of which *Anti-Oedipus* is the first volume – 'Capitalism and Schizophrenia'. Therein lies the problem for Marxists who read Deleuze and Guattari: they are threatened by a form of schizophrenia, inscribed in the 'and' of the title. Yes, there are machines (a concept which does not leave Marxists indifferent), but they are desiring machines: an analysis of capitalism is indeed foreshadowed, but in its relations with schizophrenia. Once the surprise is over, Marxists will note with interest that the practice is consistent. Whatever the concept, however colourful its name (nomadism, assemblage, war machine), and however remote from familiar concepts – and it is often very remote – we always have the impression that there is a relationship to Marxism in Deleuze and Guattari's conceptual elaboration. Thus, the famous analysis of nomadism with its war machine (contrasted with the state apparatus), with its smooth or striated space, has a certain relation, albeit distant, with the Marxist concept of Asiatic mode of production. The whole issue is the relevance of this relationship, of the extent of the shift it involves. Marxist concepts are indeed there (not all of them, of course). But Marx would not recognise them as his offspring.

There are various historical reasons and some contingent biographical reasons for this proximity. It is difficult for a French philosopher formed in the immediate post-war period not to have – or have had – a relationship with Marxism, even if in the form of a critique. It will be recalled that Michel Foucault burst into tears when he learnt of Stalin's death – which did not prevent him from declaring that Marxism was a storm in a teacup. And, if Pierre Bourdieu refused so vehemently to declare himself a Marxist, it was doubtless for reasons of proximity. The spectre of Marx haunts French philosophers – even the greatest of them.

Guattari was a Marxist. For a time, he was a member of the PCF and, for rather longer, was linked to oppositional left-wing groups: he never denied this heritage. For his part, Deleuze was not, even if he sometimes gave it to be understood that he was. In his youth, he was too busy to join the Party, preferring philosophical work to smoke-filled meetings. In his maturity, he performed all the tasks of what he called 'ordinary leftism', from the Groupe d'Information sur les Prisons (GIP) to Coluche's presidential candidacy – places where (as is well-known) he formed a friendship with Foucault. However, this is not the main thing: what interests us is conceptual proximity, not the political opinions of the authors of those concepts.

But, in order to assess this proximity, or this distance, I need a yardstick or a set of criteria. I need to state what a Marxist in search of a soul mate expects from a text, in a conjuncture where the erstwhile certainties of *diamat* are dead and buried, but where the discourse on the end of grand narratives is not acceptable either – at least, not for those who call themselves Marxists. I am, therefore, going to take some risks and propose four Marxist theses or themes in as strict a sense as possible.

From a Marxist text or position I expect: (i) an analysis of capitalism in terms which, however attuned to current tastes, are inspired by the concepts of *Capital*; (ii) a political programme deduced from this analysis of capitalism (it is not enough to anticipate the advent of the revolutionary event as a divine surprise; it is necessary to prepare for it); (iii) an overall conception of history that tells me how the seeds of the future are contained in the present and the past: as a Marxist, I am suspicious of sectoral analyses, even if they are indispensable, and seek to adopt the standpoint of the totality (to use Lukácsian language). The danger of this concept of history is obviously teleology: Marxist have long suffered from it, but through no fault of Marx's;[17] (iv) a conception of time, centred on the concepts of conjuncture and moment of the conjuncture, and guiding political action, by distinguishing strategy from tactics, the urgent from the more long-term, the principal aspect of a contradiction from its secondary aspects: this, as we have seen, is Lenin's contribution to Marxist theory.

These four theses or themes are of immediate concern to political activists, economists, and historians. However, one can be a Marxist without belonging to any of these categories. One can be interested (as I am) in literature, linguistics, the philosophy of language. I therefore need some broader theses for Marxists who do not spend their time directly analysing the current situation of capitalism. I am going to propose six, in the shape of six dichotomies which form a correlation – a philosophical technique I borrow from Gilles Deleuze, who was fond of it.

First dichotomy: the standpoint of the collective rather than methodological individualism. We know that the latter refuses to consider society other than as an aggregate of individuals making rational choices whose resultant explains social dynamics. For its part, Marxism works with collective entities – class or party – which are social subjects, social agents. *Second dichotomy*: subjectivation as a process of production of the subject, rather than the subject/person/centre of consciousness. This dichotomy correlates with the preceding one: if the 'subject' is collective, pre-eminence will not be assigned to the individual subject (a historically dated product), author, speaker, or moral agent. *Third dichotomy*: ideology as a necessary framework rather than ideology as mystification. This dichotomy is situated within Marxism, the

---

[17] See Bensaïd 2002.

ambivalence of the concept having adversely affected the Marxist theory of ideology (take, for example, the history of the concept in the work of Althusser). A Spinozist conception of the positivity of error (whose significance lies in its inevitability and the explanation it elicits), or a conception (borrowed from the work of Judith Butler)[18] of 'enabling constraints' (constraints that do not only oppress, but which enable and guide action), will make it possible to understand the framework in which subjects are produced. *Fourth dichotomy*: materialism rather than idealism. Naturally. This option will be regarded as a thesis of philosophical demarcation (let us choose sides – in which case, the concept of 'matter' will remain vague), but even more as a series of positions that form a system. In the domain of the sciences of language, for example, we will stress the materiality of the body of the speaker (excluded by idealism from the 'language system' and from a concept of communication that turns its speakers into angels), but also the materiality of institutions and rituals and the practices which they frame (interpellation, counter-interpellation). *Fifth dichotomy*: historicism contra naturalism – or why Chomsky's philosophy of language (regardless of the sympathy his political positions elicit) is unacceptable. As we have seen, in anchoring language in the frozen time of evolution, it rejects any possibility of historical change affecting language. This has the dual disadvantage of excluding the majority of phenomena from the field of science and precludes, under the rubric of 'synchrony', understanding the complexity of what a Marxist will be tempted to call a 'linguistic conjuncture'. *Final dichotomy*: the standpoint of *agon* as opposed to that of *eirene* – the standpoint of (class) struggle against that of peaceful co-operation (a utopian ideal – in the positive sense – rather than current reality). If the class struggle is the motor of history, then linguistic practice is not foreign to conflicts, the establishment of power relations, the hierarchisation and attribution of 'places' to speakers. The principle of co-operation in Grice, or the communicative competence of Habermas, takes our desires for reality. The first dialogue in the history of humanity brought together Cain and Abel: we know how it turned out.

I am aware of the fact that these ten theses, or positions, or themes are open to challenge; and that they say more about this particular Marxist than about Marxism in general. But I believe that, if none of my six dichotomies

---

[18] See Butler 1995.

is the exclusive property of Marxism, their conjunction determines a generally Marxist position, which I am going to use to elaborate a Marxist philosophy of language. How do Deleuze and Guattari stand with respect to these theses? The answer is: in a relation of distance or proximity, but always in a relation.

Let us take the strict theses. It is clear that *Capitalism and Schizophrenia* seeks to provide an analysis, however surprising, of the functioning of capital, and not only – as in Derrida – of a 'new world order' that, of necessity, remains vague. And a relationship to Marxism there most certainly is: a relation of translation, or addition, which includes and focuses on what Marxism ignored: the issues posed by madness, sexual orientation, and so on – issues which are treated as *social* questions and not merely individual ones (for Deleuze and Guattari, the wanderings of the delirious patient are not the product of her individual anguish: the whole of history is the object of her delerium). In a sense, Deleuze and Guattari are part of a tradition of extending Marxism: they continue *The Origin of the Family* by other means. This analysis of capital involves, if not a programme capable of guiding an organisation, then at least a *line* or *lines* (as everyone knows, the concepts of plane of immanence, line of flight, and rhizome are essential in Deleuze and Guattari).[19] These multiple lines (here we have a difference with Marxism: the line of organisation, as Leninism dictates, is one) found a politics of desire, often characterised as *anarcho-désirant*. And, in truth, Marxists have difficulty making sense of this (just as they previously found it difficult to approve of the concrete political options of Deleuze and Guattari – e.g. their support for Coluche's presidential candidacy in 1981). But they will acknowledge that it is derived from an analysis of capitalism. According to their usual tactics (we know their pronounced hostility to metaphors), Deleuze and Guattari take the metaphor of the body politic literally. And every reader of Hardt and Negri's *Empire*[20] knows that this politics, far from being a curiosity of the immediate post-'68 period, has its extensions in the current conjuncture.

We also find in Deleuze and Guattari an overall conception of history, in the typically Marxist form of a periodisation. Not, certainly, in terms of modes of production, but of régimes of signs – a concept peculiar to them (which is bound up with their concepts of flow and code). Here the shift, which is not

[19] Cf. Lecercle 2002.
[20] See Hardt and Negri 2000.

a copy, is clear: the task of the philosopher of history is to periodise; the content of the periodisation varies. Finally, I will have more difficulty showing that their conception of temporality approximates to that of Marxists: rather than concepts of conjuncture and moment, we find syntheses of times in Deleuze that owe more to Bergson than Marx.

The harvest is even richer when we pass to the six broad theses. Although preoccupied by the personal dimension of the political, Deleuze and Guattari, who have a decided contempt for Anglo-American philosophy (in an effusive moment in *Abécédaire*, Deleuze even treats Wittgenstein as an assassin of philosophy[21]), do not succumb to methodological individualism. For them, the origin of utterances is not the individual speaker, but the collective assemblage of enunciation. This term, which displaces the study of language from the result – the utterance (fetishised into an object of scientific study) – to the process of enunciation (a stance they share with the linguists of enunciation, Benveniste and Culioli), also effects a shift from the individual to the collective: the individual speaker is dislodged from her habitual central position. In fact, Deleuze is one of the philosophers who pushes the relegation of the concept of the subject furthest: in his work, the subject is not quartered to the four corners of a schema in the shape of a Z; it is not the result of a process of interpellation; it is absent. In its stead, various concepts do the same philosophical work: the collective assemblage of enunciation, haeccity, impersonal, non-individual, non-subjective singularity (a *haiku* and a shower of rain are examples), the body without organs. We are no longer in the sphere of the personal subject, centre of consciousness and source of action; we are in the machinic assemblage and what Deleuze and Guattari call the *socius*. And, if we no longer need interpellated subjects, we do not need an interpellating ideology either. In its Althusserian version, the concept is explicitly rejected. But it is replaced: collective assemblage, with its ontological mix of bodies, discourses and institutions, performs the same role. Relegating the subject, Deleuze and Guattari refuse any form of transcendence: they are very far removed from idealism and decidedly close to the pan-somatism of the stoics, which informs Deleuze's *Logic of Sense*. Closer, therefore, to the strict materialism of the pre-Marxist tradition than the expanded materialism of the philosophy of *praxis*: we find no materialism of institutions in them,

---

[21] See Deleuze and Parnet 1997, 'W, c'est Wittgenstein'.

but a materialism of corporeal assemblages, of combinations, without metaphors, of desiring machines. They can hardly be accused of naturalism: in their work, human nature appears in none of its forms, but history is ubiquitous. Finally, they explicitly opt for the standpoint of the *agon* (which they characterise as 'philosophical athleticism' in *What Is Philosophy?*[22]) against that of *eirene*. In their work, the basic utterance is not the proposition/judgement/assertion, but the order-word. The object of interlocution is, therefore, not a co-operative exchange of information, but establishing a power relation.

Deleuze and Guattari thus clearly do have a relationship to Marxism. In order to think through this mixture of distance and proximity, we shall avoid the religious idiom of filiation and haunting; and to the term post-Marxism, which implies succession and supersession, we shall prefer *para-Marxism*, which implies displacement by translation.

Accordingly, I shall propose a series of six shifts (the number is once again arbitrary).

First shift: a change in periodisation. As we have seen, *Capitalism and Schizophrenia* is a historical fresco marked by an almost obsessive desire to periodise. However, we find no mention of modes of production, productive forces, and relations of production, but a parallel series – and hence one translated from the Marxist original: régimes of signs, flows of libidinal energy, coding. A Marxism that is virtually unrecognisable, because it has been both semiotised and corporealised. And we understand that Deleuze and Guattari's main objection to Marxism is its attachment to the vertical model, with its separation of ontological planes, of base and superstructure.

Second shift: the transition from history to geography. It is as if Deleuze and Guattari are interested in capitalism, which they are attempting to analyse, but not in previous modes of production (the feudal assemblage is nevertheless employed as a canonical example) – except in the most marginal of them, the one situated outside of the historical sequence: the Asiatic mode of production. This is also the only one whose name assigns it a geographical, not a historical, basis. In fact, we are dealing with a re-interpretation of the Marxist periodisation from the perspective of its most eccentric element, which produces a series of new concepts that are 'geographical' and no longer simply historical (we

---

[22] Deleuze and Guattari 1993, p. 8.

know the significance of the concept of 'plane' of immanence or coherence in Deleuze's thinking: smooth or striated space, *nomos* and war machine, cards and strata, decalcomania). The displacement of the series of modes of production is therefore twofold: by translation from the economic into the semiotic and the corporeal, in the form of a correlation; and by inversion of centre and periphery, with a correlative change in the plane of organisation (space and no longer time). This shift, while it might leave Marxists wondering, will not surprise readers of Wallerstein or Braudel. And, here, we see how the concept of *socius* is not the same as the concept of society. It involves rendering the metaphor of the body politic literal (a tactic our authors are fond of): the social body is as material/corporeal as the body of the earth; it is traversed by energy flows, segmented by coding operations. And this material body is, of course, a collective body whereas society – in its dominant liberal version at least – is a collection of individuals. But it will also be noted, with a resignation tinged with regret, that the concept of class has paid the price for this dual shift.

Third shift: from labour to desire. This is because the concept of class is based on the productive structure of society, the contradictions that propel it forward, and the struggles that this entails. And the productive structure foregrounds labour as the basic human practice and as the measure of value. Deleuze and Guattari – such was the climate of the time – are hostile to productivism, the appropriation of nature by humanity (as is well known, towards the end of his life, Guattari, independently of Deleuze, attempted to develop an ecological philosophy that had hardly any resonance). We therefore pass from the centrality of labour as *praxis* to that of desire, as the motor of energy flows. It must be admitted that this concept of desire is not uninteresting. Contrary to the Freudian concept, predicated on lack and hence negative (it is of the essence of desire never to be satisfied, never assuaged, except by the death of the subject, which puts an end to it), it is a positive concept: an energy traversing and animating a machine. In *Abécédaire*, where the letter D is devoted to desire, Deleuze insists on the fact that there is no desire except within an assemblage. We can see how the subject is once again erased. A transitive binary relation – a subject desires an object – gives way to the complex structure of an assemblage. Desire is the energy that holds together the assemblages and circulates in them. We understand the new meaning assumed by the concept of machine (which, in one of his first texts, Guattari opposed to that of structure):[23] not an instrument, a complex tool marking a necessary yet transient stage in the metamorphoses of the commodity, but an organ 'excentric to the subjective fact', inhabited by what Guattari (in his Lacanian period) still called 'the subject of the unconscious', charged with cutting up and coding energy flows. One thinks of the eccentric machines of the English caricaturist William Heath Robinson, or Tintin threatened with being swallowed by a huge corned-beef machine, whose 'input' is a succession of ruminating cows and whose 'output' is a series of tins of corned beef.

Fourth shift: from ideology to assemblage. As we have seen, Deleuze and Guattari are wary of the concept of ideology, above all in its Althusserian structuralist version, in that it implies a separation between base and superstructure, a world of objects and a world of representations. They have a reductionist view of the concept, but it is clear that the coupling of desire/machine (effected in what they call 'machinic assemblages of desire') transcends this separation. The advantage of the machine over the structure is that it functions, it works, it is positioned from the standpoint of the process and not the classification of objects. But Deleuze and Guattari need a concept to do the philosophical work attributed to the concept of ideology in its necessary aspect (and not simply in its pejorative sense of mystified consciousness): subjectivation – the production or interpellation of subjects. The concept of assemblage is charged with this task. An assemblage has two aspects: a material-corporeal aspect, which I have just referred to (machinic assemblage of desire) and an institutional-social aspect (hence likewise material in its way and yet also ideal) – the collective assemblage of enunciation. These two aspects are indissociable, even if Deleuze and Guattari are more forthcoming on the second than the first. Their indissociability explains the most important characteristic of an assemblage: the ontological mix that is effected in it. Deleuze and Guattari's canonical example will enable us to understand it. The feudal assemblage is composed of a certain number of physical bodies (manors, horses, armour, knights and chatelaines, without forgetting the villeins and a few priests), of a corpus of texts (e.g. courtly love poems), of a body of laws and decrees, myths and beliefs, and of the institutions (in both their material and their ideal aspects) that manage them (courts of

---

[23] See Guattari 1972.

justice, convents, etc.). This involves an organization of space (from the manor to the cathedral), a hierarchical social body (the King, his vassals, etc.), a body of rituals and practices. I shall stop there, for the whole of feudal society is in danger of being swallowed up by the concept. But its interest lies elsewhere: precisely in the ontological mix, in the materiality of the processes that produce discourses and their speakers. It is thus that, although Deleuze and Guattari do not mention it (no doubt the French translation of the text was too recent), their concept of collective assemblage of enunciation is proximate to Bakhtin's chronotope (the difference lies in their stress on the '-tope' as opposed to the 'chrono-').

Fifth shift: from party to group. Deleuze's most explicitly Marxist (or para-Marxist) text is his preface to Guattari's *Psychanalyse et transversalité*, entitled 'Trois problèmes de groupe'. The preceding shifts are already made in germ in it. And it is explicitly a question of shifts, Reich and Guattari being at the outset saluted as embodying the coincidence of political activist and psychoanalyst. In this text we find a critique of the theoretical and political positions of the Communist Parties (it dates from 1972). Thus, the theory of state monopoly capitalism is analysed as a compromise formation between the internationalism of capital and the defence of the national framework of the state. The degeneration of the Soviet Union is described in prophetic terms, which (vaguely) recall certain analyses of state bureaucratic capitalism. The main thing is the distinction between *subjected group* (as the Bolshevik Party became after 1917 and as were – and still are – communist organisations and parties), which is obsessed by its self-perpetuation and only offers a skeleton of reified organisation, and *group subject*, which is in a constant state of flux, always hastening to announce its own dissolution. Here, we find the political equivalent of the contrast between machine and structure, under the rubrics of party and *groupuscule* (we have already mentioned Deleuze's attachment to 'ordinary far leftism'). Even if the dissolution of the concept of party is difficult for a paleo-Marxist like me to accept, this analysis poses a real problem of crucial significance: how are we to prevent the vanguard from substituting itself for the body of the army, or transforming itself into a permanent high command, cut off from the infantry in the trenches and despatching them to be butchered?

Sixth shift, which in fact covers the whole series: from the molar to the molecular. These are two central and well-known concepts of *Anti-Oedipus* (even though, whether in the work of Deleuze or of Deleuze and Guattari, they scarcely survived beyond it). Expelling the subject from its central position, the philosophy of assemblages (as they say, 'philosophy of *praxis*') is hardly indulgent towards the individual subject of bourgeois liberalism. But it has no more sympathy for the mass subject of Marxism (class as a collective subject). The origin of action – the agent – is, here, the non-structured, as yet non-reified group, in a constant state of variation or metamorphosis. This savours of May 1968, understood as an anti-authoritarian revolt. And this (something that is wholly positive) makes it possible to take account of the emergence of new political subjects (women, psychiatric patients in hospitals, prisoners, immigrant workers). Some of these subjects have faded away; others occupy the front of the stage: the balance-sheet of the priority accorded the molecular remains to be drawn up. But this pair of concepts, through a shift internal to the work of Deleuze and Guattari, gave rise to two other concepts, which, in my view, are far more important: the concepts of majority and minority. Here, it is no longer a matter of social molecularity, or of political minority, but of linguistic and literary minority. A major language, such as what is called standard English (or rather a major usage of the language), is constantly rendered minoritarian by a multitude of minor dialects, registers, and styles. A minor literary text (the canonical example is Kafka)[24] has no need to call with all its heart for socialist revolution, or to describe in detail the most deleterious effects of capitalist exploitation; from the outset, it is collective, political, and deterritorialised.

In Deleuze and Guattari, we are therefore dealing with a systematic displacement of Marxist concepts. They think within Marxism, certainly more directly than the Derrida of *Specters of Marx*, even if their wanderings or lines of flight lead them rather far from this starting-point. To be convinced of this, it is enough to compare the treatment of Marx and Freud in *Capitalism and Schizophrenia*: the former is practically never mentioned, but provides an intellectual framework; the second is referred to on virtually every page, in person or in the shape of one of his avatars – but is subjected to a systematic, often ferocious critique.

If readers will grant me this displacement, and hence point of origin, a question remains: why undertake this journey and what have we to gain, as

---

[24] See Deleuze and Guattari 1986.

Marxists, from following philosophers who do everything in their power to warrant the sobriquet *anarcho-désirants*? Rather than engaging in this reading against the current, would it not be better to abandon them to the 'anarchist' reading of their work, which has the advantages of being obvious and immediate, and is not bereft of lessons for a Marxist (e.g. the Deleuzian concept of event, developed in *Logic of Sense*, or the critique of representation, including political representation)? In the list of most frequent citations in Daniel Colson's *Petit lexique philosophique de l'anarchisme*,[25] Deleuze comes second, behind Proudhon but before Bakunin. My answer is simple: if there is a domain where Deleuze and Guattari have advanced critical thinking, it is that of language.

As we have seen, the fourth plateau of *A Thousand Plateaus* proposes a vigorous critique of the dominant philosophy of language and of the linguistics that derives from it. But, underlying the negative theses, marked by the conditional of the propositions expressing the four postulates of linguistics (*le langage serait informatif et communicatif*), there are positive theses. Proceeding rapidly, I shall formulate six of them:

The basic utterance of language is not the declarative, assertive and constative sentence ('the man hit the ball'), but the *order-word*.

The fundamental type of speech is not direct speech, which is supposed to refer to the world and to offer communicable information about it, but reported speech – what is called *indirect speech*.

The fundamental sector for the study of language is not phonology (as in the original structuralists), or syntax (as in Chomsky), but *pragmatics* – a pragmatics that is nevertheless different from that of Anglo-American philosophers in that it is basically *political*.

In that they are order-words, speech acts exercise *power* and have a specific *effectivity*. This effectivity takes the form of *incorporeal transformations*.

Utterances are produced not by individual speakers, but by *collective assemblages of enunciation*.

If a language is not a homogeneous system, it is because it is shot through with contradictions. The principal contradiction lies between the *major dialect*, or *major usages* of the language, and *dialects* or *minor usages*.

---

[25] See Colson 2001.

We can already see the proximity of these theses to those that have been extracted from the Marxist tradition: the stress on order-words, inspired by a reading of Lenin; on the political nature of pragmatics; on the effectivity of speech acts; and on the contradictions that constitute what is understood by a language and make language a set of social, historical and political phenomena. The negative principles heralding abandonment of the dominant philosophy of language (non-immanence, dysfunctionality, opacity, materiality, partial systematicity, and historicity) are employed in these theses (the incorporeal character of the transformations takes nothing away from the material character of their effectivity: as we know, slogans exercise a material force when they seize hold of the masses).

I am going to comment briefly on five of these six theses (thesis three – on the political character of Deleuze and Guattari's pragmatics – will be discussed in Chapter 7).

The *first thesis* states that the basic utterance is the order-word. This is to be regarded not as an origin (in the sense that Chomsky's declarative sentences yielded, via transformation, interrogative sentences, etc.), but as a co-substantial relationship: in a crucial regard, every utterance, whatever its form, is an order-word. This is obvious in the case of political utterances, even when they are couched in the form of 'information' (when the prime minister, for example, 'informs' the French people about pensions), and advertising slogans. But Deleuze and Guattari generalise the thesis to the whole set of utterances: the most innocuous utterance, the most simple example of a declarative sentence – in the canonical example of the early Chomsky, 'the man hit the ball' – must be regarded as an order-word. In truth, the point is not difficult to appreciate, since it involves an example of grammar. Barthes's example will be recalled: *quia ego nominor leo* – a Latin sentence that tells us by denotation 'because my name is lion', but which also informs us by connotation: 'I am a grammatical example meant to illustrate the rule about the agreement of the predicate'.[26] The order-word in a grammatical utterance functions like a connotation: it signals that every utterance of this type exercises power, marks a form of power. The schoolmaster does not inform, he teaches – that is, he commands the pupil, commands her to respect and apply the rule. And this command is not added on to a piece of information, is not its consequence:

---

[26] See Barthes 1972, p. 116.

it is consubstantial with it. Hence this famous formula: 'A rule of grammar is a power marker before it is a syntactical marker.'[27] We have already had a similar experience with the most innocuous question – for example, 'What time is it?' Every request for information is an assertion of the right to pose the question and a demand for a response. And there is no need to imagine a police interrogation to bring out the point: variations of intonation will make my banal question express a polite query or a sign of irritation, a sardonic commentary, an aggression, and so on. In short, '[l]anguage is made not to be believed but to be obeyed, and to compel obedience.'[28] The recent conjuncture of the run-up to the war in Iraq indicates that the imperialists are fully aware of this maxim.

Accordingly, 'order-word' does not designate a type of utterance, but an aspect of every utterance, just as for Anglo-American pragmatists illocutionary force does not only consist in speech acts which, like insults, explicitly exercise power, but is a component of every linguistic act:

> We call *order-words*, not a particular category of explicit statements (for example, in the imperative), but the relation of every word or every statement to implicit presuppositions, in other words, to speech acts that are, and can only be, accomplished in the statement. Order-words do not concern commands only, but every act that is linked to statements by a 'social obligation'. Every statement displays this link, directly or indirectly. . . . The only possible definition of language is the set of all order-words, implicit presuppositions, or speech acts current in a language at a given moment.[29]

The *second thesis* follows from the first. If language is nothing but the set of order-words presupposed in a given conjuncture, it follows that there is no direct speech, that every utterance is always-already an indirect utterance. We see how Deleuze and Guattari converge on this point with Voloshinov, whom they had possibly read (but do not cite): there is a link between the polyphonic and dialogical conception of language and the stress on the priority of indirect language, just as there is a link between the importance of order-words as a constitutive component of utterances and the same stress on indirect speech. An utterance is always-already in indirect speech because it

---

[27] Deleuze and Guattari 1988, p. 76.
[28] Ibid.
[29] Deleuze and Guattari 1988, p. 79.

is a link in a chain of utterances. This recalls Lyotard's serial montage, which he contrasts with the parallel montage of divine revelation and the compulsive return to the truth of the original text: in the serial montage of narrations, there is no author who is the origin of the utterance, but a listener who, in turn, becomes a speaker, who repeats but also embroiders and embellishes.[30] For Deleuze and Guattari, this absence of origin is constitutive: for them, language does not proceed from something seen to something said, from a perception to an expression, but always from something said to something said – the narrative is always a 'hear-say'. Hence the primacy of indirect speech, which is an absence of origin: here, the separation between original literal discourse and secondary figurative discourse is not inverted but displaced. For nor is metaphor original: it is only an effect of secondary discourse. We can detect here both Deleuze and Guattari's well-known hostility to metaphor ('no metaphors, metamorphoses' is one of their favourite watchwords, meaning: no representation – even of a figurative kind – but interventions); and the possibility of a non-trivial theory of metaphor, which (imitating Sperber and Wilson and their theory of irony as mention)[31] might be called the theory of metaphor as mention: like irony, a metaphor is then the trace of another discourse, another voice. But, above all, we shall note – something scarcely surprising on the part of Deleuze – a Nietzschean inspiration, more precisely Nietzsche's conception of metaphor: this primacy of indirect speech is the effect of a fundamental property of language – its capacity not for representation but for *translation*. Language does not reflect, it displaces; it does not directly state the world, but translates a first displacement, which is that of perception. This at least has the advantage of putting the issue of translation at the centre of the study of language. As we have seen, what poses a problem in the utterance *Chirac est un ver* is that it is not really translated, that it speaks English in French. This suggests that what we have here is an example of indirect speech. This explains why the French reader does not recognise the description (in the text accompanying the title-slogan) of the president of the republic (whatever one's opinion of him): a chain of utterances in the English language – i.e. English culture – is presupposed by this insult (e.g. the nursery rhymes I cited in Chapter 1). But

---

[30] See Lyotard 1977, pp. 64–5.
[31] See Sperber and Wilson 1978.

the most important aspect of this thesis arguably lies elsewhere. It consists in the conclusion that follows from the primacy of indirect speech and which links it to the first thesis: there is no individual author of the utterance, only a speaker interpellated to her place and counter-interpellating from this place. To put it in Deleuze and Guattari's terms rather than mine: 'There is no significance independent of dominant significations, nor is there subjectification independent of an established order of subjection. Both depend on the nature and transmission of order-words in a given social field.'[32] As an Althusserian Marxist, I have nothing to add to this formulation.

The *fourth thesis* follows from the first. It poses the question of the kind of power exercised by order-words. We have seen that we cannot make do with the weak (because mainly classificatory) version of the Anglo-American theoreticians of speech acts. Deleuze and Guattari's answer to this question is of the utmost interest, even if it seems to distance them from Marxism. For them, the order-word effects an *incorporeal transformation*. On 4 July 1917, a correct slogan directly transforms the situation, just as the sentence pronounced by the judge immediately and radically transforms the situation of the accused, who is now a convict: he no longer has the same rights, the same expectations, and the same hopes; and this incorporeal transformation has an impact not only on his social status, but on the body of the condemned man. We therefore have a mixture of the incorporeal and the corporeal: thus it is that the first-class passenger suddenly becomes a hostage. There is, in the correct slogan, something that pertains to the event, in the sense in which the latter (e.g. in Alain Badiou's theory of the event)[33] revolutionises the situation in which it rings out like a thunder clap. We are not far removed from a religious language (the event is an epiphany), either in Badiou or in Deleuze and Guattari: trans-substantiation is the canonical example of an incorporeal transformation. But the interest of the thesis goes far beyond this: it enables us to understand that language is not the vector of representation but a weapon of intervention. As Deleuze and Guattari put it, we 'tell things straight'; we operate a transformation on them which is a veritable metamorphosis, which produces a new mix of bodies. Here, the philosophical idiom turns stoic and *A Thousand Plateaus* takes up Deleuze's reading in *Logic of Sense*: incorporeal transformation

---

[32] Deleuze and Guattari 1988, p. 79.
[33] See Badiou 1988.

is *ascribed* to bodies, it makes itself corporeal, just as a chemical precipitate appears in a transparent solution. This 'incorporeal' is indeed the incorporeality of the stoics, to whom Deleuze's attention had been attracted by an article of Bréhier's.[34]

The *fifth thesis* follows from the two preceding ones. If an order-word has no individual author, and if it is effective in the conjuncture and on bodies, it is because the source of the utterance is a *collective assemblage*. I have already mentioned Deleuze and Guattari's standard example: the feudal assemblage. It will be recalled that an assemblage has two sides or aspects – a machinic assemblage of desire and a collective assemblage of enunciation; and that the interest of the concept resides in the ontological mix it seeks to think. In it we can see the two aspects of the power exercised by order-words: a material aspect of intervention on bodies (the order-word operates like a machine, it transmits an impulse, it communicates in the physical sense of communicating power); and an immaterial, incorporeal face, in that the assemblage is also a collective assemblage of enunciation. Here, Deleuze and Guattari explicitly polemicise against orthodox Marxism, whose architectural metaphor of base and superstructure they reject. For them, utterances intervene in the base and are not restricted to the ideological superstructures: the production of meaning is a production in a non-metaphorical sense. Marxism makes the base-superstructure relation a relation of representation, encapsulated in the notorious concept of reflection. They prefer to think the relation between machinic assemblage and assemblage of enunciation as an expression, in the sense assumed by this term in Spinoza (it will be recalled that Deleuze had the warmest admiration for Spinoza and that his secondary thesis was devoted to the concept of expression in Spinoza).[35] In as much as it is material and machinic, assemblage does not refer to the production of goods, but to a precise state of the mix of bodies in society (the example that Deleuze and Guattari give, which I paraphrase here, is the stirrup, which favours the symbiosis between man and horse within the feudal assemblage). In as much as it is enunciative, assemblage is not concerned with some productivity of language, but by régimes of signs and machines of expression. Against Marx and against Chomsky, we therefore have an assemblage that knows no

---

[34] See Bréhier 1982 and Deleuze 1990a.
[35] See Deleuze 1990b.

distinction between base and superstructure, or between deep structure and surface structure: all dimensions of the assemblage are flattened onto a single plane of consistency. This concept of assemblage is crucial, including for a Marxist philosophy of language: it definitively extricates us from liberal individualism; it enables us to think the collective other than metaphorically. It is not enough to adopt the Heideggerian metaphor 'it is language that speaks', even if it offers views on the functioning of language that mainstream linguistics precludes. We need to think this interpellation of the speaker as a subject by language. And this is what Deleuze and Guattari do when they denounce in the 'system' of *langue* a fetishisation and proclaim the primacy of the assemblage over *langue* and over utterances.

The *sixth* and final thesis likewise introduces an essential concept: minority. This is the concept that enables us to understand how language is not only a material, social and historical phenomenon, but also a political one. This thesis is opposed to the structuralist thesis of the homogeneity of the language system. It is not enough to decide that the 'language' (a given language) is a set of heterogeneous phenomena in a state of continuous variation. We also need to explain why linguists fetishise this heterogeneity into a homogeneous, or, rather, homogenised, system. The answer is simple: there is a homology between the scientific model of the language system and the political model which makes the centralised national language a vector of power. Bourdieu in *Ce que parler veut dire*, and Renée Balibar and Dominique Laporte in *Le Français national*, have offered fine descriptions of this phenomenon in the case of French. In Deleuze and Guattari's terms, it involves wresting over the proliferation of minor dialects, registers and language games a language of power, major because dominant. On a world scale, this is called the language of imperialism. And we understand why we need to argue with Chomsky, albeit not for the same reasons, that English does not exist (or not in a way relevant for science); and, paradoxically, against Chomsky that it has a massive, inescapable existence. For the major language – 'standard English' – is an artificial construct, imposed by ideological apparatuses for the purposes of domination. So it is non-existent in the natural state (what exists is a multiplicity of dialects), and yet only too existent, as a set of power markers. This is indeed why it mainly, but not exclusively, exists in English grammars. But it will also be recalled – as my first chapter sought to demonstrate – that this situation, being contradictory, is not stable: that the language of imperialism is also the language of empire and is subject to all the vicissitudes that this involves. The centrifugal forces that are acting on it will end up dismantling it. In reality, 'major' and 'minor' refer not so much to two types of language as to two possible ways of treating the same language, two usages or functions of the language. This is why the hero of the process of becoming-minoritarian for Deleuze and Guattari is Kafka, a Jewish author writing in Prague in German; not a popular writer, but nevertheless 'of the people'; a political writer in that his practice of language renders the major language – German – minoritarian and (according to the concept developed by Deleuze) makes it stammer. It is thus that literature has a directly political function: not in that it represents the exactions of rampant capitalism in 'realist' novels, but in that it renders the standard language minoritarian and helps to subvert its domination. To render the language minoritarian is to have an immediately collective, deterritorialising, and political conception of it. In this interest in Kafka's polyglottism there is not only a return of the nostalgic myth of pre-World-War-One *Mitteleuropa*, with its multilingualism and cultural richness, or even a slightly exaggerated conception of the power attributed to literature. There are also two concepts which provide for thinking about language in an original way and weapons for the concrete analysis of conjunctures that are not only historical but also linguistic.

Since all this is decidedly abstract, I shall end with an example. In June 2003 the walls of the Paris metro were covered with adverts extolling the virtues of the temping agency ADIA. There were three posters, respectively representing a young woman, a young man, and a middle-aged man. The subjects had been chosen because they did not correspond to the typical fashion model: instead, they represented a slightly comical version of Ms. and Mr. Average. Each poster carried the beginning of a sentence in block capitals, readable from a distance – i.e. from the end of the corridor – and the end of it in lower case, which had to be approached to be deciphered. Here are the three sentences:

CETTE FEMME EST BONNE . . . dans son travail [this woman is good . . . in her work]

CETTE JEUNE EST UN DROGUÉ . . . de travail [this young man is addicted . . . to his work]

CET HOMME EST UN OBSEDÉ . . . du travail bien fait [this man is obsessed . . . with a job well-done]

It seems to me that these utterances perfectly illustrate Deleuze and Guattari's theses. They are, in fact, order-words. This is hardly surprising, since they are advertising slogans. But I observe that they do not have the privileged grammatical form of the order-word – the imperative ('choose wisely, etc.'); and do not contain the usual laudatory words. (Since we are talking about the Paris metro, I cannot resist the nostalgic pleasure of recalling a slogan from my childhood, for I have reached the age when, like Perec, I remember: 'Dubo . . . Dubon . . . Dubonnet'.) The order-word here takes the form of a declarative sentence, which is apparently constative. Even so, it is an order-word. As such, it is the fourth thesis: it exercises an incorporeal transformation on the spectator; it interpellates her in the fashion of a wink, but also by identification. In as much as I belong by definition to the category of Mr. Average, I find myself ironically flattered by this praise and, if I am sufficiently cynical not to be impressed, I am nevertheless interpellated as an accomplice in the mental exercise. (These slogans are based on the stylistic device called 'dual syntax', which offers a provisional meaning, in a sentence that is seemingly complete but in fact unfinished, only to change it completely when the sentence continues and concludes.) My smile, and my memory of a campaign that was by its very nature ephemeral, attest to it. Unless, of course, I am a woman and scarcely feel like smiling, the sexist allusion of the first slogan not being in the best taste, and the interpellation (as in witticisms according to Freud) putting me in the position of the victim of the joke. Moreover, I seem to have observed that this poster disappeared more rapidly than the other two. These utterances – and this is thesis five – have no individual author, but are produced by a collective assemblage of enunciation. Not only in that such slogans are commonly, if not written, then at least modified and finalised, by groups, but in that they presuppose a whole assemblage, a whole machinery: the selection of images, the choice of strategic positioning so that the slogans can be read (they must first of all be seen from afar and hence head-on), but also the market research – in short, the enormous social machinery that ends up generating a successful slogan. And obviously – thesis two – these utterances are in indirect speech, even if they bear no mark of it: in addition to resorting to the device of dual syntax, they are part of a tradition, they operate on presuppositions shared by the reader, who in order to understand the slogan identifies two different discourses, the first of which – in upper case – rests on clichés – that is, on the immediate recognition of what has already often been said. Finally, it might be thought that thesis six is not illustrated here, for the slogans – composed in standard French – scarcely cause the language to stammer. And yet . . . The sexual allusion of the first slogan functions in a vulgar register, immediately denied by the end of the sentence: here, two dialects contradict one another for expressive purposes. That this vulgarity is bound up with a sexual allusion only illustrates the functioning of the standard usage of the language as an instrument of domination.

In short, it seems to me clear that Deleuze and Guattari, despite their distant and critical relationship to Marxism, provide elements for constructing a specifically Marxist philosophy of language. The next chapter is going to develop its six main theses.

Chapter Six
Propositions (1)

1. Six theses

The construction – or reconstruction – is already under way. To re-read the texts of Marxist thinkers on language as a tradition, even if they are sometimes mere fragments, indicates a framework for what a Marxist philosophy of language should look like. This is the framework I am now going to try to flesh out. And, since I am an old Althusserian Marxist, I am going to proceed by theses – six in all: a main thesis, four positive theses that develop the main thesis, and a concluding thesis. I shall state them at once: this and the subsequent chapter will be devoted to commenting on them.

Main thesis: language is a form of *praxis*.
First positive thesis: language is a historical phenomenon.
Second positive thesis: language is a social phenomenon.
Third positive thesis: language is a material phenomenon.
Fourth positive thesis: language is a political phenomenon.
Concluding thesis: language is the site of subjectivation through interpellation.

The formulation of these theses will not surprise anyone who has read the previous chapters. Negatively, they abandon the dominant philosophy of language, from Saussure and Chomsky to Habermas; positively, albeit implicitly and in disorderly fashion, they are already present in the Marxist or para-Marxist authors to whom I have referred. The fact that the grammatical subject of my four theses is 'language [*langage*]', and not 'the language-system [*langue*]' or some other scientific construct (e.g. Chomsky's 'I-language'), signals this shift. And readers should not take umbrage at the singular form of the predicate 'is *a* phenomenon': I am aware that if language is something, it is a set of phenomena. The formulation has the function of indicating a characteristic of language and a field in which we must account for linguistic phenomena. Accordingly, we shall not be able to speak of language without referring to history, society, bodies (among other material entities), and politics.

2. Language is a form of *praxis*

This thesis is not original. It informs the work of Voloshinov and is explicit in Raymond Williams's book on Marxism and literature.[1] My Marxist philosophy of language will therefore be situated in a tradition. But, if the thesis is not original, its implications warrant development. In fact, to regard language as a form of *praxis* is to *change standpoints*. It involves considering language from the standpoint of process rather than outcome, social interaction rather than the individual speaker, history rather than synchrony, the totality rather than exclusion or separation (of what is, and what is not relevant, to science), power relations rather than irenic co-operation.

So, the first implication of the main thesis – the first *change of standpoint* – is that the study of language must adopt the standpoint of *process*, rather than of 'things' or 'facts'. (We can find in Roy Harris, a linguist who has already been cited, a powerful critique of the notion of 'linguistic fact'.[2]) In other words, the thesis involves a non-fetishistic view of language, which aims to go beyond the fetishised objects that are 'words' and 'sentences', and the fetishised facts that are statements and grammatical rules, in order to account for the totality of linguistic phenomena in terms of processes. Obviously, it is not a question of giving up the notions of words, sentences, utterances or rules bequeathed to us by the linguistic tradition. However, it definitely is a

---

[1] See Williams 1977.
[2] See Harris 1998, Chapter 6.

question of no longer regarding them as stable or static things or facts, but as dynamic processes: a 'word' covers a series of semantic, morphological and phonetic variations each of which has its own history; an 'utterance' is not the inscription of an ideal proposition, but the site of a polyphony whose result is multi-accentuality; and a language – English, for example – is not an ideal type realised in individual speech acts, but (as we have seen) a fluid, dynamic set of dialects, registers and styles. Alternatively put, language is no longer conceived as a stock of words (like *langue* in Saussure), or of rules (like Chomskyan competence), but as a system of variations – a formulation which (as we have seen) is not as paradoxical as it might seem. Here is what Vygotsky, the Soviet psychologist, has to say about the meaning of words:

> The discovery that words' meanings evolve leads the study of thought and speech out of a blind alley. Word meanings are dynamic rather than static formulations. They change as the child develops; they change also with the various ways in which thought functions.[3]

And Vygotsky adds: 'The relation of thought to word is not a thing but a process, a continual movement back and forth from thought to word and from word to thought.'[4]

The first quotation seems to be a matter of plain good sense: we know very well that the meaning of words changes all the time and we are used to resuscitating these superseded meanings and telling these stories, in all their nuances, for the benefit of younger generations, who pay no attention to them. The second quotation indicates the enemy by negation: a positivist conception of language that wants to isolate and fix facts so that they are more readily manipulable by science. To replace these 'facts' by processes is to affirm that the object of the 'science of language' is not to discover the laws of nature, but to describe pragmatic maxims, of the kind 'do not say x, say y' – or indeed 'if you say x, then you must also say y' – where it is clear that power relations obtain and that these 'rules' are made to be challenged, exploited, changed. This means that what are called 'exceptions' (leaf/leaves, mouse/mice, etc.) are not so much defects of grammatical construction, which a refinement of the rules will soon suppress, as indices of a semantic and

---

[3] Vygotsky 1962, p. 124.
[4] Vygotsky 1962, p. 125.

pragmatic struggle in which the 'rules' are at stake. This is why I propose to place at the centre of the study of language pragmatics, which replaces the language of Kant's first critique – that of 'pure' or theoretical reason – the language, principles and maxims of the second – i.e. that of *practical* reason. We thus pass from the formulation of a natural law ('every' sentence is composed of a subject and a 'predicate') to that of a practical maxim ('be relevant': such is the maxim of relation in Grice):[5] a transition that is scarcely innocent, because it avoids the naturalism and fetishism of abstraction through the exclusion of a major part of linguistic phenomena.

This implication of my main thesis – the transition from the standpoint of fetishised 'things' to that of processes – has consequences, which are so many changes of standpoint.

The *second change of standpoint* leads to tackling language from the standpoint of *social interaction*. For language is no more situated in the individual speaker (in her mind/brain as in Chomsky, her faculties, her consciousness or unconscious) than aesthetic creativity resides in the irrepressible individuality of the artist. Obviously, this does not mean that I am denying that it is you and me who speak; like every speaker, I am highly impressed by the profound originality of what I say and write. What I mean is that this irreducible individuality is not the source of my language, but its effect; and that the language which is mine is such only because it is collective in the first instance. Methodological individualism in the field of politics and economics has never prevented multinationals from behaving like collective entities, rather than as the democratic sum of individual choices. In the field of language, it feeds the illusion of the subject's mastery over her speech and of equality of opportunity in the domain of communication.

People have a natural tendency to speak of 'language' or of 'the English language' as if they were things, for reification is profoundly inscribed in our common sense. But these 'things' are not things: they are processes of social interaction; they are the object of learning processes within social practices, like family life or relations at work. The subject becomes a speaker by appropriating a language that is always-already collective – which means that she is appropriated by it: she is captured by a language that is external

---

[5] See Grice 1975.

and prior to her, and on which she will leave her mark – possibly even a lasting mark – through linguistic or literary creation. Possession here is a transitive relationship, something clearly marked by the ambiguity of the word: I possess the language in as much as I am possessed by it, just as people were once possessed by the devil.

We can see why the Heideggerian expression *die Sprache spricht* (the language speaks) – a formula that contrasts with the 'I speak the language' of common sense – is not necessarily (or not only) a flagrant example of linguistic fetishism (I hypostatise the language, which rebounds on me to oppress me), but, rather, the expression of a dynamic process of subjectivation: subjection to language is, at the same time, the active creation of subjectivity. The apparent fetishism of the expression is a symptom of the fact that language, as a social process, is manifestly not the result of the composition of individual choices and calculations. We certainly have the impression that we 'use' language like an instrument at our disposal. But this relationship is dialectical, for, if we reflect on it, we shall come to understand that the hammer guides the hand which wields it: we 'use' language within strict constraints and our ability to transform it by a deliberate decision, while not completely non-existent, is highly restricted. The history of feminist attempts to invent or impose an epicene pronoun, especially in English, is instructive in this respect: they have largely failed to invent a pronoun to replace the un-marked 'he' that refers to the reader or author whatever their sex. But they have, in the English-speaking world at least, completely succeeded in imposing the equal use of 'she' and 'he' in epicene contexts (i.e. contexts where the sex of the referent is not specified). The same might be said of official attempts, laid down in decrees, to erase any trace of franglais from our beautiful French vocabulary: today, who in France says *baladeur* rather than 'walkman' and who, outside official documents, characterizes her email as a *mel*?

The *third change of standpoint* involves adopting the standpoint of *history*. The semi-frozen time of evolution is not enough for me, nor is the time of the system, which, in its natural course, transforms Old English into Middle English and then Modern English (this 'natural bent of the system' is obviously a retrospective construction on the part of science). If language is a form of human *praxis*, its time is that of the history of human beings and the societies they form. Accordingly, the history of language is not the immanent history of a system – what post-Saussurian linguistics marginalises under the rubric of diachrony; it is that of the totality of a social process: it is interwoven with the history of culture, of class struggle, and of the common sense which conserves its traces and monuments (in clichés, dead metaphors, processes of grammaticalisation).

Here, we can see how the concept of synchrony is deficient. It corresponds to what Althusser's analyses under the name of 'essential section', which is, once again, a form of fetishisation of language. Synchrony transforms dynamic processes into things; it arbitrarily arrests the development and variation of the different elements that make up a language (sounds, words, and sentences): it pins them down the better to study them, rather as one does insects – which implies making them expire. Above all, it crushes the differences of temporality between the different strata of language (for each has its own time, like the different layers of the social structure in Althusser), replacing them by the fixed image of the pyramid of language (phonology, morphology, syntax: the pyramid threatens to collapse when we reach semantics, because we do not really know which level to assign it to). But language, as a historical process, has its own dynamic and is oblivious of the stratifications imposed by science. We are constantly dealing with shifts, rhizomatic dispersions, heavy mixtures, when supra-segmental phenomena like intonation invade syntax, when iconicity subverts the arbitrariness of the sign – i.e. the arbitrariness of dual articulation. And we note with a smile that the model of stratification adopted by most research programmes in linguistics shares the architectural metaphor with the most deterministic version of Marxism.

The *fourth change of standpoint* leads us to adopt the standpoint of the totality. As is well known, this concept enables Lukács to criticise and avoid fetishism. And we have seen that in the dominant philosophy of language this fetishism took the form of the principle of immanence defining an internal linguistics, in which language is separated from the rest of the phenomena that make up the world. This reification of language is two-fold: it makes it a fixed *object*, object of manipulation and contemplation on the part of the linguist, as the etymology of the term has it (the linguist is an entomologist); and it posits a reified *subject* – the speaker – who possesses her language and uses it like an instrument. Hence the dominant metaphors (that of instrument is the most frequent) and habitual dichotomies (*langue* and *parole*, competence and performance). This entails certain consequences – especially a tradition of mistrust of natural languages (for it must be acknowledged that language is a highly imperfect instrument, which betrays the speaker's intended meanings, makes her say what she did not mean to say or did not know that she was saying: when it comes to instruments, the great watch-maker could have done better); and a valorisation of artificial languages, which have the advantage over natural languages of logical coherence (we now understand the metaphorical fantasy that leads people to think about language in terms of computer programs).

We must, therefore, view the relations between collective linguistic processes and a community of speakers in non-fetishistic fashion, understand the processes of interpellation that make individuals speaker-subjects, who, in turn, help the language change, develop and vary, through their linguistic practice, which comes down to a form of counter-interpellation. As I speak, I counter-interpellate the language that interpellates me to my place as a speaker, which makes me what I am. I exploit the potentialities of meaning that it provides me with, I play tricks with and on it, I accept or reject the names with which it assigns me a place in the community of speakers or excludes me from it (the study of insults offers an antidote to the dominant philosophy of language). For the fact that language is a collective practice must not be understood in a determinist sense: the speaker acts on and in language by using it. Every speech act, no matter how humble or conventional, by virtue of being an act, an action in a historical conjuncture, shifts the language, makes it advance, millimetre by millimetre, on the path of its history – even if the language in a global sense is out of the range of any individual action. The same is true of language as of the whole of society: I am well aware that my individual action will not change the capitalist social relations in which I am caught, but there is no reason for this to induce resignation in me.

The *fifth and final change of standpoint* leads to adopting the standpoint of *power relations* – something I have often had occasion to characterise as the standpoint of *agon* as opposed to *eirene*. This change of standpoint is the natural consequence of the other four. Even if, as the most plausible myth of origins would have it, language has its source in the exigencies of communication, not in any circumstances whatsoever (but in social interaction when, in the relations that govern labour in common, it is necessary to arrive at an understanding about what to do and to indicate the objects on which theses actions bear), this cannot be its only source. For affects also stand in need of expression – for example, when expressive exclamations become orders and are thereby transformed into articulated language; or in the rhythmical sounds accompanying labour in common and finding a mode of aesthetic expression in dance. For the 'heave-ho!' theory of the origin of language, to which I alluded in a previous chapter, is not the only candidate: there is also the 'ding-dong' theory which attributes a musical origin to language, but also the 'come hither darling' theory in which humanity accedes to language in the context of sexual intercourse, which it prepares for and accompanies. These mythical theories, which at least have the merit of unbridled imagination, are also interesting and not manifestly less plausible than the usual theory, which I propose to call the 'pass me the leg of mammoth' theory. All these theories postulate both a co-operation in, and a division of, labour in the broadest sense – that is, the assignment of a system of places (who are you to talk to me like that? Who am I to address you in this fashion?). From this system of places to a system power relations is but a short step; and Marxists know that humanity took it: language is caught up in this history and its history – as a social process and despite Stalin's good sense – is also that of class struggle.

Treating language in terms of *praxis* raises a number of issues. For example, what is the relationship between this form of *praxis* and other practices, productive or superstructural? I risk getting lost in the paradox of the chicken and the egg: I need language to explain the emergence of relations of an economic type, and yet my most plausible myth of origins tells me that language is generated out of labour in common – that is, from the most primitive form of relations of production. Contrary to linguists who obey the principle of immanence, however, Marxists are not afraid of the question of origins, as we saw in the case of Engels, even if they know that the problem has only a speculative solution – i.e. no solution or rather a solution which is an act of ideological partisanship. For only a myth can release us from the vicious circle and allow us to think, *with the help of the concept of praxis*, the contemporaneous emergence of relations of production and language in the context of action in common, be it the fabrication of tools, hunting, agricultural work, or the sexual division of labour. In other words, even if they do not entertain too many illusions, Marxists cannot be indifferent to the type of analysis that seeks in the domain of language to produce the equivalent of Engels's *Origin of the Family* – a text which is not at the forefront of anthropological research, but has lost nothing of its philosophical and political vigour (especially when dealing with the relations of domination of one sex over the other).

It is in this spirit that I want to return to the work of the Vietnamese philosopher Tran Duc Thao, a work that is neglected today and unjustly forgotten. He is the author of two books, one devoted to a critique of phenomenology and the other to studies of the origin of language and consciousness.[6] The second, written in Vietnam under the civilising influence of American bombs, and without its author having access to contemporary anthropological research except in the form of outdated articles published in Soviet journals, seeks to propose a Marxist theory of the origins of language, in which the contribution of the particular philosophical origins of Tran Duc Thao – i.e. phenomenology – is apparent.

Tran Duc Thao starts out form the famous nineteenth-century thesis of Haeckel, whom he cites via Engels, that ontogenesis recapitulates phylogenesis: the origin of language is therefore to be studied through its emergence in children. This is combined with a phenomenological thesis, according to which consciousness is consciousness of something before being self-consciousness (this is Husserl's thesis on intentionality); and a Marxist thesis, which makes language the source of a consciousness, a source that is material (the language of 'real life', language as material *praxis*), collective (language emerges within a group of hunters), and social (the beginnings of work in common and the division of labour).

His central thesis is that what distinguishes the human being from its immediate ancestor is the use of *indicative gestures*: language and consciousness emerge from these gestures. This is where the theory becomes original.

From this main thesis there follows a set of theses on the origin of consciousness. (1) The immediate reality of consciousness is language (verbal or gestural). (2) Conscious perception is perception that apprehends the external object as external (this is a materialist thesis, which recognises the externality and priority of the world vis-à-vis consciousness). (3) The indicative gesture makes its appearance in the context of the summons to labour in common; and its original function is collective and social. (4) This gesture rebounds on the subject, who indicates himself as it were. The summons to

---

[6] See Thao 1951 and 1973.

order becomes an order to the self: it is thus that the isolated hunter, separated from the rest of the group, urges himself on. At this stage, consciousness is still contingent and sporadic. (5) The dialectic of internalisation of the external sign constitutes consciousness as a relation of the subject to himself. (6) Consciousness thus becomes not only consciousness of the external object, but constant self-consciousness. (7) When the indicative gesture thus internalised by the individual is internalised by the whole group, it can serve to designate not only the subject, but any object in its absence: it then becomes a sign. (8) The generalisation of signs within the group confirms its members as individual subjects.

The emergence of consciousness, the first *conscious realisation*, therefore passes through three stages: the sporadic use of indicative gestures to refer to oneself, which induces the appearance of the first forms of self-consciousness; the generalisation of this self-consciousness via the appearance of signs – a generalisation that is the acquisition of a group consciousness, consciousness of belonging to a collectivity; and the dialectical return to self-consciousness through the intermediary of the collective, which leads to the transformation of sporadic self-consciousness into stable consciousness, making the member of the group an individual subject. All this contains echoes of the process that Althusser describes under the rubric of interpellation (of which Tran Duc Thao was unaware), by means of an indicative gesture addressed towards the outside and returning to the self by being internalised in the form of consciousness.

Where is the birth of language in this picture? Language is born at the same time as consciousness and has its origin in indicative gestures, in the original form of economic activity: hunting in bands. Faithful to his starting-point, Tran Duc Thao analyses the emergence in the child of what he calls 'syncretic language' – the transformation of indicative gestures into words-sentences. The first words-sentences accompany gestures – for example, goodbye gestures. These words-sentences are limited in number and polysemic. The crucial moment is situated here. Not only when the same gesture is used for diverse objects or situations, but when it sets about designating objects *in their absence*, thus leading the child to graduate from presentation to representation – that is when it becomes a sign. This transition to representation involves a form of subjectivity: by producing signs even when they are alone, primitive hunters recognise themselves, *provided that these signs become public.*

It is in the same way that their descendents – today's children – become persons.

We have here a very attractive myth. But a myth none the less: the latest developments in anthropology, genetics, and primatology probably preclude us from considering this description of the origin of language as corresponding to the facts. And yet, in addition to the 'facts' being (perhaps irretrievably) out of our reach in this instance, I note that recent American studies of the issue offer solutions which, while they ignore the role of labour, are not so far removed from Tran Duc Thao's analyses. For they suggest that the origin of articulated language is to be found in the gestures of primates or in their becoming carnivorous, when it is not via socialisation by delousing.[7] But a myth does not need to be 'true' in the sense of positive science to be effective, as is clearly demonstrated by the Freudian myth of *fort-da*, which is not unrelated to this one. It is enough for it to be relevant to our philosophical concerns and, so far as possible, *correct*. And this myth, which claims to show us what we can never see, renders explicit, by contradicting it, what the dominant philosophy of language leaves implicit (doubtless because this embarrasses it): naturalistic and/or individualistic myths of the origin of language.

Tran Duc Thao's myth of origins is therefore to be regarded as an anticipation of truths to come, in a Hegelian manner, and as evidence of the intimate link between language and social *praxis*. We can, for example, read Tran Duc Thao in the light of Vygotsky's theories about the relations between language and thought, in which Vygotsky identifies two separate functions. Vygotsky is not directly interested in the origin of language, but in the acquisition of language by children, the emergence of internal language as an internalisation of public language, via the intermediate step of what he calls egocentric language. As in Tran Duc Thao, however, his starting-point is the collective, public, interlocutory aspect of language. Like him, he has a *historical* view of the relations between thought and language and the development of human consciousness. The following quotation is typical: 'We found no specific interdependence between the genetic roots of thought and of word. It became plain that the inner relationship we were looking for was not a

---

[7] See Liebermann 1998 and Dunbar 1996.

prerequisite for, but rather a product of, the historical development of human consciousness.'[8]

This means that the myth of origins, in reality, refers us to the central role of fetishism in capitalist societies. Myth projects onto the origin of language its real functioning in conditions of capitalism, whereas the metaphors of money, market and commodity applied to language indicate that language furnishes us with a unique and archetypal example of fetishism, just as it is a unique and archetypal form of *praxis*. For language is indeed the archetypal form of *praxis*, in that it affects the core of human practice in the process of subjectivation.

Perhaps it is time for me to indicate more precisely what I mean by *praxis*. More precisely, what is the relationship between this Marxian concept and the more usual Marxist concept of 'practice'? For the idea that language is a form of *practice* is not obvious, if we accept the famous definition of practice given by Althusser in *For Marx*:

> By *practice* in general I shall mean any process of *transformation* of a determinate given raw material into a determinate *product*, a transformation effected by a determinate human labour, using determinate means (of 'production'). In any practice thus conceived, the *determinant* moment (or element) is neither the raw material nor the product, but the practice in the narrow sense: the moment of the *labour of transformation itself*, which sets to work, in a specific structure, men, means and a technical method of utilizing the means.[9]

It is difficult to subsume language under this definition of practice. Unless we are prepared to say that language transforms 'ideas' into 'words', which would involve a regression to an idealist conception of the relations between thought and language where thought precedes language and uses it as an instrument of expression – that is, unless we revert to the dominant philosophy of language – I do not see how language can be characterised as a 'practice': thought is not the 'raw material' of language and language is not the technical means for its transformation into words.

---

[8] Vysgotsky 1962, p. 119.
[9] Althusser 1969, pp. 166–7.

But Althusser's definition of practice is not faithful to the Aristotelian origin of the concept; in other words, Althusserian 'practice' is not *praxis*. Aristotle does not simply contrast *praxis* and *theoria*, as Althusser opposes practice and theory (as we know, he adds that theory is a specific form of practice): a distinction is made in Aristotle between three terms – *praxis*, *theoria*, and *poiesis*. What corresponds to Althusser's definition of practice is *poiesis*, not *praxis*. It is *poiesis* that transforms a raw material into a product, which 'fabricates', whereas *praxis* is not fabrication but action in common, whose canonical example is political action. And it will be recalled that, on the first page of his *Politics*, Aristotle defines man as a political animal *in that he is a speaking animal*.

In the Aristotelian sense, then, language is indeed a form of *praxis*: it is the medium of political action (programmes, slogans, pamphlets, laws and decrees, but also, in the classical definition of democracy, debates). It is language that imparts material force to the ideas that it embodies and which have no existence aside from the words that formulate them, which enable them to persuade the masses and rouse them to action.

We find a contemporary version of this idea in the Italian philosopher Paolo Virno, who makes the intervention of language in production a characteristic of the phase of the capitalism he calls 'post-Fordism' (he thus assimilates Althusserian 'practice' to Aristotelian *praxis*). In this stage, he tells us, which is the current stage, language is no longer a mere instrument of communication or stock of signs that are so many tools. In the post-Fordist stage, language is directly involved in the process of production. The worker is also, *as a worker*, a speaker and an important part of her labour is devoted to communication with complex machines, with the complex structure of the production process. This means that the role of the worker is not confined to traditional *poiesis*, but involves *praxis*. The labour process becomes a process of open, public interlocution, whose direct analogue is political action. In short, Virno tells us, the worker is no longer a simple producer but in a way a virtuoso, whose production is inseparably an interpretation in the musical sense of the word. Virno encourages us to re-read the *Nicomachean Ethics*, where the distinction between *poiesis* and *praxis* is explicit; he even encourages us to re-read this opposition in the light of the Saussurian opposition between *langue* and *parole*, or of the concept of enunciation in Benveniste, in that it marks a transition from the standpoint of the result (the utterance as product) to the process (enunciation as public *praxis* of interlocution). In this theoretical framework, language is indeed a form of *praxis* and the best way of accounting for it is a version of *pragmatics*. The following quotation, in which he criticises Hannah Arendt, is typical:

> I am claiming that in today's work we rediscover 'exposition to the gaze of the other', a relation with the presence of others, the beginning of original processes, a constitutive familiarity with contingency, the unforeseen, the possible. I am arguing that post-Fordist labour, labour productive of surplus-value, subordinate labour, involves qualities and exigencies which, for an age-old tradition, belong instead to political action.[10]

Virno bases his interpretation on a passage in the *Grundrisse* where Marx develops the concept of the 'general intellect'. And we find similar conceptions in Marazzi, the Swiss economist on whom Hardt and Negri draw.[11] I have some serious doubts about the 'linguistic turn' of the economic and the politicisation of the workplace through the virtuoso use of language by the set of worker-speakers. To read Deborah Cameron's book on the standardisation and control of workers' language in enterprises, and not only in service enterprises, is salutary here.[12] But it clearly demonstrates, *a contrario*, the strategic importance of linguistic *praxis* and the acute awareness of this on the part of the class enemy. I am therefore going to develop my central thesis in the form of four positive theses.

3. First positive thesis: language is a historical phenomenon

My thesis has two aspects: language (a determinate natural language) *has a history*, which the theory of language is not entitled to ignore or treat as a marginal phenomenon; and language *is history*.

Contrary to what might be said of it by a positivism which describes the development, the expansion, the convergence, the corruption, and the retreat of a language which ends up being transformed into a different language, the history of language, such as it can be grasped through the history of natural languages, is not a long, tranquil stream. (One might take as an

---

[10] Virno 2002, p. 44.
[11] See Marazzi 1997.
[12] See Cameron 2000.

example the history of Latin as traditionally narrated.) For the temporality of change in a given language is complex and uneven, because the various elements that make up a language develop at different speeds.

Thus, the vocabulary of a language changes very quickly, year by year, generation by generation. In his youth my father smoked *sibiches* [ciggies]; in mine we smoked *seiches* [butts] and then *clops* [fags]; I do not know what today's adolescents smoke (or I know only too well), but I have heard the word 'nuit-grave', which has the advantage of cutting up and re-semanticising the deterrent slogan that every packet of cigarettes must carry in France (*nuit gravement à la santé*). This shows that linguistic invention is not the preserve of poets and that we must assume a poetic voice of the people which I have elsewhere proposed to call the 'unknown coiner'.[13] This very rapid change, which has something to do with the dialects of social groups and generations, obviously does not involve the vocabulary in its entirety: the spoken changes more rapidly than the written; the lexicon of a language has a more stable central component, to designate natural kinds like 'gold' or 'tiger', and everyday objects to the extent that (and as long as) they do not change, like 'house'. Naturally, we understand that emotive words or *argot* change more quickly than others. But what interests me here are the different speeds of evolution of the different dialects, registers, jargons, and language games, which render any synchronic essential section decidedly random.

It will be objected that what evolves so rapidly is the most superficial aspect of language – its spoken vocabulary – and that the core of the structure – the syntax and grammatical markers – does not shift. But they definitely do shift, even if they take rather longer. There is a history of markers, which explains the complexity and nuances of their contemporary usage. Thus, all Anglicists are interested in the form 'be + ing', mark of the continuous aspect ('she is eating' contrasts with 'she eats'); and theoretical explanations of the values of this marker, which are sometimes of a Byzantine complexity, are not wanting. But this marker also has a history, whose traces are still inscribed in contemporary English. To arrive at the form 'she was reading', where we simply have a modification of the main verb by a marker of aspect, things have passed from 'she was on reading', where the main verb is in reality a verbal noun, and 'she was a-reading', corruption of the previous form, which

---

[13] See Lecercle 1991.

heralds the contemporary one, and which is still to be found in the archaic language of ballads.

Syntax also evolves at its own pace, slowly but perceptibly. Contemporary English knows a solecism called the 'unattached participle', which makes it possible to use a participial proposition without a subject, whose implicit subject is not the same as that of the verb of the main clause, thus contravening one of the sacrosanct rules of deletion of grammatical subjects, which are no doubt inscribed in the genetic inheritance of the species – at least if Chomsky's naturalism is accepted. 'When writing, the paper should be kept flat': *En écrivant, le papier doit rester à plat*. My translation is deliberately clumsy, so that we can grasp what does not work: logic (the logic which the grammarian seeks to impose on the language) prompts me to think that it is the paper – not me – which does the writing. But I note that the ambiguity is artificial: in reality, this sentence is understood straight away. And the recent history of the language tells us that, up to the end of the eighteenth century, use of the unattached participle was so common that it could pass for the norm. It is precisely the grammarians who, by codifying their rules and imposing this straitjacket on the diversity of usages, transformed an innocent construction into a 'solecism'. (In English, this word is used more widely than in French and also refers to a gaffe committed in company: we are dealing with social and hence historical constraints, not with laws that are natural or dictated by the logic of the system.) So, if one is interested in the history of syntax, one will have to take an interest in the history of the grammars that have sought to codify, and thus alter, it – and sometimes succeeded in so doing. Obviously, change is not always deliberate: we shall also interest ourselves in the phenomena that linguists call 'grammaticalisations' – for example, the appearance in French of two-term negation, the *ne . . . pas*, where *pas* originally meant 'a step', in the sense 'would you like to take a few steps?'. It was therefore what is called a 'natural complement' of a verb of motion: *il n'avance pas* [he is not advancing] meant *il n'avance (même pas) d'un seul pas* [he is not even advancing by a single step]. The history of the construction would show us how this *pas* has been generalised to all verbs, losing its lexical meaning and acquiring a grammatical sense of negation. We still find a trace of the old construction in *il n'y voit goutte* [he does not see a thing], whose literal meaning (readers will agree) is obscure, but which becomes clearer if we regard it as a corruption of *il ne boit goutte* [he does not drink a drop].

Finally, there is the history of the language as whole, of what is called 'English'. As we have seen, this name is an ontological metaphor, which transforms a chaotic variety of phenomena into an object and is therefore a historical and political construct – a historical process of unification of different dialects and registers. (Striking traces of it remain in the importance of regional, class, and even generational accents in contemporary British English.) In Chapter 1, I referred to the centripetal and centrifugal forces affecting the language of imperialism: to study these processes is a more important and more urgent task for linguists than to produce the umpteenth explanation of the contrast between the deictics 'this' and 'that'. If, for example, we read Paul Fussell's admirable book on the language and literature of the Great War, we will appreciate the direct influence of a historical event (in truth, not any event) on the language of its actors.[14]

Here we can see the origin – and the sole interest – of the architectural model of language as a pile of strata (phonetic, morphological, syntactical, etc.) to which linguistics is attached: in the form of an essential section, it fetishises the different temporalities of language. A language changes at different speeds according to its different regions or sectors. Here the same is true of language as of the whole of society, at least according to Althusser's image of it – the image of a structure each of whose elements develops according to its specific time, thereby generating phenomena of survivals (of a previous mode of production within the new mode of production), but also of anticipation (of the mode of production nascent within the one that is still dominant). We therefore have linguistic survivals (words and constructions sediment former states of the language: what are called exceptions and archaisms) and linguistic anticipations (one of the main function of the language games grouped under the name of literature is to be attentive to linguistic change – i.e. to the new language that is being born within the old one). And this also enables us to understand the relationship between language in general and a particular language, which we will no longer conceive as the relationship of a faculty (inscribed in our genetic programme) to its embodiment in a particular system, but as the relationship between a human *praxis* and the variety of forms it takes in determinate conjunctures. Marxists describe a particular society (say,

---

[14] See Fussell 2000.

French society at a particular moment of its history) with the aid of the concept of *social formation*: this aims to conceptualise, in some historical conjuncture, the precise distribution of survivals and anticipations, the complex mix of elements of different modes of production coexisting in this conjuncture. If we extend our analogy, we have a definition of what *a language* is: a *linguistic formation*, an unstable state of tensions and contradictions affecting the *praxis* of language in a given historical and cultural conjuncture (the term 'cultural' being intended to delimit the geographical, and not merely historical, limits of the conjuncture). So, a language is not a relatively stable system that evolves exclusively according to immanent systemic constraints, but a system of variations, which changes with the change in historical conjunctures. Language is indeed a historical phenomenon.

If historical events – e.g., as Fussell shows, the Great War – can have a direct impact on the language, in defiance of Stalin's good sense, and even if this impact is not identical in the domains of the lexicon, semantics, phonetics and syntax, it is because of a characteristic of language whose universality simply reflects that fact that it is a social practice, a set of processes and not a result or a system. This characteristic is the tendency to *metaphorical drift* that affects the meaning of words because they are immersed in the history of those who utter them and develop with conjunctures. Let us attend to Gramsci on this point:

> Usually, when a new conception [of the world] replaces the previous one, the previous language continues to be used but is, precisely, used metaphorically. The whole of language is a continuous process of metaphor, and the history of semantics is an aspect of the history of culture; language is at the same time a living thing and a museum of fossils of life and civilizations. When I use the word 'disaster' no one can accuse me of believing in astrology, and when I say 'by Jove!' no one can assume that I am a worshipper of pagan divinities. These expressions are however a proof that modern civilization is also a development of paganism and astrology.[15]

And, a little later, Gramsci affirms that '[l]anguage is always metaphorical', a thesis which has Nietzschean accents, but which is firmly historicised, for the metaphorical relation links the contemporary meaning of the word and

---

[15] Gramsci 1971, p. 450.

the aura of sedimented meaning that inscribes 'the ideological content which the words used had in preceding periods of civilization'.[16]

Vygotsky's explanation of concept-formation in children furnishes an excellent description of this metaphorical drift. It begins with what he calls 'complexes' – that is, associations of objects in the perceptual experience of the child ('[i]n a complex, individual objects are united in the child's mind not only by his subjective impressions but also by *bonds actually existing between these objects*').[17] These associations tend to form chains, but without there being a centre from which all the associations stem. Instead, there is a drift, which passes from one element of the chain to another, the set possessing the coherence of what Wittgenstein calls 'family resemblances'. A chain complex consists in 'a dynamic, consecutive joining of individual links into a simple chain, with meaning carried over from one link to the other'.[18] It is here that the association of objects in perceptual experience becomes linguistic, becomes an association between a word, with its meaning, and not a singular object but a chain complex. And this is not due to some spontaneous decision on the part of the child; it depends on her interaction with adults, in the course of an elementary form of social *praxis*: 'in real life complexes corresponding to word meanings are not spontaneously developed by the child: The lines along which a complex develops are predetermined by the meaning a given word already has in the language of adults'.[19] Vygotsky explains how the child gradually passes from associated pseudo-complexes to chain complexes to complexes proper – that is, how she acquires the collective meaning of the 'words of the tribe'. What interests me here is that his explanation attributes a radically metaphorical character to language. Meaning does not develop through a leap from one reified meaning to another reified meaning, but though metaphorical slippage:

> What are the laws governing the formation of word families? More often than not, new phenomena or objects are named after unessential attributes, so that the name does not truly express the nature of the thing named. Because a name is never a concept when it first emerges, it is usually both

---

[16] Gramsci 1971, p. 450.
[17] Vygotsky 1962, p. 61.
[18] Vygotsky 1962, p. 64.
[19] Vygotsky 1962, p. 67.

too narrow and too broad. For instance, the Russian word for cow originally meant 'horned', and the word for mouse, 'thief'. But there is much more to a cow than horns, and to a mouse than pilfering; thus their names are too narrow. On the other hand, they are too broad, since the same epithets may be applied – and actually are applied in some other languages – to a number of other creatures. The result is a ceaseless struggle within the developing language between conceptual thought and the heritage of primitive thinking in complexes.[20]

What is interesting about a genetic approach of this sort is that it inverts the usual relationship (adopted by the dominant philosophy of language) between the literal and the metaphorical, between denotation and connotation. The literal (the concept) is the result of a process of literalisation of the metaphorical (which restricts or expands what was originally too broad or too narrow): thus the complex, the purely verbal meaning, the pseudo-concept yield to the concept. *Metaphor* is, therefore, the motor of the history of the meaning of words, which it causes to drift, just as *metonymy* is the synchronic motor of the meaning of the sentence, when the nodal point – the moment when the meaning is revealed – closes the sentence and retrospectively impose a meaning on it ('So that was what it meant!'), which sequential processes in a Markov chain construct word by word. (I shall return to this point at the end of the chapter.)

I announced a second aspect of my first positive thesis: language not only has a history, it *is* history. If we accept Gramsci's thesis that every language contains a conception of the world, we shall draw from it the conclusion that language is sedimented history. It is in the work of Raymond Williams that this thesis is set out most powerfully.

Williams devotes one of the chapters of his book *Marxism and Literature* to language: language is one of his 'basic concepts'. He begins by deploring the absence of a Marxist tradition in thinking about language and attempts to construct a Marxist concept of language, largely inspired by Voloshinov. The following two quotations illustrate his starting-point and conclusion respectively:

---

[20] Vygotsky 1962, p. 74.

The key moments which should be of interest to Marxism, in the development
of thinking about language, are, first, the emphasis on language as *activity*
and, second, the emphasis on the *history* of the language.

Thus we can add to the necessary definition of the biological faculty of
language as *constitutive* an equally necessary definition of language
development – at once individual and social – as historically and socially
constituting. What we can then define is a dialectical process: the *changing
practical consciousness of human beings*, in which both the evolutionary and
the historical processes can be given full weight, but also within which they
can be distinguished. . . .[21]

The first quotation confirms my positive theses, which therefore belong to a
tradition starting with Marx and passing via Williams. The second seems to
me to be unduly motivated by a desire to compromise. In conceding the
necessity of conceiving language as a 'biological faculty', Williams reverts to
the dominant philosophy of language; and his position must be taken as a
symptom of the respect too rapidly accorded to positive science by literary
critics. However, since I do not want to deny the facts, and according to the
gradient set out in Chapter 2, I am prepared to grant him the opposition
between language as *constitutive* (chimpanzees do not speak) and language
as *constituting* (i.e. as interpellating individuals as subjects), provided that we
are also aware of the fact that language is *constituted* in historical *praxis*.

What is interesting about Williams's position is that he did not merely
theorise the historical constitution of language, but practised what he preached –
a practice that anticipates the Marxist theory which I have just evoked – in,
for example, his best-known book *Culture and Society*.[22] This practice culminates
in *Keywords*, a book that is presented as a vocabulary, but an untypical one
in that it is concerned not only to give the current meanings of words, but
also and especially their history and the metaphorical slippage to which they
have been subject, which has produced their contemporary meaning. So what
Williams analyses are not words or meanings, but *formations of meaning*.
Originally, the work was to be a glossary attached to *Culture and Society*, but
it rapidly became an independent text: 'Every word which I have included

---

[21] Williams 1977, pp. 21, 43–4.
[22] See Williams 1958.

has at some time ... virtually forced itself on my attention, because the problems of its meanings seemed to me inextricably bound up with the problems it was being used to discuss.'[23] And in order to understand these formations of meaning, it is necessary to go beyond the usual practice of dictionaries, even when they are historical dictionaries. Ranging beyond '"proper meaning"',

> We find a history and complexity of meanings; conscious changes, or consciously different uses; innovation, obsolescence, specialization, extension, overlap, transfer; or changes which are masked by a nominal continuity so that words which seem to have been there for centuries, with continuous general meanings, have come in fact to express radically different or radically variable, yet sometimes hardly noticed, meanings and implications of meaning.[24]

The words that figure in *Keywords* are obviously not the concrete words referring to the objects of everyday life, are not the names of natural kinds like the word 'cat' or the word 'gold' (i.e. the words on which analytical philosophy, from Kripke to Putnam, builds its theory of naming). It is the words that enable us to live our social existence – words like 'family', 'culture', 'industry', 'class', or 'subject':

> The kind of semantics to which these notes and essays belong is one of the tendencies within *historical semantics*, where the theoretical problems are acute indeed but where even more fundamental theoretical problems must be seen as at issue. The emphasis on history, as a way of understanding contemporary problems of meaning, is a basic choice from a position of historical materialism rather than from the now more powerful positions of objective idealism or non-historical (synchronic) structuralism.[25]

The term 'objective idealism' refers to the critique of Saussure conducted by Voloshinov, whereas the implicit possibility of a 'historical structuralism' is doubtless an acknowledgement of Lucien Goldmann. As for the historical semantics thus announced, it has not really seen the light of day beyond the dictionary entries that make up *Keywords*: the task is still before us.

---

[23] Williams 1976, p. 13.
[24] Williams 1976, p. 17.
[25] Williams 1976, pp. 20–1.

But the sketch presented by Williams gives us an excellent idea of what we need: a concept of *linguistic conjuncture* to replace the inadequate concepts of synchrony and diachrony. The linguistic conjuncture is the context in which meanings are formed, within the social practices of speakers (the expression 'formation of meaning' has an active sense here), and within which they are reified into formations of meaning (here the expression no longer refers to a process, but to its outcome), which form so many points or forces in a semantic field. The operation of fetishism tends to fix or freeze these formations, to give words a stable meaning, to isolate them from the processes in which their meaning is active or living, in the way that we refer to a living metaphor as opposed to a dead metaphor. This fixing of meaning, which transforms the language into a cemetery of dead or forgotten meanings, cannot halt the processes that constitute language. To arrest the language – which is what the synchronic section tries to do – can only be an arbitrary coup de force, of temporary interest at best. This is why we also need the Leninist concept (Hegelian in origin) of *moment* of the conjuncture, which obliges us to regard language as a series of processes in a state of constant variation.

To name the moment of the conjuncture and fix its temporal limits has nothing arbitrary about it, as we have seen with the moment of the slogan 'All power to the soviets!'. It depends on the situation of the one who names, who constructs the theory of the situation; and this theory is an intervention in the situation, not a contemplation or external observation. The theoretical thesis does not emanate from a subject separated from its object, but from an activist immersed in the object that she theorises – which means that the formulations of the theory possess a performative aspect, that they are speech acts which contribute to the constitution and, ultimately, the existence of their referent. And because situations are multiple and diverse, there will be multiple, diverse moments of the linguistic conjuncture: the moment of literature is not the same as that of political interventions (the two types of language game do not develop at the same pace); and the moment of political intervention is not that of generations or social milieus. The upshot is that an analysis of a linguistic conjuncture in its constitutive complexity will analyse tensions, contradictions, power relations. It will involve not only an analysis of institutions and their role (in so far as these institutions are collective transmitters of discourse), their explicit linguistic policies (Deborah Cameron's book analyses the linguistic policies of enterprises or educational institutions:

it shows that language is not a neutral object intended for scientific contemplation, but subject to attempts at control – something that has not escaped employers).[26] It will also analyse the power relations between the various apparatuses (schools, media, state), the role of economic and technological change which influences linguistic change (the influence of text-messaging from mobile phones on the language of future generations can be foreseen), and, naturally, the role of globalisation not only in that it renders English the language of imperialism, but in that it alters the balance of power within the conglomeration called 'English': everyone knows the attractiveness of American argot for British adolescents. All of this pertains to a form of socio-linguistics – a historical semantics *à la* Raymond Williams – but also to a linguistic politics – that is, a Marxist philosophy of language whose basic concepts are those of *linguistic conjuncture, moment* of the conjuncture, and linguistic *power relations*.

4. Second positive thesis: language is a social phenomenon

At first sight, this thesis would seem to be a tired platitude. Everyone knows that languages presuppose communities of speakers and that human beings live in societies. Almost no one challenges Wittgenstein's argument against the existence of a private language, even if its precise philosophical objectives remain obscure; and the myth of origins which (as we have seen) is preferred by Marxists – the 'heave-ho!' theory – clearly assumes that language is the product of labour in common and the division of labour. Whether language is grounded in inter-subjectivity, or conceived as an effect of interlocution in the objective framework of labour in common, a form of society is required.

In truth, however, the assertion is not as obvious as it seems: it shifts the centre of interest from the individual speaker to the community of speakers, makes the individual a subject-speaker in that she is interpellated by a language that is always-already collective. In so doing, it runs counter to the dominant philosophy of language and the research programmes in linguistics inspired by it (which means most linguistics: generative, enunciative, pragmatic, etc.). For, as we have seen, the dominant philosophy of language presupposes already constituted subjects to whom language is always-already given in the form of a faculty.

---

[26] See Cameron 2000.

So my thesis is not trivial in that it ejects the individual speaker as the source of utterances and meanings from the front of the stage. The question that then follows is: what is she to be replaced by?

Previously, I explored the Heidegger-style response that consists in saying: *by language itself*. It is the language that speaks and which interpellates the individual as a speaker. From it, I derived a theory of the violence of language whose main concept is *remainder*.[27] This recourse to the entity 'language', and to the ontological metaphor that calls it into being by naming it, risks making me succumb to the same fetishism that produced the concept of *langue* as object of science, by excluding the rest of the phenomena. There is a difference, however, over and above the fact that naming by abstraction is a necessity and a basic characteristic of language, which is therefore not only the instrument but the source of fetishism – a fetishism that becomes inevitable and not always harmful: this 'language' is not some human creation transmuted into a thing and rebounding on humanity to oppress it, but, rather, marks the introduction of the standpoint of the totality of *praxis*. Unlike the concept of *langue*, it does not exclude any linguistic phenomena but enables us to think the totality of linguistic *praxis*. This is the totality that subjectifies the subject. To say that it is the language which speaks is to put the subject back in its place, which must also be understood in a positive sense: it is to assign the subject a place. We can compare the concept of language thus formulated with the Marxist concept of class, which is an example of abstraction but not of fetishism, precisely in that it does not refer to entities fixed prior to the class struggle, but to a process of struggle that produces the classes in struggle – which presupposes adopting the standpoint of the social totality, of society as a set of processes. The same is true of individual speakers: they are produced by interlocution just as classes are produced by class struggle. They are, therefore, products of the whole of the language and, by this token, are spoken by the language.

We have seen one of the consequences of such a position in the materialist pragmatics of Deleuze and Guattari: they replace the concept of individual speaker by that of collective assemblage of enunciation. But we have also seen how hostile they were to the concept of ideology, at least in its Althusserian version. However, this is concept that I am going to try to breathe life back

---

[27] See Lecercle 1991.

into, by examining the proximity – even the inseparable links – between language and ideology.

In a passage of *A Theory of Literary Production*, Pierre Macherey suggests, in the course of a sentence, that language and ideology are the same thing.[28] He does not linger over the point, doubtless because it is too general. I am nevertheless going to try to give it a non-trivial meaning and ask how ideology is linguistic in character and how language is ideological. The name of Macherey cited here is not innocent. As Marxists are only too well aware, the concept of ideology is highly polysemic and it is open to doubt whether ideology constitutes anything outside of the theory that constructs its concept. (This situation should not concern us: it is true of all ontological metaphors and that also means 'language' and 'human being'.) To speak of ideology in non-trivial fashion is therefore first of all to state which theory of ideology is being referred to. The one I am referring to here is the theory – or rather, theories – of ideology to be found in the work of Louis Althusser (this distinguishes my argument from Williams's thesis 'ideology is linguistic' in *Marxism and Literature*).

That ideology in the trivial sense is not only conveyed by words, but consists in words, had already been apparent to numerous thinkers, from George Orwell (to whom Chomsky refers in a passage I quoted in Chapter 2) to Althusser in his first theory of ideology – the one formulated in *For Marx* which suggests that ideology functions by playing on the meaning of words, which are in a way political puns. We can even define the term in this trivial sense by saying that it describes any situation where the words do not correspond to the deeds or the facts. The history of colonialism and imperialism abounds in manipulations of this kind, with colonial wars currently being re-baptised 'peace-keeping operations', intervention to save a genocidal government in Rwanda 'humanitarian intervention', and aggression against Iraq and its occupation 'liberation' (which the 'liberated', out of sheer perversity, resist with weapons in their hands), and so on. The commonest terms in our political vocabulary, like 'freedom' and 'democracy', are (as everyone knows) the privileged sites of these ideological operations – a process that is not unimportant in the current disaffection with politics in Western countries.

---

[28] See Macherey 1978, p. 52.

I think we can go beyond these formulations, which form part of our common sense, by turning to the second theory of ideology proposed by Althusser, as formulated in the famous essay on 'ideological state apparatuses', which I have already tried to interpret in terms of language in my book *Interpretation as Pragmatics*.[29] We are familiar with the success of this theory and the difficulties it creates (it refers to ideology in the singular, when the term is usually declined in the plural; it argues that ideology has no history – which is paradoxical coming from a Marxist; and so on). At the heart of this theory is the concept of interpellation (ideology is what produces subjects, in that it interpellates each individual as a subject). I propose to interpret the Althusserian chain of interpellation in linguistic terms. This allows me not only to assert that ideology is language, but to define this mysterious ideology declined in the singular: it is the power that circulates across the whole length of the chain of interpellation, the illocutionary force conveyed by utterances, which does not only characterise some particular speech act, but has a material effect in producing subjects.

This chain, at the end of which the individual is interpellated as a subject, runs from institutions to rituals, from rituals to practices, and (in my interpretation at least) from practices to speech acts:

Institution – ritual – practice – speech act – subject

The subject is, therefore, not only interpellated by ideology – which is the core of Althusser's theory – but subjectified by the language that speaks it. And at each link of the chain, ideology and language are indissolubly involved.

We therefore begin with the massive materiality of institutions as producers of discourse. They are material in that their apparatus involves a certain number of bodies (the bodies of the functionaries of the institution, the buildings in which they operate, etc.). But they are also material in a broader sense, in that they produce laws and decrees which assign places to the subjects produced by their apparatuses. And they are, if I may risk the expression, *linguistically* material in that they are the source of ready-made (one should say: 'ready-to-be-spoken') discourses and expressions, which speakers tirelessly repeat because they recognise themselves in them. By this, obviously, I mean the clichés and dead metaphors which, in Lakoff and

---

[29] See Althusser 1984 and cf. Lecercle 1999b.

Johnson's apt phrase, 'we live by'.[30] These dead metaphors are the only ones that are truly living in that they are constantly transmitted in linguistic exchange, in that they define the common sense which enables us to apprehend the world and share this understanding with others: a common sense that is always in danger of congealing into good sense, the authorised way which attests that we are indeed, as subjects, in our rightful place.

I speak of subjects as if they were directly interpellated by the institutions that give them their identity. But the process is more complicated: the subject is an end-of-the-chain production and its interpellation first of all passes through *rituals*, which precisely have the role of attributing an identity to the subject – that is, a place, a role in the social division of labour and collective action. This is the privileged moment of the performative speech act, when the judge adopts a solemn tone (in Britain he used to don a black cap) to condemn the defendant to death: it is the moment of the instantaneous incorporeal transformation, to speak in the manner of Deleuze, which produces notable effects on the bodies that it affects. We are all concerned by such rituals, which punctuate our daily lives and make us the social character we are, by determining the place from which we speak. Had I had not, in the distant past, participated in such academic rituals, it is a safe bet that you would not be paying the same attention to my words (and this in a directly material sense: I would have had difficulty finding a publisher). It will be noted that the subject who emerges here is more collective than individual: a ritual is not accomplished in solitude and the titles and the qualifications that make me an authorised author have been personally awarded to me, but I am not their only holder, as the very name of 'national qualifications' indicates. The issue is therefore at what point the individual subject separates off from the collective subject. And the answer is: when the ritual becomes a practice.

So a *practice* is here something that transforms the solemnity of the collective ritual into the banality of the daily life of the individual – the everyday life of the young married people once the ritual of the great day and the exceptional phase of the honeymoon are over. Here, collective ideology, with its clichés and metaphors that we live by (and which form a system: Lakoff and Johnson calls this 'structural metaphors' and their canonical example is 'argument is

---

[30] See Lakoff and Johnson 1980.

war'), is distributed or dispersed between individuals, as they go about their business. It is here that individual action makes its appearance, negotiating (adapting to, resisting, getting round) the constraints of the field: to each subject-actor her strategy, which means that she emerges from the position of subjected subject. Such individuality has its limits, but I am not proposing that we should lapse into determinism (an accusation often levelled at Althusser's theory of ideology). That is why I propose to complete the Althusserian concept of interpellation with that of *counter-interpellation*, which is inspired by the work of Judith Butler on insults and other forms of hate speech.[31] And it is precisely the linguistic character of ideology which enables us to understand that we are not dealing here with the unauthorised reintroduction of a subject who is fully in control of her actions, hence an irreducible liberty, and so on: in short, the subject of idealism. For the speaker is undeniably constrained by the language she speaks, which is prior and external to her, and to which she must adapt. But this has never prevented anyone from expressing themselves freely, and sometimes creatively. The speaker is therefore interpellated to her place by language, but, in so far as she makes the language *her* language, she counter-interpellates it: she plays with it, pushes it to its limits, accepts its constraints in order to subvert them, just as the participant in a conversation in Grice's co-operative model acknowledges the universality of the maxims in that she exploits them for expressive purposes. Hence the interpellated one counter-interpellates the ideology that interpellates her.

But we have now reached the last link of the chain: *speech acts*. These acts are irreducibly individual and, even if they can be classified by kinds (which is what Searle applies himself to),[32] there is an indefinite number of them. This is the source of methodological individualism in linguistic matters that fetishises the individuality of conventional acts, which depend on conditions fortunately supplied by a context that is always collective. For the individual speaker is indeed responsible for her speech act, she does indeed speak the language that speaks her, and can if needs be transform a performative misfortune into a stylistic felicity. The same is true of clichés: these provide opportunities for parody, pastiche, irony, quotations, and all the dealings in

---

[31] See Butler 1997.
[32] See Searle 1969

which the speaker can engage with the language for her pleasure. But she can only do so within the limits of what is furnished by her language – that is, the linguistic conjuncture she finds herself in. Her linguistic freedom is, therefore, as limited as the chimerical imagination in Plato: for a chimera – e.g. the Socratic goat-stag – is a mad creation of the free imagination, but its elements belong to reality. The griffin is constructed out of the eagle and the lion.

With the speech act we have thus reached the end of the chain, the moment of full subjectivity: the moment of expression in its infinite variety and whose name is *style* – a term that has the great advantage of containing the two poles of this dialectical relationship between the collective and the individual. For the style is the man in what is most unique and inimitable about him: every artist has a style that makes it possible to identify him and we speak unreservedly of Cézanne's style. But the history of painting shows that this inimitable style makes forgers happy precisely in so far as it is all too readily open to imitation. And it is not only imitated by forgers, for it can characterise a group or a school. We therefore do not hesitate to refer to a post-impressionist style. Accordingly, style is at once individual and collective, a sign of interpellation of the individual by the group and of her emancipation from the group in the process of counter-interpellation. The chain of interpellation tells us that one does not escape the collective (of the language, of ideology in as much as it is language), which is simultaneously liberating and oppressive; it also tells us that at the end of the chain, one does not escape the individuality of the speaker become a subject.

Ideology is therefore language – by which is to be understood more than the trivial assertion that, since ideology manifests itself in discourse, language is always involved in it: in this sense, every practice involves language. I do not practise bungee jumping by launching myself into the void before the order 'go!' has been uttered. But this does not make bungee jumping a linguistic practice. I am postulating a stronger bond, a constitutive link, between ideology and language, which means that the distinction between the two terms is an effect of theory. The whole chain of interpellation, not only the speech act that crowns it, is linguistic: institutions are collective assemblages of enunciation; at the heart of the ritual is the performative utterance that it stages; and practices are shot through with language in that they are social and language is the medium and motor of social interaction.

My thesis has its converse, which states that not only is ideology linguistic, but language is ideological. What are we to understand by this?

At its simplest level, it means that there is no neutral language uncontaminated by ideology (in its trivial sense). Ideology here is declined in the plural, allowing Lenin to defend the idea that there is a 'socialist ideology'. His contribution to the tradition, with the concept of slogan, especially as generalised by Deleuze and Guattari, says nothing else: the most innocent grammatical markers are power markers. (In reality, it also says something else, which was the subject of the previous paragraphs: the link between ideology, construed in the Althusserian sense, and language is much deeper and much closer than is assumed by the fact that 'ideas' need 'words' in order to be expressed.)

The linguistic tradition has not always ignored this state of affairs. Take, for example, the work of Roland Barthes, who in his youth was more than somewhat Marxist,[33] and especially two of his concepts: connotation and ideosphere.

Connotation – a term adopted from Hjelmslev – is at the heart of the concrete analyses contained in *Mythologies* and the theorisation undertaken in the concluding essay, 'Myth Today'.[34] Barthes wants to show that in natural languages (in contrast to artificial languages) there is no denotation without connotation. His two canonical examples are well known. The first is an example of Latin grammar, *quia ego nominor leo* ('because my name is lion') The translation indicates the denotation of the phrase, whose connotative meaning is: 'I am a grammatical example meant to illustrate the rule about the agreement of the predicate.' To which, having read Deleuze and Guattari and Renée Balibar, we can add:[35] 'and if you do not obey my implicit commands, you will get a bad mark for Latin translation'. The other, still more famous, example is a *Paris Match* cover which, in 1956, represented a Senegalese infantryman saluting the French flag. The meaning of the denotation of the image is given by the sentence describing its content. Barthes shows that its connotative meaning, which is the real reason for the choice of this

---

[33] On Barthes's relationship to Marxism and his abandonment of it in favour of semiotics, readers are referred to Milner 2003.
[34] See Barthes 1972.
[35] See Balibar 1974.

image for the cover of the weekly, has something to do with what he calls 'French imperiality'. The historical distance allows us to grasp the relevance of his example with the utmost clarity. This image is informed by an implicit slogan – 'we must defend the French empire' – which, on the eve of decolonisation, is a dramatic irony. It might therefore be said that connotation is the ideological aura of language: not a superfluous addition, but an essential aspect of its functioning. We even come to suspect that the distinction between denotation and connotation, like the distinction between the literal and the metaphorical, is an ideological distinction.

The concept of 'ideosphere' features in Barthes's course at the Collège de France devoted to 'le neutre'.[36] The term is created from 'ideology' and aims to replace it, or, rather, to make explicit the idea that 'all ideology for me is only language: it is a discourse, a type of discourse'.[37] In Barthes, ideology has a rather different meaning from Althusser's. For him, the term is declined in the plural: there is not a single structure, outside of history; there are systems of ideas and these systems are in no way independent of language. The concept of ideosphere states this dependency. With this concept, which, in reality, signals an exit from the Marxist tradition of thinking about ideology, but which strongly suggests that there are no thoughts and no 'ideas' without language, the copula that separates 'language' and 'ideology' in the two aspects of my thesis becomes fully reversible: ideology is wholly linguistic and language is wholly ideological. This becomes apparent when we consider the characteristics assigned to the ideosphere by Barthes (the distance from Marxism will likewise become apparent): the ideosphere is plural (there are always several and the question arises as to whether reference to a 'dominant ideology' still makes sense); it determines a *doxa*; it is eponymous, in that it has an attributable author (Freud and Marx are the names of creators of ideospheres); it 'sets' like mayonnaise and it sticks like chewing-gum, for it is bound up with error (we see how this differs from the Althusserian theory: the ideosphere is illusion, not allusion); it involves a *pathos* (it is the object of an addiction); it passes itself off as nature (as did myth formerly); its action is regulatory, constraining for the subject's thinking; it serves as a relay between power and the individual; it functions by violence and is transmitted by

---

[36] See Barthes 2002, p. 122 ff.
[37] Barthes 2002, p. 122.

unconscious imitation. The last two characteristics are the most interesting for us: in ideology, language is indefatigable (Barthes notes the link between *dire, dicter* and *dictateur*) and it produces the 'idiosphere' – i.e. the individual subject – in the form of internal language. Even if we must regretfully conclude that Marxism is only one ideosphere among others (I had already observed that it sticks to me like chewing-gum), the set of theses that I am defending is present here, at least implicitly; and it has become impossible to separate language and ideology in that they fulfil the same function, which is the production of subjects-speakers.

It is evident that the two aspects of my thesis are not equivalent. 'Ideology is linguistic' is to be construed as a development of the Althusser's second theory of ideology – the theory of subjectivation (he would say 'subjection') via interpellation. 'Language is ideological' refers instead – and this is clear in Barthes – to the common meaning of ideology, whose main characteristic is a pejorative conception of ideology (as the opposite of science or as false consciousness). This conception is too rooted in our common sense for us to be shot of it by theoretical *fiat*: it is at least a symptom and it too tells us something about the operation of language. But I cannot help regarding the development that led Althusser from his first to his second theory of ideology as an advance, or, at least, as a clarification.

Since all this is highly abstract, I would like to end this section with a short example, by way of illustration. Take the highly innocent-looking sentence, 'the cat is on the mat'. It has everything to please linguists: it is a simple, active and declarative sentence; out of such building-blocks are splendid grammars constructed. It will also please philosophers: it is unambiguous; it expresses a proposition whose reference is amenable to verification by assuring ourselves of its conformity to the facts. With it we might believe ourselves to be in the intellectual universe of Tarski: '"the cat is on the mat" if and only if the cat is on the mat'.

This innocence and philosophical good health are confirmed by the fact that the sentence is used as the first part of the formulation of what is called 'Moore's paradox': 'the cat is on the mat, but I don't believe it is'. Moore wants to get us to see that claims presuppose beliefs and he does it with this grammatically correct and semantically bizarre sentence. A hint of anxiety emerges here, for if even the most innocent sentence can find itself mixed up in the shady business of paradox, we cannot be certain where the drift towards semantic incoherence is going to stop.

But where did our philosopher find this sentence, which he did not invent? In a primary school manual, where its simplicity and clarity are paedagogical virtues. They are also good examples of the reification of processes into things: this coloured, purring mass is indeed a cat and this rectangular, brown shape is, in fact, a mat. And this reification extends to the perceiving subject whom the language absents – if readers will forgive me the term – from her utterance, in order to transform a process of perception into a series of things, i.e. objects and positive facts. For this sentence in the third person contains no indication of its subject of enunciation: seemingly limiting itself to the registration of a fact, without indicating any standpoint, it affects not to have one. And it possesses another glaring characteristic which, following Antoine Culioli, I shall formulate as follows: the likelihood of it occurring in real interlocution is virtually nil. For, in a real dialogue, no one will pronounce a sentence of this kind, not because it is singularly trivial, but because it is artificial. The example Culioli likes to use is 'the dog barks' – a sentence likewise innocently grammatical, but which it suffices to compare with 'there's the dog barking', 'dogs, they bark', or any other real sentence, to appreciate that it does not exist outside of a teaching situation, outside of the grammar that provides an elementary syntactical analysis of it, or of the philosophical work that takes it as a pretext for discoursing abstractly on the supposed functioning of language. To adopt the language that I have just been using, my sentence is rich in connotations, setting its speaker and listener within an institution – i.e. a relationship of places ('we lay down the rules of grammar here', just as elsewhere they say 'we ask the questions here') and hence a power relation. It imposes on both of them the self-evidence of its transparency (which is a symptom of ideology in the traditional pejorative sense of the term), starting with the child who must copy it, illustrate it, and learn it by heart at school. This sentence clearly illustrates that ideology is language and language ideology; it is the product of a collective assemblage of enunciation (it does not – and never will – have an author); it has served to interpellate generations of school kids as speakers. Finally, it illustrates the two aspects of linguistic fetishism: its necessity – that of naming and abstraction – which makes it possible for the sign to stand in for the referent in its absence; and that of the imposition of a power relation through the reification of processes into nameable things.

Methodological individualism in linguistic matters has at least one advantage: it readily explains the construction of the meaning of the utterance, which for it is a function of the speaker's meaning. All things being equal, I say what I say because I mean to say it; I put my linguistic resources to work in the service of my intended meanings. Making language a collective and social phenomenon before it is an individual one renders the issue less easy to resolve. So how is the social construction of the meaning of the utterance to be conceived? At the end of the previous section, I accounted for historical change in language in terms of metaphorical drift and suggested that the systematic construction of the meaning of the utterance was effected along a Markov chain – a chain that is interrupted, or rather completed, at the moment of the retrospective provision of meaning, from the nodal point. A Markov chain is a mathematical entity which takes the form of a series of finished states such that the choice of the first is wholly free, that of the second determined by the first, and so on, with the choice of the final state being constrained to the maximum. Applied to language, this means that the speaker's freedom of expression diminishes as the sentence advances, from left to right, along the line of language. But a Markov chain does not only unfold according to the internal constraints of language, be they syntactical (a transitive verb is followed by a direct object noun), syntactico-semantic (in French a feminine article precedes a feminine noun), or semantic (which explains why Chomsky's famous sentence, 'green ideas sleep furiously', is grammatical but meaningless). It is also constrained by the socio-collective constraints of public meaning (and meaning is always public). To take the standard example in English, take the beginning of the sentence 'pride comes before a . . .'. The appearance of the final word, which is going to complete the sentence, obeys syntactical constraints (it must be a noun; any one will do), and semantic constraints (here not any noun will do: it must be compatible with the preposition 'before'). But it is above all constrained by the encyclopaedic knowledge that readers have of the proverb, which leads them to expect as a matter of course the word 'fall' at the end of the sentence. For in English proverbial pride always comes before a fall, just as in French the Tarpeian Rock follows the Capitol (the height of glory is close to the nadir of disaster). The speaker is therefore interpellated to her place, summoned by her language to be a speaker of the proverb. Naturally, however, nothing prevents her from counter-interpellating it, from playing with it by playing on the proverb. Nothing prevents me from saying, wholly unexpectedly: 'Pride comes before a vote of impeachment' – which will force my listener to exclaim internally (and readers will note the use of the imperfect): so he was intending to refer to Nixon or Clinton! In uttering this sentence, I accept my place as authorised speaker of the proverb and at the same time challenge it – i.e. exploit it for expressive purposes. The nodal point, moment of the retrospective provision of meaning ('yes, it's obviously . . .'), re-interprets a sentence that is always-already interpreted – that is, always-already endowed with a public meaning, which enables the speaker to recognise its meaning. At the nodal point, the social meaning being guaranteed, the interpellated speaker becomes the fully-fledged subject of her enunciation, for ideological-linguistic constraints are at once implacable and defeasible, and as fated to be exploited as syntactical and semantic constraints are.

Chapter Seven
Propositions (II)

1. Third positive thesis: language is a material phenomenon

At first sight, this thesis seems to be caught in an antinomy. Language is certainly a set of material phenomena, in the sense that it consists in sounds emitted by human organs (here, we might cite what I have called the Castafiore principle: these sounds have a material impact on bodies, those of listener and speaker alike). And, when presented in written form, it consists in a certain number of traces, marks on a white page. But, in addition to the fact that technological progress is leading to an increasing immateriality of language (I am writing this text on a computer screen: so its materiality is not the same as that produced by the quill pen I used until last year), language has always had an immaterial or ideal aspect: *phone* is insufficient to yield language if there is not also *logos*. Language is not screaming. The object of this section is to escape this antinomy and to do so via materialism, which will not surprise anyone.

I am going to do so in two stages: language involves materialism in the strictest sense in that it involves *speaking bodies*; and it involves a broader materialism, with which Marxists are familiar – that of institutions and apparatuses, in that they produce discourses and speech acts. I have already broached this issue in Chapter 5, when I referred to Deleuze and Guattari's concept of collective assemblage of enunciation, which (it will be remembered) is characterised by an ontological mix of bodies (agents and instruments), institutions (buildings, decrees and rituals), and texts (literature, etc.). And I broached it in Chapter 6, when I evoked the Althusserian chain of interpellation, which involves the same kind of ontological mix and the same type of materiality. Here, I am, therefore, going to concentrate on the problem of the body which, as we saw when referring to *Anti-Oedipus*, has been largely ignored by Marxists.

We still need to agree on the concept of the body, by posing the question: what concept of body do I need in order to understand the functioning of language? For there are several candidates.

The most obvious is the *biological body*. After all, language is physically produced by our physiological organs, even if we at once add that it is also the ideal product of the functioning of our brain. But even this aspect can be reduced, as is the tendency in Chomsky's phrase 'the mind/brain', which aims to reduce the difference (hence the solidus) while denying this reduction (hence the preservation of the term 'mind' alongside that of 'brain'). After the First World War, reference used to be made to regions of the brain; today's cognitive science talks in terms of neuron circuits and – soon – of genes. Even the 'embodied language' of the West-Coast linguists Lakoff and Johnson does not wholly escape this physicalism, which Marxists will tend to regard as a return to the mechanistic materialism of the age of Enlightenment. We have seen where the problem lies. By reducing language, in the form of a faculty, to the body of the individual speaker, these conceptions lapse into methodological individualism and preclude themselves from understanding how language is a historical phenomenon and a social phenomenon. By comparison with Saussure's system, this is a regression.

Let us consider a second candidate: the *phenomenological body*. Here, the body is the body of the speaker, in as much as it is the site of enunciative or cognitive operations. I am referring here to various linguistic theories – those of Benveniste and Culioli in France, or Langacker and Lakoff and Johnson in the USA – which are closely or remotely influenced by phenomenology (a philosophical field in which, from Husserl to Merleau-Ponty, we find extremely interesting reflections on language).[1] I am doing a partial injustice to Lakoff

---

[1] See Benveniste 1966 and 1974; Culioli 1990, 1999a, 1999b and 2002; Langacker 1987 and 1991; Lakoff and Johnson 1999.

and Johnson, who take their distance from phenomenology, in that they employ a concept of the unconscious, which is nevertheless closer to Leibniz's 'minute perceptions' than the Freudian unconscious. The phenomenological body is at once conscious of itself and active. It orients itself in the world that surrounds it, its *Umwelt* which is also a *Lebenswelt*. Lakoff and Johnson thus describe a type of metaphor that they call 'metaphors of orientation'. The ball is behind the rock not because the rock has a front and a back, like a car, but because it is situated between the ball and my body: if I walk around it, this 'behind' becomes an 'in front'. And it is involved in the elaboration of systems of metaphors (characterised as 'structural' by Lakoff and Johnson), which interpret what is new on the basis of what is known – that is, starting from the concrete of perception.[2] As for the third kind of metaphor – 'ontological' metaphors (i.e. abstractions such as 'inflation' or 'revolution') – it embodies language's tendency to fetishism (which, as we have seen, is both necessary and deleterious), to the transformation of processes (e.g. inflation) into things. But this abstraction is grounded in the body, which is its necessary starting-point. Thus, according to Lakoff and Johnson, our conception of the world is constructed on the basis of metaphors of the situation of our body in space, which yields, for example, the Metaphor of Temporal Orientation: the localisation of the body of the observer is linked to the present, the space situated in front of the observer to the future, and so on.[3]

This kind of analysis rapidly reaches its limits (and we remember the ferocious critique to which Bergson subjected metaphorical thinking about time in terms of space). To realise that the conception of time set out here is rather simplistic, it is enough to consider the elaboration of notion of aspect in Benveniste or Culioli. But this view of an embodied speaker, in which the object of analysis is not the utterance as result but the process of enunciation, has the signal merit of saving us from physicalist reductionism or Chomskyan naturalism. To revert from Chomsky to Merleau-Ponty (and his dichotomy between the speaking word and the spoken word)[4] is insufficient, but it helps us to advance. The phenomenological body is more relevant for our analysis than the 'natural', purely biological body which, in linguistic matters, always

---

[2] See Lakoff and Johnson 1980.
[3] See Lakoff and Johnson 1999, pp. 140–3.
[4] See Merleau-Ponty 1973 and 1968.

proves to be an abstract ideal construct. And it also enables us to avoid the 'principle of immanence' on which structuralist linguistics is based, to reconnect language and the world, to forget the ideality of the ideal system. The body of phenomenological experience is not so far from the body of *praxis*, as the work of Tran Duc Thao has shown. It is the body in which consciousness and subjectivity emerge. But it is not the only body.

The third candidate is the *erotic body*. By this, I obviously mean the body as psychoanalysis seeks to think about it. And, because we have read Lacan, we know that this body has something to do with language. This body is corporeal in a more precise sense than the phenomenological body, at least such as linguists implicitly refer to it (we are not dealing with Merleau-Ponty's philosophy here). For we ask which body is the site of these cognitive and enunciative operations that are sometimes dubbed 'psycho-grammatical'. In this respect, physical reductionism at least possesses the advantage of clarity. As does psychoanalysis, with its conceptual apparatus of primary and secondary processes, dream-work and the operation of jokes. And this conceptual apparatus produces effects in the field of language. With the help of the concepts of primary and secondary processes (more than a little tampered with, it is true), the pre-Guattari Deleuze of *Logic of Sense* constructed what he called a 'logical and psychoanalytical novel', offering not only a general conception of the functioning of language, but what is, in my view, the most interesting theory of the construction of meaning available in a well-supplied market.[5] I have myself attempted to show that Lacan's famous texts on language enable us to construct an agonistic pragmatics that is much more interesting than Anglo-American irenic pragmatics.[6] In truth, Freud was a great linguist, like his prophet Lacan: in the previous chapter, I used the concept of nodal point [*point de capiton*] as the moment of the retrospective provision of meaning (however, we must make it clear that this concept pertains to the first Lacan – Lacan the linguist – and that thereafter, with the development of his doctrine, it underwent a metaphysical drift rendering it inapt for describing language). Finally, we can cite the work of Serge Leclaire, with its inscription of the letter on the erotic body; that of Luce Irigaray (another early work) on phantasy and the relations between subject and

---

[5] See Deleuze 1990a and see also Lecercle 2002.
[6] See Lecercle 1987.

language; and that of Jeanne Favret-Saada on sorcery in the copse (where language is very directly involved).[7] This is an impressive corpus.

The problem is that the erotic body, in its relations with language, is theoretically unstable: we have just seen this with the history of the concept of nodal point in Lacan. The turn that saw the Lacanians move from thinking about language to thinking about *jouissance* does not help the philosophy of language (which is not obliged to judge its relevance here). The erotic body, nevertheless, remains of crucial importance for us. We owe it the concept of 'mother tongue' – an expression that the psychoanalysts did not invent, but to which their theories impart a meaning. For the speaker is not an angel (this is how Milner describes the ideal speaker posited by the Saussurian schema of communication): she possesses a body, ensnared in the famous triangle: she is inhabited by the language of her mother (this is only too clear in the case of Wolfson, the literary madman who could not bear his mother tongue – English);[8] and she is spoken by her mother tongue. A direct link exists between the erotic body and accession to language.

If it is a good candidate, however, the erotic body is not the only one. There is a *fourth* one: the *labouring body*. This expression is not current in French. The reason is simple: the theory of it has been elaborated by a Canadian Marxist, David McNally, in his book *Bodies of Meaning*. The concept of 'labouring body' in McNally owes more to Benjamin and Bakhtin (especially his book on Rabelais) than Voloshinov. This has some problematic aspects, but McNally's general position cannot leave us indifferent. This is how he formulates it in his introduction:

> One overarching argument runs through these pages: that postmodernist theory, whether it calls itself post-structuralism, deconstruction or post-Marxism, is constituted by a radical attempt to banish the real human body – the sensate, biocultural, laboring body – from the sphere of language and social life. As a result, I argue, these outlooks reproduce a central feature of commodified society: the abstraction of social products and practices from the laboring bodies that generate them. . . .

---

[7] See Leclaire 1968; Irigaray 1985; and Favret-Saada 1977.
[8] See Wolfson 1970.

> Central to the critical materialism that informs this book . . . is the insistence
> that the concrete bodies, practices, and desires, which have been forgotten
> by idealism, perform a return of the repressed. Invariably, these things return
> in devalued form, as 'the excrescences of the system,' as the degraded and
> discarded elements of refuse which 'show the untruth, the mania, of the
> systems themselves.' The task of critical theory is produce a knowledge
> built out of these excrescences, a knowledge derived from attending to the
> fragments which have escaped the imperial ambitions of linguistic idealism.
> And this means starting from the body. . . .[9]

We can welcome this philosophical programme in that it adopts a materialist
position. The labouring body is what linguistic idealism, which prefers angels,
excludes; and it does indeed reappear in the outgrowths of the system, which
subvert its ideality (as the inventor of the linguistic concept of 'remainder',
I cannot but sympathise with this viewpoint). The origin of the idealist
conception of language is clearly attributed to a basic feature of market society,
in which we have no difficulty recognising fetishism. At this stage, the concept
of 'body' is still vague, and not wholly distinct from the erotic body of the
psychoanalysts. But it becomes more precise when this body becomes labouring,
when the 'labouring body' emerges, introduced in the most classical Marxist
terms (with a feminist nuance):

> Of course, bourgeois discourses have to admit the body at some stage of
> the game. But they do so by 'cleansing' it of the sweat of labor and the
> blood of menstruation and childbirth. The bourgeois body is a sanitized,
> heroic male body of rational (nonbiological) creatures: it does not break
> under the strain of routinized work; it does not menstruate, lactate, or go
> into labor; it does not feel the lash of the master's whip; it does not suffer
> and die. The bourgeois body is, in short, an abstraction.[10]

I like the direct language that uses the adjective 'bourgeois' unreservedly.
And the lyricism of this passage owes something to the North-American
conjuncture: McNally plays on the ambiguity of the word 'labour' (work and
parturition) and signals a solidarity, which has something obligatory about
it but can only arouse our sympathy, with the struggles of women and blacks.

---

[9] McNally 2001, pp. 1, 4.
[10] McNally 2001, p. 5.

And we are not far removed from the pathos of the *incipit* of *Anti-Oedipus*, where the body evoked shits and fucks. At this stage, NcNally's labouring body is not distinguished from Deleuze and Guattari's body without organs – that is, the body of desire, in a conception of desire and affects that is neither phenomenological nor psychoanalytical. Accordingly, we shall not be surprised to find a chapter on Bakhtin's Rabelaisian carnivalesque body in his book. And this body soon becomes more explicitly socio-historical:

> To talk about human bodies and the practices in which they are immersed need not entail treating the body as a timeless object of nature. The human body, as I hope to show, is inherently historical. True, bodies have a relatively fixed biological constitution. But the evolutionary history of the human body also involves the emergence of cultural practices and social history. To talk meaningfully about the human body is to talk about bodies that are the site of dynamic social processes, bodies that generate open-ended systems of meaning. It is, in other words, to talk about relations of production and reproduction, about languages, images of desire, technologies, and diverse forms of sociocultural organization. All of these things operate on the site of the body and its history.[11]

By comparison with phenomenological and psychoanalytical conceptions of the body, the advantages for us of this one are obvious: this body is no longer simply individual, it is a social body fashioned by social forces and relations; it is an irreducibly historical body, the 'biological endowment' – itself the product of history – being modified by history; it is not only the agent of a social *praxis*, but also the product of the processes that constitute this *praxis*.

We have here an explicitly materialist position, grounded in the materiality of the human body, with its *pathos* in the etymological sense (this body is not only the seat of reason, but also of affects). But, for me, its importance consists in the fact that it also makes it possible to envisage a broader form of materialism, that of institutions, of ideas as embodied in discourses – for example, the slogans that set the masses in motion. We can see how ideology is material: because it is the force that circulates all along the chain of interpellation, in which each link is material (material institutions, material rituals, material practices, material speech acts: buildings, assembled bodies,

---

[11] McNally 2001, p. 7.

regulated behaviours, material transformations – the Althusserian definition of practice – and communication which is communication in the physical sense: the communication of a power). We understand the power of insults and their impact on the body of the victim; we understand how the words of the English language caused Louis Wolfson, to whom I referred earlier, physical pain. Finally, we understand what the subject that emerges at the end of the chain of interpellation is: a body to which linguistic interpellation assigns a place, a socially and historically situated body, the 'labouring' body of *praxis*. Before being fetishised into an ideal system facilitating the communication and exchange of ideas transmitted with the aid of words, language is a system of places, a site of struggles and power relations, but also of processes of subjectivation through the assignment of places (an operation described by François Flahault in *La Parole intermédiaire*).[12]

Phenomena that illustrate this social materiality of the body are not wanting. I have referred to insults and to what Judith Butler calls 'hate speech', which fix the body of the victim rather as the pin fixes the butterfly, but which are the site of a possible counter-interpellation when the victim seizes hold of the insulting word to appropriate it or turn it against the aggressor (numerous examples will be found in the case of homophobic words). But we can generalise this implication of the materiality of the body to all language games: even the practice of philosophy is not void of affects, which are not (one hopes) as devastating as amorous passion (on the other hand, . . .). This enables us to understand why it has been possible to claim that order-words are the basic utterances; and readers will find excellent illustrations of this in Favret-Saada's work, where sorcery is a question of words even more than of rituals, and where these words sometime have devastating physical effects on the bodies to which they are addressed. Finally, we can understand why we do not need to decide which – language or labour – came first: as attributes of the social body, they presuppose one another. They are both derived, in a dialectical embrace, from social *praxis*.

---

[12] See Flahault 1978.

2. Fourth positive thesis: language is a political phenomenon

This thesis appears to be self-evident and possibly also a paradox.

A paradox: when, for example, it takes the form of a science of language, theory is neutral. Science does not engage in politics and Stalin's polemic against Marr, and especially its reception in the West, can only be understood as an abandonment of the opposition between bourgeois science and proletarian science and the relief this created among specialists, scientists above all, but also linguists and philosophers. There is only one physics; and to say that language is a political phenomenon is to renounce science. This does not prevent the linguist being an activist – witness Chomsky. However, the two activities are strictly separate (even if some critics murmur that Chomsky's naturalism and his libertarian political convictions have something in common – i.e. his belief in a human nature defined by linguistic creativity).

Naturally, it is not certain that linguistics, if it is a science, is a science *like physics*: notwithstanding Milner's claims, it is not obvious that linguistics does not have more to do with sociology than physics. This comes down to asking whether the 'human sciences' are, in fact, sciences. By constructing its concepts through exclusion, under the rubric of *langue* or 'I-language', internal linguistics seeks to protect itself against such contamination. But we have seen that there is a heavy price to be paid for this purification. We can now give it a name: abandoning regarding language as a form of *praxis*. All the more so in that the politics expelled by 'science' tends to come back in through the back window: this is called methodological individualism, which has a worrying resemblance to bourgeois liberal individualism.

The external linguistics that I am defending does not therefore detect a paradox in the thesis. On the contrary, it sees in it what risks being an obvious fact, or, rather, two. The first obvious fact is that politics occurs mainly in the medium of language: programmes, tracts, speeches, motions, slogans, laws, and decrees. Above all, if this politics claims or wishes to be democratic: its essence is debate. Obviously, politics does not consist exclusively in discourse, but it will be granted that the relation between politics and language is closer than that between cooking and language: I can cook without recipes, but political activity without words is war, which is (as we know) the continuation of politics by other means – that is, something other than politics. In the United States, there are specialists in political philosophy who describe war as a malady of language and language – e.g. that of international conventions –

as the way to defuse antagonisms. This position is familiar to us: it grounds the distinction in Habermas between communicative action and strategic action.

The second obvious fact is that there are linguistic policies and political movements whose demands are in part – and sometimes in the main – linguistic. There is, therefore, a politics of the national language, just as there is a politics of dialects and regional languages. As we have seen, the concepts of 'linguistic imperialism' and 'becoming-minoritarian' are useful for describing such situations.

So language has a close relationship with politics. However, my thesis wishes to argue that this relationship is not contingent. Let us take the example of the relations between language and war. If war is a non-politics, it is possibly because it not only replaces communicative action by strategic action, but also acts directly on language. Elaine Scarry argues that war causes the collapse of language, by reducing it to propaganda and cries of pain; that its objective is the national self-description of the participants: it is a question of imposing one's own self-description and destroying the enemy's (the forces of Good against the forces of Evil). In short, war constitutes an operation of 'verbal unanchoredness'.[13] However, this is not enough: this analysis makes language the victim of politics (of a form of undemocratic politics) and does not suggest that the link between language and politics is constitutive.

Yet acknowledgement of such a link is age-old. In fact, it dates back to Aristotle. We have seen that he defined *praxis* as action in common and that the cardinal example of *praxis* is political action. If we re-read the famous opening of the *Politics*, we come upon the following passage:

> [M]an is a political animal in a sense in which a bee is not, or any other gregarious animal. Nature, as we say, does nothing without some purpose; and she has endowed man alone among the animals with the power of speech. Speech is something different from voice, which is possessed by other animals also and used by them to express pain or pleasure; for their nature does indeed enable them not only to feel pleasure and pain, but to communicate these feelings to each other. Speech, on the other hand, serves to indicate what is useful and what is harmful, and so also what is just and what is unjust. For the real difference between man and other animals is

---

[13] See Scarry 1985.

that humans alone have perception of good and evil, just and unjust, etc. It is the sharing of a common view in *these* matters that makes a household and a state. . . . It is clear . . . that the state is both natural and prior to the individual.[14]

We recognise the distinction between *phone* and *logos*: animals are endowed with *phone*, but they do not possess *logos*. The humanity of man consists in the fact that he speaks. As is the case for Chomsky too, except that, in Aristotle, it is a question not so much of a biological capacity (defended by Chomsky's sole argument – i.e. the child's rapid acquisition of language, under-determined by experience), but of a 'logical' capacity – that is, the capacity to go beyond emotions and the cries they provoke and to distinguish between good and evil (ethical capacity), the useful and the harmful (pragmatic capacity), and the just and the unjust (political capacity). It even seems that his last capacity has priority over the other two, since the first object proposed by nature is the state. The linguistic bond is, therefore, indissolubly a social bond – i.e. a political bond. We remember that the barbarians – those excluded from the city – were thus named because they spoke gobbledygook – i.e. an idiom that the Greeks did not understand. Whoever does not speak the language of imperialism is a barbarian.

So the issue of the politics of the language is not a contingent aspect of a set of political questions: it is essential to politics. In our modernity, it has taken the privileged form of the issue of the national language. It is here that we begin to take the *methodological collectivism* of Marxism seriously (I use this expression by contrast with the methodological individualism of the dominant philosophy of language and to recall its links with liberal individualism). For, as we have seen, methodological individualism fetishises the individual speaker. But language involves subjects living in society – what Lucien Goldmann called 'trans-individual' subjects[15] – before interpellating the individuals that we all are as subjects-speakers. We can, therefore, speak metaphorically, but with a metaphor that hits the nail on the head, of a collective speaker: this is called a national language. This metaphor, which is, in reality, a synecdoche, tells us that one speaks a language only as a member of a linguistic community which is also, inseparably, a political community,

---

14 Aristotle 1981, pp. 60–1.
15 See Goldmann 1970.

a *polis*. I am aware that if this *polis* has something to do with the nation-state of our modernity, it is not reducible to it: the English-speaking world covers numerous states; the francophone world extends beyond the borders of the Hexagon. The concept of 'national language', which is intimately bound up with that of 'natural language', transcends the historical limits of the constitution or dissolution of nation-states. But it plays a key role in what Benedict Anderson calls an 'imagined community' – i.e. a nation:[16] a régime of distribution of social capital, assigning places – i.e. identities – to subjects, creating communities, and organising ideological consensus. This role is due to the fact that man is a speaking animal in that he is a political animal (for provocation's sake I invert Aristotle's formula); that inter-subjectivity emerges from interlocution, which has a relationship of mutual presupposition with social relations, the relations of labour and the division of labour, which are also power relations.

We can see how Chomsky's grammatical universalism, his refusal to consider natural languages in that they are national languages, is profoundly mistaken: English is something quite different from the few parameters more or less which gradually make us slide from German to Dutch and from Dutch to the language of Shakespeare. For this is the veritable unity of English, over and above the dialects, registers, levels of language and language games that make it up: a political unity in the broad sense – that is, the ever-unstable, ever-consolidated result, in a historical conjuncture, of a power relation. This is how a theoretician of translation, Lawrence Venuti, formulates the point:

> There can be no question of choosing between adhering to the constants that linguistics extracts from language or placing them in continuous variation because language is a continuum of dialects, registers, styles, and discourses positioned in a hierarchical arrangement and developing at different speeds and in different ways. Translation, like any language use, is a selection accompanied by exclusions, an intervention into the contending languages that constitute any linguistic conjuncture. . . .[17]

This text owes something to the conception of language that we have described in Deleuze and Guattari (to refer to the extraction of constants as opposed

---

[16] See Anderson 1983.
[17] Venuti 1998, pp. 29–30.

to a process of continuous variation is to speak the language of *A Thousand Plateaus*: we detect an echo of the concepts of 'minor language' and ' becoming-minoritarian of the major or standard language'). This language has the great advantage of enabling us to formulate the first two moments of the dialectical process clearly. On the one hand, there is only continuous variation, a multiplicity of dialects, of the languages of small communities, united in common practices, like Tran Duc Thao's hunters. But, on the other hand, there is a hierarchy, which is a political hierarchy, between these dialects and registers, at whose summit is enthroned 'standard English' – this political fiction, this imagined linguistic community which serve as a national language, this sedimented aggregate of past and present political struggles, always subject – which is what makes it living – to a process of subversion and becoming-minoritarian by dominated dialects.

The national language is, therefore, in a dialectical relationship with the constitution of nation-states. But, being dialectical, this relationship works in both directions. The language is national because it is elevated to such a status in the context of the political struggles leading to the creation of a nation-state. But it intervenes in these struggles and thus contributes to the emergence of what causes it to emerge, for these political struggles often take the form of linguistic struggles. The role of the Tuscan written by Dante in the creation not only of Italian as a national language, but also of the unified Italian state, is well known. The same could be said of the English of Shakespeare (as long as we add to it that of the King James Bible): this English, which even British Anglophones find it increasingly difficult to understand today, plays an essential role not only in the transformation of 'Shakespeare' into a national myth, but in the constitution of the United Kingdom (as its name suggests) into a nation-state. We appreciate the significance of the old witticism: a language is a dialect equipped with an army. A nation is an army united by a language.

I am going to illustrate this situation by taking two examples. The first has been the object of famous studies and analyses: the constitution of French as a national language, and its triumph over dialects, in the era of the Revolution. Historians possess an extremely valuable document, the Grégoire report, the first survey of the extension of French within what it is henceforth called the national territory. We have two analyses of this report – by Renée Balibar and Dominique Laporte and by Michel de Certeau, Dominique Julia and Jacques

Revel.[18] I am not going to go into the divergences between these analyses here, or the polemics they provoked, and will rapidly summarise the main points. Abbé Grégoire was, in a sense, the Convention's education and culture minister. In 1790, he sent a series of correspondents, individual or collective (various Jacobin clubs), a questionnaire on the use of the patois in their region. As his correspondents were spread across the whole country, we have the first survey of the state of French in France. The result is instructive. It appears that, of the 24 million French, 12 million did not speak the French language at all, 8 million spoke it badly, as a second language that they had learnt, and only 4 million (or one-sixth) spoke it fluently.[19] What the French spoke was foreign languages (German in Alsace, Italian in Corsica, Dutch in Flanders, Breton, Catalan: as we can see, there was still no notion of 'regional language'); or patois that were distinct from French (Picard or Poitevin patois, both patois derived from langue d'oc). This linguistic division was not only geographical; it coincided with a social division: French was spoken in towns by bourgeois and petit-bourgeois; in the country, by aristocrats and the clergy. Patois were therefore decidedly rural and peasant.

Abbé Grégoire's questionnaire, which gave rise to a report on the situation of French and the Convention's tasks in this regard, was obviously not neutral. The questions are slanted and various political orientations emerge: they are hostile to patois, which are an object of concern. There were many reasons for this. On the one hand, there was the Enlightenment universalism that desired a united nation and people, and united in and by a language. There was the preoccupation of the democratic statesman who wanted the laws to be understood by all those to whom they applied. There were the concerns of the militants of the Revolution, who, as representatives of the new, were opposed to age-old traditions, customs and superstitions, of which patois was the privileged vehicle: a unified language was required for the Revolution to diffuse its ideas, to conduct propaganda. There was also the desire to combat the hitherto dominant ideological apparatus – the Church – which, tendering to the faithful a discourse in a language they did not understand,

---

[18] See Balibar and Laporte 1974 and de Certeau, Julia and Revel 1975.
[19] These figures are from Balibar and Laporte 1974, p. 32. Dalby 2003, p. 135 gives significantly different figures: 26 million inhabitants, 11 million French-speakers, plus an additional 3 million who spoke French as a second language, leaving 12 million non-French-speakers in the national territory.

adapted very well to the patois when it needed to make itself understood: it said mass in Latin and prayers in the patois. Finally, by a typical ruse of reason, Abbé Grégoire was also the representative of the rising bourgeoisie, a class that required an efficient, mobile army of labour for the emerging industrial revolution: this unification via proletarianisation also took the form of unifying the language, just like the defence of the Revolution by a conscript army. The result of this complex set of factors, in addition to offering a snap-shot of the linguistic state of France, was a policy of national education – the first of the kind – which Napoleon was to implement and of which we remain the inheritors. The objective, which was obviously not realised straightaway, was seemingly modest: to establish in each village a teacher holding classes in French. That glorious figure of our not so distant past – the teacher of the Third Republic – was already planned.

So, patois was the enemy that had to be eliminated. A little over two centuries later, it will be noted that this policy was very largely successful, even if it took a long time to establish the institutions and apparatuses capable of completing the task: a conscript army, courts of justice, and especially the educational state apparatus that replaced the Church as the principal ideological state apparatus (this is Althusser's thesis, which Balibar and Laporte develop). Only the foreign ex-languages still resist, with varying degrees of success. The situation has, it is true, become complicated with the melting-pot of the twentieth century and the appearance on the national territory of new foreign languages – Spanish, Portuguese, Arab. The problem of linguistic diversity persists and, with it, the necessity of a politics of language. The language is at the heart of the political issue that continues to haunt us – the nation: to be convinced of this, it is enough to see the role assumed by questions of European integration, regional decentralisation, immigration and assimilation, and not only the issue of state schools and what they teach, in our everyday political life. But it is clear that the 'question of the national language', which refers to the imbrication of language and politics, actually names the contradictions that make up this complex: to the progressivism of a language that delivers the masses from the dark night of superstition and facilitates international co-operation corresponds the linguistic nationalism that plagued thinking about language throughout the nineteenth century and for part of the twentieth. These contradictions were already present in exemplary fashion at the time of Abbé Grégoire. Witness this extract from a speech by Barère dating from 1794:

We have noted that the dialect known as Low Breton, the Basque dialect, and the German and Italian languages have prolonged the reign of fanaticism and superstition, they have guaranteed the domination of the priests, nobles and lawyers, they have obstructed the advances of the revolution into nine large departments, and they are capable of favouring the enemies of France. . . .

Federalism and superstition speak Low Breton. Emigration and hatred of the Revolution speak German. Counter-revolution speaks Italian. Fanaticism speaks Basque. We must smash these tools of sabotage and delusion. . . .

Our enemies turned French into a court language, and thus they brought it low. It is for us to make it the language of peoples. . . . It is the destiny of French, alone, to become the universal language. That ambition, however, we leave to the genius of the French language to fulfil, as indeed it will. For ourselves, we owe it to our fellow citizens, and we owe it to the strengthening of the Republic, to ensure that the language in which the Declaration of the Rights of Man is written will be spoken across the whole territory of the Republic.[20]

It is clear that here we are not only dealing with the expression of a centralising mania: a complex political struggle, in which the survival of the Republic was at stake, but also its internationalist ambitions, is registered via the issue of the language. But we can see that the triumph of the Rights of Man takes the form of denying the right of the majority of the French population to practise its mother tongue. This irony of history has frequently been repeated. Thus, the country of liberal free choice – the USA – has shamelessly practised a glottophagic politics that destroyed the Indian languages, whereas the USSR of the dictatorship of the proletariat pursued, at least at the start of its existence, a policy of protecting and developing minority languages. In 1925, the US authorities burnt dictionaries of Chamorro, the mother tongue of the inhabitants of the island of Guam; in the same years, cohorts of Soviet linguists were employed providing a script for spoken languages threatened with extinction (this is an opportunity to salute the greatest of them, Polivanov, who was killed during Stalin's purges).[21]

Accordingly, it is clear that this stress on the question of the national language is not exaggerated, even if, of the five thousand languages spoken

---

[20] Quoted in Dalby 2003, pp. 133–4.
[21] See Dalby 2003, p. 141 and the whole of Chapter 4.

throughout the world, only 130 are national languages – that is, if we accept the most current definition, the official language of a political entity. For the linguistic question is irrevocably a political question. The class struggle is so closely mixed up with idiomatic struggle that the fact of being, or not being, a national language crucially affects all languages, including (and perhaps especially) those that are going to die. Hence my second example, selected for reasons that are more biographical than scholarly, and directly inspired by my quotation from Barère's speech. It revolves around an issue whose directly, and explosively, political character will be obvious to every French person: is Corsican an independent language? This slanted question, which anticipates a positive response, is recent. It was not posed in Abbé Grégoire's time, or until the middle of the twentieth century, when Corsican was a dialect of Italian, certainly closer to the Tuscan that gave rise to standard Italian than many other dialects (e.g. Venetian or Bergamask), but scarcely more than a patois spoken by illiterate peasants. And linguists are indeed obliged to acknowledge that Corsican and Italian are mutually intelligible, that they have parallel morphologies and similar syntaxes, and that they share a good deal of their vocabularies – in particular, the stable part that names natural kinds and everyday objects. The differences, which obviously do exist, concern pronunciation (Corsican has palatalised phonemes that do not occur in standard Italian: but this might be regarded as a mere difference of accent, since French is not spoken in the same way in Lille and Marseilles) and vocabulary, which are increasingly diverging.

But the fact that the question has been posed in the last forty years and has received a positive response cannot be ignored – any more than the fact that it is bound up with the emergence (or re-emergence) of a Corsican nationalism. A language is now not a dialect equipped with an army (Corsicans do not have one), but a dialect promoted to the status of a language because an imaginary community has decided to find its unity in it or to base its unity on it. (This aspect of a political decision is important in the case of Corsican, which is divided into several dialects, whose grammars carefully distinguish between the speech of the south and the north of the island: one sometimes has the impression, when opening a Corsican grammar, of learning two languages for the price of one.) The irony of this situation is that the accession of Corsican to the status of independent language owes much to French – a language that threatens to liquidate Corsican; to the language itself and the French educational apparatus. To the French language in the first instance.

Corsican has been politically separated from Italian for more than two centuries and Italian, which was the language of administration and civil society, receded to the point of completely losing these functions: until the end of the 19th century, Italian was the language in which notaries operated and young Corsicans often pursued their university studies in Italy. To my knowledge, Corsica is the only 'country' where the national anthem is sung in a 'foreign' language – namely, Italian. French having become the official language and the written language (until the return of Corsican as a language in the last forty years), it influenced the Corsican language, which has developed by distancing itself from standard Italian (which is now only taught in secondary schools as a foreign language) and approximating more closely to French, through lexical loans and syntactical loan-translation. The vocabulary of public life and administration is French, by loans or Corsicanisation, as is the vocabulary of new technologies of all sorts, producing sentences such as: *Vo à fà e legne cù a mo tronçonneuse* (*je vais faire le bois avec ma tronçonneuse* [I am going to do the wood with my chainsaw]).[22] This hybridisation, which is the commonest thing in the world (English as we speak it is derived from a hybridisation of French and Anglo-Saxon), is what makes Corsican a language equidistant from French and Italian (I exaggerate: the mutual comprehension is with Italian) and distinct from both. But this is insufficient: to assert itself as such, this language still needs at least the beginnings of institutional recognition. This has been the case for some decades: papers and journals in Corsican, polyphonic songs, publishing houses, the Assimil method of Corsican, a renascent literature – the language as culture and conception of the world is in the process of reappearing. But this is still not enough, and here is the irony: the language must still be sufficiently fixed to be transmitted paedagogically. This is the role of the educational apparatus, with its grammars for secondary schoolchildren and its anthologies of texts. Encouragement for the teaching of Corsican, the creation of a competitive exam for recruiting secondary schoolteachers in Corsican, and hence a body of functionaries in the Corsican language appointed by the state, have played a key role in the survival and potential development of the language.

All this has not occurred without political struggle. And it may be that the picture I have just painted is unduly optimistic. For it involves survival

---

[22] See Perfettini 2000, p. 19.

measures, which are deliberately limited (we are aware of the resistance to the legal recognition of the notion of a Corsican people and the mandatory character of the teaching of Corsican at school) and lack the political consensus required for their extension. The sad truth is that traditional Corsican society, based on a mountain agriculture, is in the process of disappearing; that the new Corsican society is primarily urban; and that the urbanised young generations speak French – the language of administration but also of modernity – much more readily than they do Corsican. French solicitude for Corsican is a form of suffocation. One of the reasons for the success of this suffocation is that the number of Corsican speakers has not reached the critical mass required to impose political changes: the comparison with Welsh, which, although threatened, has resisted the language of empire much better, is instructive in this regard.

It appears, then, that the history of a language, starting with its accession to the status of independent language, is a political history: for Corsican did not separate from Italian on account of the immanent weight of its phonetic, morphological or syntactical system. Optimists will describe this situation in terms of mutual presupposition; pessimists, in terms of a vicious circle: for Corsican to emerge as a 'natural language' – i.e. as a national language – Corsica must be a nation. But for Corsica to have the possibility of becoming a nation, Corsican must be a natural language.

The relations between language and politics in the broad sense nevertheless go beyond the contribution of the language to the constitution of the nation-state, for they are much more profound. The language permeates civil society; it forms part of the fabric of everyday life. We shall not be astonished to see that this is how Gramsci describes the spontaneous philosophy not of the scientist, but of the man or woman in the street. For him, everyone is spontaneously a 'philosopher' and this philosophy is contained in:

> 1. language itself, which is a totality of determined notions and concepts and not just of words grammatically devoid of content; 2. 'common sense' and 'good sense'; 3. popular religion and, therefore, also in the entire system of beliefs, superstitions, opinions, ways of seeing things and of acting, which are collectively bundled together under the under of 'folklore'.[23]

---

[23] Gramsci 1971, p. 323.

Conceived thus, language is the language of the *polis*, the repertoire of the reasons people have for believing and for acting according to their beliefs. It is the inscription and sedimentation of popular culture – hence Gramsci's interest in folklore, common sense, and popular religion. It is language that causes the individual agent, with her idiosyncratic perspective on the world, to be always-already preceded by a collective agent, which shares with the rest of a linguistic and/or national community a 'conception of the world', a form of common sense, a 'natural' philosophy (which is obviously a cultural and historical construct), a religion. We see why Gramsci's conception of language is intimately bound up with the process that I have called 'metaphorical drift', to what Lakoff and Johnson (as we have also seen) call 'metaphors we live by'. And we also understand why the concept of linguistic imperialism is not simply a grandiloquent slogan or an insult: it expresses the intricate links and state of mutual presupposition between language and politics. A standard language – that historico-social construct – is at once the vehicle of linguistic imperialism, which in its triumphal progress condemns minor languages to disappear, and imposes its grammatical markers of power (from modal auxiliaries to Lara Croft's grunts) on speakers on the other side of the planet; and also a dialect, which is constantly being rendered minoritarian, always running the risk of devaluation (the metaphor of language as currency is age-old), if not of degeneration. On these two points, the same is – or will be – true of English as was true of Latin in its time. Hence the unexpected importance that Marxists or para-Marxists – Voloshinov, Pasolini, Deleuze – have attributed to the concept of style. For linguistic imperialism, like the broader imperialism of which it is a component and the expression, provokes resistance and this resistance, which the concept of minor dialect seeks to conceptualise, is inscribed in the style of speech, conceived not as the culmination of the speaker's creative originality, but as the inscription in the utterance of the clash of contending dialects. This is what Voloshinov calls the 'multi-accentuality' of the word. This is what the concept of polyphony in Bakhtin is attempting to grasp: a way of describing the linguistic class struggle. Here, we can leave the last word to Bakhtin:

> Languages are philosophies – not abstract but concrete, social philosophies, penetrated by a system of values inseparable from living practice and class struggle. This is why every object, every concept, every point of view, as

well as every intonation [finds its] place at this intersection of linguistic philosophies and [is] drawn into an intense ideological struggle.[24]

To summarise. The thesis that language is a political phenomenon contains a certain number of propositions.

First proposition: human beings are political animals because they are speaking animals. Language is the requisite, even constitutive, medium of politics. *Agôn* – this generalised 'athleticism', as Deleuze and Guattari call it[25] – is the archetypal form of the political relation. For Deleuze, this is the essence of democracy, in the form of democratic debate. For Marxists, this is the essence of struggle (which is also class struggle) in that it initially, and inevitably, takes the form of a linguistic struggle.

Second proposition: the converse is also true. Human beings are speaking animals because they are political animals. Political action is the canonical form of *praxis*, at least it is for a tradition of political philosophy from Aristotle to Habermas; and, for us, linguistic *praxis* is the archetypal form of *praxis*. This comes down to saying that language and politics are inextricably interwoven. Language is at once the expression and form of constitution of the human collectivity; it attests to the fact that, among human beings, one never begins with the individual, but always with the *socius*, from which the individual emerges through a process of individuation which is a process of subjectivation by interpellation. The umbilical cord, which is also the social bond, uniting the individual to the *socius* is language. We understand why Marxists have never been afraid to have truck with the mythical question of the origin of language – to which, naturally, they suggest different answers, from the collective practice of the hunt in Tran Duc Thao to the division of labour in Marx.

Third proposition: ideas become material forces when they seize hold of the masses. They do so only because they are embodied in language – because, in reality, they are language (what is called order-words). For political ideas do not pre-exist order-words, which they do not 'translate' into a language that is more accessible to the masses: they *are* order-words that inscribe them on the body of the *socius*. We have seen that, in his early works, Marx emphasised the materiality of language as a sensory reality. The ideas that

---

[24] Bakhtin 1984, p. 471.
[25] Deleuze and Guattari 1993, p. 8.

take hold of the masses draw their effectivity from this material existence as words and order-words, from their insertion into a collective assemblage of enunciation, whose main characteristic, as we know, is its ontological mixedness. So ideas do not become 'material forces' by some process of transmutation: from the outset, they are material, for they are the words which 'express' them (here, as usual, the metaphors of the dominant philosophy betray us). We understand why Lenin, in a moment of extreme political urgency, found the time to write a text on slogans: the correctness of a political line in a given conjuncture is not an abstract theoretical question, but the practical outcome of the linguistic selection of good slogans.

Fourth proposition: if the origin of language is to be sought in the exigencies of the division of labour, and if this myth is effective, it is because language is intimately involved in the division of society into antagonistic classes and in the struggles that produce this division. For language is the source of the illusory generalisation (i.e. ideology in its traditional pejorative sense) whereby humanity conceals the real relations between the families, tribes and classes that make up society and fetishises them in the form of the state (which is due to disappear one day). But it is also the terrain on which the struggles implied by these relations are conducted. The task of a revolutionary critique – that of Marx and his successors – is, therefore, to make language descend from its philosophical heights (Marx is especially virulent about the philosophical pretensions of Max Stirner, whose post-Hegelian puns pass for concepts) to the materiality of the real world. Thus we will pass, in the words of Marx's famous formula, from the language of philosophy to the 'language of real life'.

Language is the terrain of the class struggle. This statement can be construed in two ways. The first is obvious: the class struggle passes (in particular) *through* language. The second is less clear: the class struggle is situated *in* language. An example will permit me to impart a more positive sense to this second formulation, which comes down to giving a meaning to the old Marxist saw: 'the dominant ideology dominates'. For the class struggle *in* language has one spectacular feature: its agents – I should say its spokespersons – do not need to be conscious either of its existence or of the fact that they are participants in it. The following utterance was to be heard on British TV news a few years ago: 'The dispute by the health workers in now in its third week'. For us, English has an advantage over French in this respect: it does not conceal the partisanship behind this seemingly factual and 'objective' news item in so far as it contains a solecism, which French also contains but not so blatantly. In fact, the grammar of the noun 'dispute' requires that it be followed by a prepositional phrase beginning with 'between'. In other words, for there to be a 'dispute', there need to be two parties: this necessity likewise applies to conflicts. And this noun cannot take an agent introduced by 'by' (this is where French is more sly, in that the *de* in *le conflit* des *travailleurs de la santé* does not so clearly mark an agent). We can draw two conclusions from this. The first is that the rules of syntax, which are not inscribed in human nature, are not as stable as all that, since my sentence has not only been uttered but is perfectly intelligible, and even adapted to its purpose, which is the subject of my second conclusion. For, obviously, this solecism is scarcely innocent: it is not *politically* innocent. By not mentioning it (the fact that the passive verb takes an agent phrase as its complement transforms the process denoted by 'dispute', which is a process with two actors, into a process with only one), it exonerates the other party to the conflict – the administrators or employers – from any responsibility, thereby making the workers exclusively responsible for the inconveniences caused by the conflict. It therefore seeks to mobilise the listeners, who are also users and tax-payers, on the side of one of the two parties to the conflict. And you will have noted that the utterance avoids the politically taboo word 'strike', which is too emotionally and politically charged. But the most interesting thing is that my analysis, which is situated at the level of the text, does not need to posit conscious, malevolent intended meanings on the part of the journalist who is the author of this sentence: whether there was, or was not, an intended meaning is of little consequence. It suffices that this solecism surreptitiously introduces the noun 'dispute' into a passive syntactical structure for the political effectivity of the utterance to be guaranteed. The passive is a weapon in the linguistic class struggle, whether the individual speaker is conscious of it or not. This gives a new meaning to what Fredric Jameson calls the 'political unconscious'.[26]

---

[26] See Jameson 1981.

3. Final thesis: the function of language is the production of subjects

Language is not only a battlefield and one of the instruments of the class struggle, but also the site and instrument of the transformation of individuals into subjects. This is even – and this is the sense of my final thesis – its principal function, which is, therefore, not that of being an instrument of communication. And the link between linguistic *agôn* and class struggle is not metaphorical or merely analogical: just as classes emerge from the struggles that oppose them (and in which they are constituted), so speakers emerge from interlocution, from the linguistic *agôn* that unites and opposes them, and which they do not pre-exist. My Marxist concepts form a system: the linguistic conjuncture gives the state, or the moment, of the linguistic *agôn*; linguistic imperialism describes the state of the power relations in this *agôn*; linguistic class struggle is the Marxist name for the *agôn*; and interpellation (and counter-interpellation) in and by language describe the outcome of the *agôn*. Thus everything ends with the chain of interpellation that I have described, and whose end product is a set of subjects. This is why methodological individualism, which is the most widely shared conviction in thinking about language, is, for me, the main philosophical enemy: in that, by a classic operation of ideology as *camera obscura*, (i.e. in its traditional pejorative sense), it turns things upside down, taking the end of the process for its starting-point. To return the process to its correct order is precisely to avoid the concomitant fetishism of language (as an abstract system) and of the subject (as centre and user of words) and to treat the process in its totality – i.e. as a process. It is to put language and the subject back in their place. The place of language is that of a historical, social, material and political *praxis*. The place of the subject is that of a becoming-subject interpellated by the language that speaks it and counter-interpellating it in order to speak it.

Contrasting Short Glossaries of Philosophy of Language

My final thesis suggests that the Marxist concepts elaborated by the tradition and developed above form a system. By way of conclusion, I am therefore going to try to assemble the main ones here. Obviously, it is not only Marxist concepts that form a system. The leitmotiv of this book has been that the class enemy is a past master in the linguistic class struggle. This is apparent in the linguistic *doxa* of which the dominant philosophy of language is the noble version. And it takes the form of a number of linguistic notions that are directly applicable politically. They warrant a book in their own right. Here, I shall only tackle three of them, in the light of works by authors who do not (always) identify with Marxism, but whose reflections are valuable in that they capture the political common sense in linguistic matters in the current conjuncture.

1. Brief glossary of Marxist philosophy of language

Assemblage

This term was coined by Deleuze and Guattari in *A Thousand Plateaus*. Assemblages have two aspects – a machinic, desiring aspect (machinic assemblages of desire) and a discursive, linguistic aspect (collective assemblages of enunciation). Their principal characteristic is the ontological mix that occurs in them. Thus, the feudal assemblage – Deleuze and Guattari's canonical example – is made up of human bodies (the knight, his lady and his vassals), animal bodies (the knight's horse), buildings and objects (the manor and the sword), but also of utterances and texts (courtly love poems, decrees of justice), and, hence, of institutions (courts of law) and rituals (marriage). This concept is important in a variety of ways. It makes it possible to go beyond the separation between material infrastructure and ideal superstructure, by demonstrating the imbrication of the material and the ideal: language is precisely the site of this imbrication. It therefore underscores the material character of linguistic phenomena. But it also stresses their social character: the source of utterances is not the individual speaker, but the assemblage of enunciation, which is collective. The individual speaker speaks in that she is spoken by the collective assemblage. This in no way prevents her discourse from exhibiting the idiosyncratic originality of a style. The court poet produces creative work in that he is spoken by a collective assemblage: in terms of literary criticism, this is called a genre, as long as we conceive a genre as an institution (a set of constraints that are both material and ideal), and not only as an abstract set of rules. Finally, the canonical example clearly shows that linguistic phenomena are historical phenomena: each assemblage has its conjuncture.

Class struggle

That language is involved in the class struggle is self-evident: I have tried to show that language is a political phenomenon. Politics finds its natural medium in language: programmes, speeches, debates, and so on. I have said enough about the specific importance of slogans, a theory of which represents Lenin's contribution to the Marxist philosophy of language, for there to be no need to return to it. But we must go further. If language is the archetypal form of historical human *praxis*, and if the history of humanity is the history of class struggles, there must be a closer link between language and class struggle, over and above the obvious linguistic divisions (dialects, jargons, styles, speech genres) analysed by socio-linguistics. In the work of Bourdieu (whose relationship with Marxism is complicated), we find a set of concepts (cultural capital, authority-authorisation, intimidation, etc.) that make it possible to conceive this linguistic sociology. But if we attend as closely as possible to language, we note that in linguistic practice the specific form taken by class struggle is the contradiction between *agôn* and *eirene*. The dominant philosophy of language, in the form of Grice's pragmatics or Habermas's theory of communicative action, thinks in terms of co-operation – a noble objective that is regrettably exploited when action becomes strategic, which it always does. For our philosophy of language, *agôn* dominates and co-operation is the unstable result of an effort, a struggle, of the establishment of a power relationship, which is also a relationship of places. This means that a principle of struggle, which I have sought to formulate in *The Violence of Language*, will be preferred to Grice's principle of co-operation.[1] The motto of this position is: there is no communicative action that is not simultaneously strategic action. The principle of struggle will have a general formulation (we speak in order to lay claim to a place and to impose one on an interlocutor) and some detailed maxims, which can be combined in a super-maxim of agonistic relevance: adapt your linguistic tactics to your strategy, never lose sight of the objective, which is to remain in control of the discursive terrain. This conception of the primacy of *agôn* is consistent with my description of linguistic *praxis* in terms of interpellation and subjectivation. It makes it possible to account for phenomena that are usually dealt with (co-operation as an equilibrium in a power relation) and those which are no less invariably excluded (whether directly aggressive language games, like insults or threats, or linguistic phenomena that escape the liberal framework of the egalitarian contract of communication, like the rhetoric of reticence, the linguistic expression of madness, or all the stylistic games that subvert the rules of grammar). But the link is closer still. To think linguistic *agôn* in terms of class struggle (and to think class struggle, at least in part, in terms of linguistic *agôn*) is to effect three inversions with respect to the dominant philosophy: it is to pass from the individual to the collective (in order to struggle, you must not be alone: you need opponents just as you need comrades in arms); it is to move from thing to process (*agôn* produces speaker-subjects as the struggle produces the classes who wage it); and it is to abandon the conception of the egalitarian contract that governs the dominant thinking (in the form of the famous Saussurian schema of communication): *la langue* is not a code equally possessed

---

[1] See Lecercle 1991.

by two interlocutors, allowing for an egalitarian exchange of words, but a linguistic formation – that is, the unstable outcome of a multitude of linguistic contests, the image, in a given conjuncture, of a set of power relations which are seemingly in temporary equilibrium but actually fluctuating.

Collectivism

The defining characteristic of the dominant philosophy of language is individualism, hallowed in the two forms of liberal individualism (the essential thing is the free choice of the individual, whose freedom of expression is unlimited, politically and theoretically); and methodological individualism (collective entities – say, state or class – have no existence apart from the individuals that compose them; and the collective actions imputed to them are simply the result of the composition of individual actions). The overwhelming majority of linguistic theories and philosophies of language share this individualism. It stands to reason that it is the individual who speaks, that it is the individual who possesses the faculty of language, which therefore has its seat in the individual. Biological, phenomenological and enunciative versions of linguistics share this individualist position, which has greatly contributed to the Chomskyan research programme becoming dominant. The only exception (albeit sizeable) is Saussure's system of *langue*, which is external and prior to individual speakers and imposed on them. For stubborn observation indicates that, when it comes to language at any rate, methodological individualism does not work. The individual speaker's ability to have an effect on her mother tongue or national language is strictly limited, even in the most favourable case – that of the literary creator. To be thought about adequately, what language needs is the collectivism of the assemblages, order-words, institutions, rituals and practices which are the source of utterances. The speaker is not the inventor of her language; she speaks a language that she has not created, but into which she is integrated to find her voice. The result is that, in an important sense, she is no longer the initiator of her discourse, except through an illusion (fortunate and necessary), but enters into a discourse that is always-already collective. Voloshinov calls this collective effect the 'multi-accentuality' of words; Baktin, polyphony. And this linguistic collectivism is not to be regarded as an intolerable determinism that condemns the speaker to producing Orwell's 'Newspeak' in *1984*: we are, instead, in the presence of what Judith Butler calls 'enabling constraints' –

that is, constraints which enable the speaker to speak, and to speak in her own right, to find her voice, which is not a given for the individual, but the result of a struggle, of the counter-interpellation that answers the interpellation of the subject by language.

Conjuncture

Selecting order-words as the basic utterance, as the quintessential utterance, has two advantages. It underscores the fact that language is a form of *praxis*, that its constitutive elements are speech acts, which, in the physical sense of the term, communicate power and therefore have an effectivity. But it also stresses the historically determinate character of these acts. A speech act takes on meaning in a conjuncture, which is not only a historical conjuncture in the broad sense, but a *linguistic* conjuncture – a set of speech acts that furnish the act with its context and determine its meaning. The meaning of an utterance is, therefore, the *moment* of the conjuncture that this utterance captures (which means, not only expresses but actively helps to constitute: in the moment of the conjuncture in which it is correct, the order-word is determinant). In other words, every utterance is an event, not in that it combines pre-constituted linguistic elements in an original way (this is the definition of rule-governed creativity in Chomsky), but in that it intervenes in the conjuncture from which it is derived and contributes to determining its moment. Here, incidentally, we have a possible definition of realism in literature, a concept of which Marxists are, as we know, fond: a literary text is realist not in as much it produces a faithful image of an already constituted reality, but in that it captures the moment of the conjuncture in which it is inserted and thus helps to alter it. Here, we need to re-read Lukács's texts on Balzac. But why posit the existence of a linguistic conjuncture and not make do with the more general term of historical conjuncture? Because language is endowed with a specific effectivity. First of all, an utterance is effectively caught up in a historical conjuncture; it expresses and therefore 'reflects' it (the quotation marks are due to the notoriously problematic character of this concept: but it is possible to conceive an active reflection, even a reflection without a mirror).[2] Next, in this historical conjuncture it sediments its past: language is famously an

---

[2] See Lecourt 1973.

instrument of memory. And, in the current conjuncture, it does not merely express the survivals of past conjunctures (in the form of metaphors, as we have seen with Gramsci); it anticipates future conjunctures: language – an old Hegelian theme – is also a receptacle of those provisional errors that are future truths (let us call this the utopian aspect of language). Finally, in the totality of the historical conjuncture, the linguistic instance possesses relative autonomy: the different strata of language have their own times, just as (in the Althusserian conception of the social structure) the different strata that make up the social formation have their own times. This means that the temporalities of language are caught up in the temporalities of change in the social formation, but that they have their own rhythm (we can see why Marxist determinism, which would have the social revolution revolutionise the language at a stroke, is mistaken). This enables us (finally) to define what we must understand by 'langue': neither a system, nor an ahistorical essence ('French'), but a *linguistic formation*, just as we refer to a social formation: a set of speech acts and language games, the struggles and contradictions that determine their relations in a given conjuncture.

Fetishism

I am not returning to the concept of fetishism in Marx and the metaphysical subtleties of the language of commodities. I am more immediately interested in the sense given to it by Lukács in *History and Class Consciousness* – a major text in the Marxist tradition, which is unjustly neglected.[3] For Lukács moves from the well-known Marxist thesis (fetishism is the reification of inter-human relations, which assume the appearance of things) to its generalisation: abstraction is the intellectual form that translates fetishism, an abstraction which is not an eternal necessity of the human mind but a reflection of the historical situation of capitalism. The forms of objectivity, the categories through which we apprehend phenomena, are also historical phenomena. The feature of fetishism in Lukács that interests me most is that it individualises the subject as it reifies the object: the subject facing the commodity fetish or the fetishised concept is aware only of a partial domain of reality (partial fact, abstract partial law): it is this partial vision that individualises her by

---

[3] On Lukács, see the excellent Löwy 1979.

separating her from the totality. The standpoint that makes it possible to elude fetishism is, therefore, the standpoint of the totality. Lukács adds that the world of fetishism is the world of the 'eternal laws of nature' and that the 'faculties' of the mind are the symptom of the alienation of a subject trapped in fetishism. We can see how the concept is important for a Marxist philosophy of language: it enables us to avoid Chomskyan naturalism and, at the same time, suggests an explanation of its emergence and scientific success. It does the same thing with individualism, which is ubiquitous in the philosophy of language. In matters of language, however, the concept produces a contradiction, but a happy contradiction, which enables us to understand the real functioning of language. On the one hand, language is the source of fetishism: words have a natural tendency to freeze processes into objects (this is the function of 'ontological metaphors' which are all words of abstraction). Thus, 'inflation' is a set of processes and human relations. Thus named, it becomes a 'thing' (the referent of a noun). It therefore becomes manipulable: we can construct a theory of it, fight it, seek to eliminate it, and so on. This natural dynamic of language – this fetishism by illusion – is the source of the dynamic whereby the 'science' of language constructs its object by separating what is pertinent from what is not and excluding the major part of linguistic phenomena. Against this fetishism of illusion, which directly counter-poses an equally fetishised subject (the subject-speaker or enunciator) and object (*la langue*), the Marxist philosophy of language must adopt the standpoint of the totality, as a set of contradictory historical relations which constitute the reality of language and the linguistic formations that we call languages. But there is a second aspect: linguistic fetishism is not only illusion, it is also allusion, like ideology in Althusser. For abstraction, the tendency to fetishise processes into objects, is essential to the functioning of language. There is no thought without abstraction – my discourse is proof of the fact – and the concept is a concrete abstraction (I refer here to Althusser's well-known analysis of the concrete-in-thought).[4] We shall observe, moreover, that fetishism is attributed by Lukács to the historical epoch of capitalism and that language did not await the constitution of capitalist relations of production before emerging. There is, therefore, a dual, potentially contradictory relation to fetishism in language; and this contradiction constitutes the heart of the functioning of language:

---

[4] See Althusser 1969, p. 182 ff.

language betrays phenomena by tending to fetishise processes into objects, human relations into things; and it saves the phenomena by making it possible to think them. Thought is a happy fetishism, by allusion; if it so readily turns into *doxa*, it is because of the slope that inclines it towards harmful fetishism, by illusion, which fixes and naturalises historical processes into natural objects. The standpoint of the totality in linguistic matters consists in thinking the two aspects of the contradiction at the same time (this is called the dialectic). To think only one of them leads either to scientistic positivism and methodological individualism, or to the romanticism of poetic expression, always betrayed in advance by language.

Imperialism

Linguistic imperialism is part of imperialism *tout court* and is one of its privileged instruments. But it possesses specific characteristics, which means that language is the site of specific contradictions (this does not mean that imperialism *tout court* is without contradictions: in reality, they are parallel but not identical). In the case of linguistic imperialism, and its most notorious consequence – glottophagy (etymologically, the devouring of one language by another)[5] – the contradiction takes the form of an opposition between centripetal forces, which reinforce the domination of the language of imperialism, and centrifugal forces, which tend to render it minoritarian and destabilise it. Thus, English is the language of imperialism in the current conjuncture because it is in the process of imposing itself across the globe, but also because it is beginning to crumble, and lives only because it is constantly subject to processes of becoming-minoritarian. This contradiction concerns not only English, which is simply the most striking illustration of it, but all languages in that they are linguistic formations. For English will make French suffer what French is making Corsican suffer. Faced with this contradiction, we can adopt one of two attitudes. If we are pessimists, we shall reckon that the battle has already been won by English and that it will not suffer the fate of Latin – the canonical historical example of an imperial language. In a singularly bitter irony, the dream of Zamenhof – the creator of Esperanto – is supposedly on the point of being realised, but not in the

---

[5] See Calvet 1974.

form of the harmony of peoples: in the form of neoliberal imperialist domination, to the detriment of the overwhelming majority of human languages –
i.e. cultures and conceptions of the world. If we are optimists, we shall think
that the triumph of linguistic imperialism is no more guaranteed than that
of imperialism in general and that English will inevitably suffer the fate of
Latin – even if this prediction, which is also a hope, refers to the long term.
In my introduction I adopted an optimistic position. It is possible that in so
doing I took my desires for realities. The converse argument will be found
in Andrew Dalby's excellent book, *Language in Danger*.[6] It rests on two
observations: the globalisation of English (whereas the imperial domination
of Latin hardly extended beyond the proximity of the Mediterranean basin);
and the fact that the usual instruments of linguistic imperialism – colonisation
(speakers of the dominated languages disappear through massacres or
epidemics), administration (the children of the survivors are schooled in the
language of imperialism), and trade (the economic survival of native speakers
involves adopting the dominant language) – have been joined by a fourth:
the global development of the media, which means that the whole world will
talk like the characters in *Miami Beach*. This argument contains a weakness:
it fetishises the language of imperialism, making it a single, stable entity.
If it is true that the extension of English, which has already led to the
disappearance of virtually all the Indian languages of America and Aboriginal
languages of Australia, will create new victims (it is calculated that half the
languages currently spoken will have disappeared by the end of the century),
it is also true that the globalised English of the media is only one of the dialects
of English and that English dialects are diversifying, to the extent that mutual
comprehension will soon become difficult. (The language of Glaswegian inner
cities is as difficult for a Londoner to understand as some forms of Québécois
French are for a Parisian: Québécquois films that reach Paris are sub-titled
for the first half-hour.) The English of the media, with its limited vocabulary
and elementary grammar, is going to become a global *lingua franca*. Despite
globalisation, however, the different dialects of English might well give
rise to a family of languages, just as Latin gave rise to the Romance languages. Marxists therefore incline towards the optimistic interpretation of
the contradiction, if not out of teleological certainty, then, at least, out of

---

[6] See Dalby 2003.

eschatological hope. Barbarism is never certain and we can always dream of socialism. Linguistic imperialism is no more stable than imperialism *tout court*; it is subject to the same kind of contradictions and there is, therefore, a space for emancipatory struggles, even for those whose professional task it is to teach the language of imperialism. All this is intended to recall that the expression 'linguistic imperialism' is not a facile insult, betraying its author's simple-minded anti-Americanism, but the characterisation of a complex situation. And we need a philosophy of language to grasp this complexity.

Interpellation/subjectivation

The term 'interpellation' derives from the second theory of ideology to be found in Althusser. It is the central concept of this theory, which tells us that ideology interpellates each individual as a subject. The parable with which Althusser illustrates the concept is well known: the traffic cop blows on his whistle and everyone looks round, convinced that this intepellation was personally directed at them. I have suggested developing the concept by extending the chain of interpellation sketched by Althusser to speech acts: institution – ritual – practice – speech act.

The subject is, then, the individual interpellated at end of the chain by the speech act. It is clear that, by extending the Althusserian chain to speech acts, I am being unfaithful to the master, who paid little attention to language (the only occasion on which language is mentioned in the ISAs essay is a footnote criticising linguists). But it is also clear that this extension is possible; what is more, I am not the only one to have had the idea. Michel Pêcheux's is based on the idea that ideology finds its material existence in language.[7] In *Language Alone*, Geoffrey Harpham translates Althusser's discourse on ideology in terms of language – a concept which for him is the major fetish of our modernity.[8] The importance of the concept is considerable. It makes it possible to ignore liberal jeremiads about Marxist determinism leading to the disappearance of the subject and the loss of the notions of freedom, responsibility and morality. A French philosopher who was to become a minister – Luc Ferry – once wrote a disastrous book on this subject. The

---

[7] See Pêcheux 1982.
[8] See Harpham 2002.

concept of interpellation has the advantage of putting the subject back in its place – an expression that is to be understood in both a pejorative sense (it dethrones the subject from its position of mastery and origin of meaning) and a positive sense (it assigns the subject its due place, by describing the linguistic process of subjectivation). It therefore makes it possible to understand both the importance of the notion of the subject in linguistic matters (after all, linguistics has recourse not to one concept of the subject, but to two, since it distinguishes between the subject of the utterance and the subject of the enunciation); and the need to invert the common sense that attributes centrality to the subject. In linguistic matters at least, it is difficult to argue that the subject-speaker, who must be integrated into a language that is prior and external to her, is the source, the centre, or the mistress of meaning. This inversion of perspective is characteristic of the Marxist tradition: it is already to be found in Voloshinov's work. In Deleuze and Guattari, the displacement goes even further and the philosophical work done by the concept of the subject is performed by different concepts – assemblage or haeccity. But to link interpellation and subjectivation – that is, to retain a concept of the subject put in its place – is to understand that language does not 'serve' to communicate, even if communication obviously occurs: it is the social *praxis* whereby individuals become subjects because they become speakers. Even so, it is important not to slip into the determinism of an interpellation that imposes on a helpless subject an identity and a discourse over which she has no control. Already, in Bourdieu, individual action is determined by the field in which it occurs, but agents have their own individual strategies with which they negotiate the constraints of the field. I have, therefore, suggested regarding the interpellation of the subject-speaker by language as reciprocal, and that corresponding to this interpellation is a *counter-interpellation*. The term, clearly inspired by Freud's counter-investment, is directly inspired by Judith Butler's reading of Althusser's theory of ideology.[9] There are some proximate concepts in contemporary philosophy: counter-identification in Pêcheux or counter-effectuation in Deleuze. The concept aims to describe the fact that, while speakers enters into a language that is prior and external to them, they appropriate it (this is called a style).

---

[9] See Butler 1995 and 1997.

Langage/langue

The Saussurian revolution took the form of extracting the system of *langue* from the totality of linguistic phenomena, the remainder being excluded from the field of scientific activity under the rubric of *parole*. Milner replaces the original metaphysical question, 'Why is there language rather than nothing?', by the question of the science of language: 'Why is there *langue* rather than nothing?'. (In fact, the question being Lacanian, it takes the form: 'Why is there *lalangue* rather than nothing?'.)[10] This means that the linguist has nothing to say about *langage*. On different bases (it has been argued that the Chomskyan research programme is a systematic inversion of Saussurianism), Chomsky arrives at the same conclusions, even going so far as to deny any scientific existence to natural languages. Obviously, this is the sticking point. First of all, because the word 'language [*langage*], is insistent, even in the titles of Chomsky's scientific works. And next because to deny that the issue of natural/maternal/national languages is of any interest is to preclude oneself from saying anything about the crucial problems posed by linguistic *praxis*: the problems of the history of languages, of social and regional variations within languages, of the disappearance of languages on account of linguistic imperialism, and hence of the politics of language. This is why the Marxist philosophy of language, inspired on this score by Deleuze and Guattari, does not consider the distinction between *langue* and *langage* to be essential. Firstly, because it adopts the standpoint of the totality (against the fetishism of positive science) and is, therefore, interested in language as a total human *praxis*, refusing to exclude any linguistic phenomena whatsoever and interesting itself in the interface between language and the world. Secondly, because it makes natural languages the privileged object of its interest. Thus, we can contrast 'English' – major system or language – with English – a linguistic formation – according to the following correlation. 'English' is single; immanent (its speakers are angels, it is separated from the world); reduced (by the exclusion of irrelevant linguistic phenomena); systematic (it is a fixed code); stable (it is fixed at a point in time and the system changes as a whole or not at all); outside time (this is called synchrony); abstract (it principally exists in the grammars that describe it and is only spoken by a tiny minority of speakers); and teachable

---

[10] Milner 1978, p. 26.

(because it has only an ideal existence). Contrariwise, English, which is the only thing we care about, is multiple; situated (it is of the world and in the world: a set of historical, political, social and material phenomena); total (its study excludes no phenomena – not gestural communication, not so-called supra-segmental phenomena, not pragmatic interactions); chaotic (there is no grammatical 'rule' that is not defeasible and defeated in at least one of the dialects: exception, exploitation, or expression); in a state of continuous variation (there is no stability in a linguistic formation, which is a temporary and transient equilibrium of tensions and contradictions: the ever-contested result of a series of power relations); changing (it sediments the history of peoples and cultures and accommodates, by anticipatory effect, the event that is going to change them dramatically); real (it exists in our everyday reality rather than in the grammars and is spoken in its diversity by the vast majority of speakers); and, finally, to be practised rather than taught. And it is clear that 'English' is only in the singular because of the abstraction-fetishisation that makes it possible to think it, at the cost of betraying it. That is why I return briefly to the multiplicity of the linguistic formation called 'English': it is made up of regional dialects, social dialects, generational dialects, languages in the process of being formed, professional registers, group languages (argots and jargons), speech genres (the term belongs to Bakhtin, but we find similar terms in Foucault – discursive formations – or Wittgenstein – language games), collective styles, and individual styles.

Minority

The concept of minor language or dialect, as opposed to major or standard language or dialect, belongs to Deleuze and Guattari. We likewise, and doubtless more appropriately, refer to minor usages of language. The concept is explained in their book on Kafka in particular.[11] A minor language has three characteristics: it is collective, it is directly political, and it is de-territorialising. Thus, Kafka, a Czech Jewish writer writing in German – the major language of the Austro-Hungarian empire – de-territorialises the language he writes in by confronting it with the minor languages that he does not write, but which he speaks or which are spoken around him. In so doing, he performs

---

[11] See Deleuze and Guattari 1986.

a profoundly political act and speaks in the name of the people, even if it can scarcely be claimed that he is a committed writer or a popular author. The term 'minority' is borrowed – obviously deliberately – from the field of politics and full of irony: the major dialect, the standard language, is, in fact, only spoken by a tiny minority of speakers. This is as true of standard English, language of imperialism, as of German in the Austro-Hungarian Empire. And, in truth, this ironic situation also concerns the field of politics, where speeches about respecting the majority often conceal policies defending minority or élite interests. But the real interest of the concept is that this ontological metaphor does not refer so much to a result as to a process: this is why, ideally, we should prefer the coinage 'becoming-minoritarian' to 'minority'. For the function of linguistic minorities – this is the form taken by class struggle in language – is to render the standard language minoritarian. By this is to be understood a dual process: the minor dialects subvert the major language, they disquiet it, destabilise it, put it in a state of continuous variation; correlatively, however, by subverting it they make it live, they cause the linguistic formation to continue to develop, to be the site of tensions and contradictions that render it active in the historical and linguistic conjuncture. In germ, here we have a theory of the specific effectivity of the family of language games commonly called literature. The concept is interesting for a second reason. It makes it possible to stress the diversity of linguistic phenomena and thereby challenge the unicity of language understood as a system. A linguistic formation is a rather chaotic set of dialects (e.g. the forms of English spoken in Scotland or Australia), even of languages in the process of being formed (what are called the 'New Englishes' – the English of Singapore, Nigeria, etc.), of social or generational dialects (the English of inner-city Glasgow, which is not only Scottish but proletarian; or what is called 'Estuary English', a dialect born on the banks of the Thames and dear to today's British adolescents), of jargons and registers (by which is understood the language of occupations and professions), of argots and other secret languages, of individual and group styles, of speech genres and other language games (the English of the media is a good example). It is this unstable, continually varying set, with each component having its own rhythm and temporality, which by (inevitable) abstraction and (far from innocent) fetishisation is called 'English'. Why is the fetishisation not innocent? Because it makes it possible to pass off, by synecdoche, one of the dialects – 'standard English' – for the whole of the linguistic formation, which has important consequences (e.g. when it comes to teaching). Finally, the concept has a direct political interest: it aims to grasp the state of the linguistic class struggle within a linguistic formation; it helps to define the moment of the linguistic conjuncture; it makes it possible to separate the emergent from the old. In short, it facilitates not only a description of the conjuncture, but also the intervention that it calls for.

Style

It is curious that so seemingly individualistic a concept ('the style is the man') should figure in a glossary of Marxist philosophy of language, where the main philosophical enemy is liberal individualism. Readers will recall that a number of Marxist or para-Marxist thinkers (Voloshinov, Pasolini, Deleuze) were fascinated by questions of style (in particular, by the problem of indirect free speech). In fact, the concept is of great interest to us, in that it makes it possible to think under the same term the collective (it is the language that speaks) and the individual (I speak the language that speaks me). The term, in fact, contains a happy ambiguity: it refers at once to aesthetic individuality and to the chosen identity of the group: the style of Henry James and expressionist style or rocker style. For style is not only a matter of language and a stylist is not only a novelist: one of the important things about the concept is that it speaks to us of linguistic *praxis* and non-linguistic cultural practices in the same terms. It therefore strongly suggests, as against the structuralist principle of immanence, that linguistic *praxis* is neither isolated nor isolable. Finally, if we adopt Deleuze's definition of style as a-grammaticality and taking things to the limit, the concept enables us to think linguistic change as a function of the historical conjuncture, which creates needs for identity and translates them into fashions and styles, and of the linguistic conjuncture: the counter-interpellation inscribed in the individual style is an intervention in the linguistic conjuncture which alters it, however marginally.

2. Short glossary of neoliberal philosophy of language

Communication

The sole thesis of the dominant philosophy of language in its quintessential form is 'language is an instrument of communication'. An ideology (in the pejorative sense) of communication, its necessity and benefits, derives from it: dare to communicate, know how to communicate – such is the watchword of our liberal modernity. The promises held out are enticing: communication is the surest means for the individual subject to flourish; she realises her freedom to the utmost in it, assumes her responsibility in it, enjoys control over her existence and her thought in it. To service such noble needs, a communications industry and institutions of communication have developed: they are regarded as the cutting edge of technological progress and stock-market enrichment (as long as the speculative bubbles do not burst). In one hand, modern man holds his steering wheel and in the other (to the great displeasure of the pedestrian who dares to venture onto a zebra crossing) his mobile, on which he is constantly communicating. For modern man is never alone and the most trivial and babbling thoughts must be communicated forthwith.

I shall stop, for I am lapsing into a jeremiad. But I observe that this eulogy of communication has its dark side and that communication ends up having a bad press – especially in the domain of politics. Who has not read or heard this ringing declaration, 'the government doesn't govern, it communicates!'. This tension is the index of the operation of an ideology in the pejorative sense – that is, an inverted image of reality. This does not preclude also regarding the ideology of communication as an ideology in the positive sense, as allusion as much as illusion – that is, as the expression of the contemporary form of interpellation of subjects in the framework of the division of labour, where language and interlocution play a novel and essential role (these are the theses of Negri and Hardt, Virno, and Marazzi).

The ideology of communication in the pejorative sense rests on the idea that communication serves the optimal development of the individual who knows how to use it: it conduces to social and even – why not? – amorous success. English expresses the point in a nice verb: communication *empowers* the subject. It increases, if not her power, than at least her potential in the Aristotelian sense – that is, her capacity to act. What is important about the work of Deborah Cameron, a British feminist linguist interested in what she calls 'verbal hygiene',[12] is that it puts this ideology to the test of the facts – that is, social relations in the world of work. In *Good to Talk?*, she studies the correspondence courses and other manuals that claim to enable everyone to

---

[12] See Cameron 1985 and 1995.

improve their ability to communicate (we have all seen enticing publicity that promises us success if we improve our linguistic skills); and she studies communications policies in service enterprises, where communication plays a key role: banks or telephone inquiry centres. What emerges from her studies is that the communications strategy of enterprises that profess it is the converse of the ideology that they diffuse. Communications policy within the enterprise and at the interface between enterprise and customer, far from favouring development through language, aims to control language and regulate it within strict limits. It is easy to understand why: the telephone operator who replies to a demand for information cannot allow herself to devote more than a certain number of seconds to each conversation, if she is to meet the objectives that have been set for her, which obey profit constraints. Far from being the site of freedom of expression and ethical responsibility, such conversations obey a fixed standard schema, whose ideal is a completely automated exchange (an artificial, but nevertheless cheerful voice encourages me, if I want to check my accounts, to press the star button). Even when the operator is still a human subject, her language is strictly controlled: tone of voice, formulae for addressing the customer and ending the conversation, vocabulary and levels of language, no expressive or stylistic choice, no personalisation of the utterance permitted. Pretend customers and real inspectors, or recording machines, will take care of verifying that instructions are properly applied, with 'evaluation' interviews on offer. Here, the practice of communication is the exact opposite of the ideology of communication: it aims to prohibit (in the case of the employee) and limit to the maximum (in the case of the customer) freedom of expression, the ethical responsibility of speech, and the irenic co-operation of dialogue as sharing and consensual search for agreement. In these conditions of rigid interpellation, the only possible counter-interpellation is the raising of the voice by the furious customer who insults an operator whom she knows is not responsible and the collective struggle of operators to improve their working conditions. For this communication, like any other, is the site of power relations.

I shall let Cameron speak. This is how she characterises what I have called the ideology of communication:

> The emphasis placed by so many communication experts on negotiation, conflict resolution, co-operation and agreement suggests that they are teaching communication skills for a world in which people's relationships are basically

egalitarian, their intentions toward one another are basically good and their interests are basically shared. If those conditions are fulfilled, co-operation may well be rational and rewarding. If they are not fulfilled, however, the norm of co-operation is likely, in practice, to favour the more powerful party.

As many commentators have noted, the existence of systemic power inequalities is difficult to accommodate within a liberal individualist framework. The liberal axiom that we are all positioned similarly and possessed of 'equal rights' leads to a view of conflict as essentially a local disturbance of the ideal, harmonious relation between individuals rather than as one instance of some more global contest between social collectivities over power. This view is one of the elements underpinning the idea that all kinds of conflicts can be resolved by helping the parties to communicate with one another better. Lack of consensus is taken to imply a failure of mutual understanding; conversely, it is often supposed that if people truly understood one another, they would not find themselves in conflict.[13]

And this is how she describes the reality of the social relations in communications enterprises:

Discourse about communication at work is . . . a locus where we may observe some of the contradictions of 'enterprise culture'. The rhetoric of 'empowerment' is in tension with a reality in which the minutiae of linguistic behaviour are obsessively regulated. There is also a contradiction between the rhetoric and the reality of 'skills'. . . . It is evident, too, that what many employers want, and what they mainly train their employees in, is not communication *skills* but rather a communication *style*.[14]

It is no accident if the word 'style' appears here: it is in questions of style that the linguistic dialectic of the individual and the collective, interpellation and counter-interpellation, is played out. The 'style' targeted here is 'house style' – that is, the most deterministic interpellation of the speaker de-subjectified by the institution.

---

[13] Cameron 2000, pp. 163–4.
[14] Cameron 2000, p. 89.

Language: wooden and woollen

The French phrase *langue de bois* [wooden language] is well known. It is a polemical expression that generally serves to refer to the language of the other, the opponent's language. When it has a content, it targets the stereotyped, repetitive language of politicians who shelter behind stock formulae. In particular, it has been used to describe the way in which the leaders of a working-class movement in decline express themselves. However, critics of wooden language ignore two features of this form of expression. It marks the desire for a collective expression that refuses the individualised expression of the emotions (and ambitions) – the preferred mode of address of bourgeois politicians, who trade on their 'sympathetic', 'frank' talking (which does not preclude utterly shameful lies), which is 'close to the language of ordinary people'. And, because it expresses a position, it also expresses an opposition: wooden language is decisive, it designates the enemy, it assembles friends and allies. Here, we are very close to the slogan. The critique of wooden language therefore invariably forms part of the dominant philosophy of language, in its two main characteristics: the individualism of speech and the search for consensus at any price. This is why bourgeois political speech, which is as stereotyped and repetitive as the other, prefers woollen language to wooden language.

This expression was coined by François-René Huyghe.[15] I broach the subject starting from a remarkable article by Marie-Dominique Perrot, 'Mondialisation du non-sens', published in 2002 in the journal *Recherches*.[16] She analyses a UN brochure published in 2000 in Geneva, *Un monde meilleur pour tous* [A Better World for All]. This is how she summarises her central argument:

> Global language, which is the only language capable, like a magician, of revealing the strange imaginary object that is a planetary-wide consensus, obtains its result at the price of an exorbitant sacrifice extracted from language: renouncing meaning, proceeding as if social actors did not exist, claiming that the improbable has the same value as experience . . . The lowest denominator thus sought ends up – when one succeeds in putting it into words – no longer meaning anything.[17]

---

[15] See Huyghe 1991.
[16] See Perrot 2002.
[17] Perrot 2002, p. 204.

This 'globalisation of nonsense' is obtained by the operation of woollen language, defined by Huyghe as follows: 'it has an answer to everything because it says nothing . . . it is a consensual language of power *par excellence*'.[18] What interests me is the *linguistic* description of this language given by Perrot. It emerges that the language of consensus is not transparent, that it does not make itself invisible, that it has a materiality and a specificity (it will be argued that the language of international institutions is English *even if the text is translated into innumerable languages*). I rapidly cite the main characteristics referred to by Perrot. First of all, we have the semantic characteristics. Naturally, they concern the construction of the consensus, according to the principle 'no meaning, no waves'. Hence the impression of a loss of meaning and the prevalence of fine sentiments. Who could find fault with the perspective of a 'better world for all'? Who, without laughing, would declare themselves opposed to human rights, to peace (even George Bush is in favour of peace), or sing the praises of poverty? This is obvious, but still too general: the lexicon of consensus lapses into facile moralism and erases – deliberately ignores – economic, social and political problems at the very moment that it promises to resolve them. What is more interesting is the very form of the language of consensus. For what must be called the ideology of consensus is also conveyed by grammatical markers. Here are some of them.

The first is *effacement*. This does not only concern the comprehensive effacement of thorny issues or words that contradict the ideology conveyed by the consensual text – which require that we engage in a symptomatic reading of it – but is inscribed in the syntax of the language. We have seen an example of it with the sentence heard on a BBC TV news broadcast: 'The dispute of the health workers is now in its third week.'

The second is the *presupposition*. We are familiar with the aggressive potential of this logico-linguistic phenomenon ('Are you still beating your wife?'). Woollen language makes great use of it, in the form of what Perrot calls 'naturalised axioms', 'subtracted from discussion automatically and in authoritarian fashion'.[19] This involves not only particular contents, but much more basic imaginative schemas. The example she gives – you will have understood why – is 'More is always better'.

---

[18] Quoted by Perrot 2002, p. 206.
[19] Perot 2002, p. 218.

The third is *tautology*. Thus, openness is good because it is open, or openness is openness.[20] Self-referentiality 'naturalises things that are self-evident'. Here, we re-encounter a magical conception of language (incantation, repetition, recitation of ritual formulae), on which woollen language is based, just as wooden language is.

The fourth is *metaphor*. Here, Perrot refers to the theory of metaphor in Lakoff and Johnson, which notes that the only really living metaphors are dead metaphors, for they are the ones which linguistic communication has adopted and reuses *ad infinitum*:[21] they thus become as undetectable as the presuppositions, as naturalised as the tautologies.

The fifth grammatical marker is *vagueness*. It is one of the basic properties of natural languages that they speak vaguely, by 'weakly defined terms', signifieds that are undecidable or used higgledy-piggledy, signifiers with plastic value, whose 'positive connotation is acquired automatically'.[22] The title of the UN brochure is composed exclusively of such terms.

A final marker is what Perrot calls the *anti-performative*, or 'when saying is not doing'. She cites the Genevan linguist Berrendoner, who claims that if an act is impossible to perform, saying that one is performing it is equivalent to performing it. Paradoxically, all the markers of the performative then become markers of inaction.

And this is the conclusion reached by Perrot:

> We are dealing with language here. Hollow words, stereotyped formulas, the mediocre or formatted vocabulary of world-speak do damage to the richness and complexity of reality, drape problematics in a veil of indifference. Form and content cancel one another out. This attack on language as creator and vehicle of meaning threatens the fragile capacity of human beings to live in society.[23]

In a sense, woollen language realises the communicative ideal of Habermas, since it aims at consensus and puts it into practice. But it is at the price of any genuine linguistic exchange – that is, of any debate. Wooden language was hewn in the wood from which bludgeons are made: it served *agôn*, that

---

[20] Perot 2002, p. 215.
[21] See Lakoff and Johnson 1980.
[22] Perrot 2002, p. 212.
[23] Perrot 2002, p. 220.

democratic athleticism, as Deleuze and Guattari put it; woollen language is so irenic that it suffocates meaning.

Spin

The word is American in origin and this meaning emerged around 1978. It is a metaphor borrowed from baseball, where the term refers to the effect that the pitcher imparts to the ball in order to induce an error in the batter. In politics, it designates the 'effect' that the presentation of information impresses on the 'facts' related. This manipulation of language, in which we hear an echo of an older English metaphor ('to spin a yarn'), has become one of the essential stakes of neoliberal politics, where the main thing is to 'communicate'. The reality of the existence of weapons of mass destruction in Iraq, and the threat they were supposed to represent, is of little moment: all that counted was the authority of the dossiers that asserted their existence and the seeming sincerity of those who claimed to believe in them. Spin is, therefore, a homage paid by vice to virtue: to demonstrable lies (which are nevertheless inevitably resorted to), it prefers the manipulative packaging of information, the 'spin' it gives to it.

In Great Britain, the development of spin is associated with the incumbency of Tony Blair. He did not invent the phenomenon, but it is agreed that he has made it one of the key aspects of his politics. The crisis in the summer of 2003, at the centre of which was to be found his 'director of communications', proved the crucial importance of spin, but also of its political dangers. For it can happen (as Lenin used to say) that the facts are stubborn.

Norman Fairclough, an English linguist influenced by Marxism, has devoted a work to Tony Blair's language.[24] In it, we find a detailed analysis of spin as a form of discourse. Fairclough bases himself on the study of a 'green paper' (a draft law reform submitted for public discussion before being proposed to Parliament) on welfare. He shows that this consultation was only apparent (we are ourselves used to this kind of thing in France); that the conclusions arrived are already inscribed in the premises; and that this operation is effected by the spin imposed on language in its lexical, grammatical and pragmatic aspects. We can draw a certain number of characteristics of spin from his analysis. Here is the list.

---

[24] See Fairclough 2000 and, more generally, Fairclough 1989 and 1992.

The first characteristic is the *announcement effect*. Calculated leaks or press articles written by politicians themselves anticipate and prepare the presentation of the draft put out for consultation. They prepare public opinion for the requisite conclusions of this consultation.

The second is the *summary*. The complex texts of draft laws are systematically summarised, translated into a language that is more readily intelligible to common mortals. This is the role of the mass circulation press, appropriately briefed by government communication agencies. These summaries are, in reality, translations – that is, interpretations of the texts which constrain their reading – and impose the conclusions even before the arguments that might back them up have been set out.

The third is the use of *reported speech*. In reporting government policy and translating it into simple language, the friendly press can bluntly say what the government wants to have understood, but does not wish to state explicitly. Thus, 'strong signals to those who abuse welfare' will be translated in terms of 'repression', even 'clear-out'.

The fourth characteristic of spin is the *manipulation of dialogue*. Consultation is couched in terms that proclaim a desire for dialogue (as the very word 'consultation' indicates), but which, in reality, aim to prevent it: the language chosen to formulate questions prevents the emergence of conclusions other than the desired ones. The three following characteristics develop this, which is the essential characteristic of spin.

The fifth characteristic is *propagandistic force*. Consultation is conducted in terms of seeking to persuade and convince; it therefore pertains to persuasion rather than exchange. One pretends to practise a Habermasian language game, based on egalitarian communicative exchange. But, in fact, one practises an unequal exchange (it is the consultant who supplies the relevant, carefully selected information), which pertains to strategic action.

The sixth is that the consultation is presented in terms of *problem solving*. The impression on the part of the consulted that the dice are loaded is due to the fact that the object of the consultation is presented as solving a problem, rather than discussing an issue. But the terms of a problem call, if not for a single solution, than at least for a very narrow range of solutions. Thus, a serious demographic situation poses French society a severe problem and dictates pension reform. Posed in these restrictive terms, the issue can only result in a reform that will invite future pensioners to tighten their belts: for 'there is no other solution'.

The seventh is the choice of *assertions* rather than *open questions*. We might expect a consultation to offer choices, to suggest an alternative. We might expect that it would proceed by open questions. Naturally, it does nothing of the sort. In posing questions, one does not encourage the consulted to propose any solutions other than the anticipated ones: assertions or closed questions ('Is it not the case that . . .?') presuppose the solutions and the answers.

The eighth characteristic is the *univocal character of the discourse*. Government communication speaks with a single voice. The main object of spin is that this voice, and hence this perspective, remain exclusive under the appearance of dialogue.

The final characteristic is *re-lexicalisation*. This is one of the most important. It is not enough to make it impossible for the consulted practically to engage in dialogue, because overly powerful constraints are visible and do not look good. The very terms of their responses must be imposed on the consulted. The vocabulary of exchange is, therefore, an essential strategic stake. Thus, consultation also has the function of establishing the vocabulary in which problems are going to be dealt with. The words of spin are not only the instruments of ideological struggle, they are also its stakes. In this instance, it is a question of shifting thinking about welfare out of the language of the right to welfare (acquitted by the welfare state) and into that of 'service', understood in the capitalist sense of the term (service industry rather than public service). The citizen then becomes a customer, has the right to be served, the duty to pay for the service, and so on. The French do not need instruction in the political importance of defending public services against the law of the market.

I shall leave the final word to Fairclough:

> Why focus on language? Because language is crucial in the politics of New Labour. Language has always been important in politics, but the way New Labour does politics makes it more so. Why for instance did the Labour Party change its name to 'New Labour'? . . . Changing the name wasn't just reflecting a shift in political ideology, it was manipulating language to control public perception. The public relations industry . . . is at the heart of New Labour, which calculatively manipulates language.[25]

---

[25] Fairclough 2000, p. vii.

We must not exaggerate the effect of these manipulations: they are visible and provoke resistance. But they should convince us of the fact that the class enemy (it is not without a certain nostalgic pleasure that I use this old-fashioned phrase) is acutely aware of the importance of the question of language; and that she defends a philosophy of language whose essential *modus operandi* this brief glossary has (I hope) illustrated: an emphasis on irenism and dialogical communication coupled with a resolutely agonistic practice that aims to prohibit dialogue or to make it unequal – a respect in which linguistic exchange barely differs from exchange *tout court*.

References

Albert, Michael et al. 1986, *Liberating Theory*, New York: South End Press.
Althusser, Louis 1969 [1965], *For Marx*, trans. Ben Brewster, London: Allen Lane.
Althusser, Louis 1984 [1971], *Essays on Ideology*, trans. Ben Brewster and Grahame Lock, London: Verso.
Althusser, Louis 1990 [1974], *Philosophy and the Spontaneous Philosophy of the Scientists & Other Essays*, ed. Gregory Elliott and trans. Warren Montag et al., London: Verso.
Anderson, Benedict 1983, *Imagined Communities*, London: Verso.
Aristotle 1981 [1962], *The Politics*, trans. T. A. Sinclair and revised by Trevor J. Saunders, Harmondsworth: Penguin.
Badiou, Alain 1988, *L'Être et l'événement*, Paris: Seuil.
Bakhtin, Mikhail 1984 [1965], *Rabelais and His World*, trans. Helene Iswolsky, Bloomington: Indiana University Press.
Bakhtin, Mikhail 1986 [1979], *Speech Genres and Other Late Essays*, ed. C. Emerson and M. Holquist, trans. V. W. McGee, Austin: University of Texas Press.
Bakhtin, Mikhail 1977 [1930], *Le Marxisme et la philosophie du langage*, Paris: Minuit.
Bakhtin, Mikhail 1980 [1929], *Le Freudisme*, Lausanne: L'Age d'Homme.
Balibar, Renée 1974, *Les Français fictifs*, Paris: Hachette.
Balibar, Renée and Dominique Laporte 1974, *Le Français national*, Paris: Hachette.
Barthes, Roland 1972 [1957], *Mythologies*, trans. Annette Lavers, London: Jonathan Cape.
Barthes, Roland 2002, *Le Neutre*, Paris: Seuil/IMEC.
Benjamin, Walter 1973 [1955], 'Theses on the Philosophy of History', in *Illuminations*, trans. Harry Zohn, London: Fontana.
Benjamin, Walter 1999 [1982], *The Arcades Project*, trans. Howard Eiland and Kevin McLaughlin, Cambridge, MA.: Belknap/Harvard University Press.
Bensaïd, Daniel 2002 [1995], *Marx for Our Times*, trans. Gregory Elliott, London: Verso.
Benveniste, Émile 1966, *Problèmes de linguistique générale*, Volume One, Paris: Gallimard.
Benveniste, Émile 1974, *Problèmes de linguistique générale*, Volume Two, Paris: Gallimard.
Biber, Douglas et al. 1997, *Longman Grammar of Spoken and Written English*, London: Longman.
Bourdieu, Pierre 1982, *Ce que parler veut dire*, Paris: Fayard.
Brandist, Craig 2002, *The Bakhtin Circle*, London: Pluto Press.
Bréhier, Émile 1982 [1908], *La Théorie des incorporels dans l'ancien stoïcisme*, Paris: Vrin.
Bukharin, Nikolai 1925 [1921], *Historical Materialism: A System of Sociology*, New York: International Publishers.
Butler, Judith 1995, *Excitable Speech*, London: Routledge.
Butler, Judith 1997, *The Psychic Life of Power*, Stanford: Stanford University Press.
Cahiers marxistes-léninistes 1966, nos 9–10, 'Vive le léninisme!'.
Calvet, Louis-Jean 1974, *Linguistique et colonialisme*, Paris: Payot.
Cameron, Deborah 1985, *Feminism and Linguistic Theory*, London: Macmillan.
Cameron, Deborah 1995, *Verbal Hygiene*, London: Routledge.
Cameron, Deborah 2000, *Good to Talk?*, London: Sage.
Canetti, Elias 1960, *Masse et puissance*, Paris: Gallimard.
Certeau, Michel de, Dominique Julia, and Jacques Revel 1975, *Une politique de la langue*, Paris: Gallimard.

Chomsky, Noam 1987, 'Language: Chomsky's Theory', in *The Oxford Companion to the Mind*, edited by R.L. Gregory, Oxford: Oxford University Press.

Chomsky, Noam 1989, *Necessary Illusions: Thought Control in Democratic Societies*, London: Pluto Press.

Chomsky, Noam 1996, *Class Warfare*, Monroe: Common Courage Press.

Chomsky, Noam 2000, *New Horizons in the Study of Mind*, Cambridge: Cambridge University Press.

Chomsky, Noam 2001, *Propaganda and the Public Mind*, London: Pluto Press.

Cohen, Marcel 1950, 'Une leçon de marxisme à propos de linguistique', *La Pensée*, 33: 89–109.

Cohen, Marcel 1971, *Matériaux pour une sociologie du langage*, two volumes, Paris: Maspero.

Colson, Daniel 2001, *Petit lexique philosophique de l'anarchisme: de Proudhon à Deleuze*, Paris: Livre de Poche.

Crystal, David 2000, *Language Death*, Cambridge: Cambridge University Press.

Culioli, Antoine 1990, *Pour une linguistique de l'énonciation*, Volume One, Gap: Ophrys.

Culioli, Antoine 1999a, *Pour une linguistique de l'énonciation*, Volume Two, Gap: Ophrys.

Culioli, Antoine 1999b, *Pour une linguistique de l'énonciation*, Volume Three, Gap: Ophrys.

Culioli, Antoine 2002, *Variations sur la linguistique*, Paris: Klinksieck.

Dably, Andrew 2003, *Language in Danger*, Harmondsworth: Penguin.

Deleuze, Gilles 1990a [1969], *Logic of Sense*, trans. M. Lester, London: Athlone Press.

Deleuze, Gilles 1990b [1968], *Expressionism in Philosophy: Spinoza*, trans. Martin Joughin, New York: Zone Books.

Deleuze, Gilles and Félix Guattari 1986 [1975], *Kafka: Towards a Minor Literature*, trans. Dana Polan, Minneapolis: University of Minnesota Press.

Deleuze, Gilles and Félix Guattari 1988 [1980], *A Thousand Plateaus: Capitalism and Schizophrenia*, London: Athlone Press.

Deleuze, Gilles and Félix Guattari 1993 [1991], *What is Philosophy?*, trans. Hugh Tomlinson and Graham Burchell, London: Verso.

Deleuze, Gilles and Claire Parnet 1997, *Abécédaire*, Paris: Éditions du Montparnasse.

Derrida, Jacques 1982 [1972], 'Signature Event Context', in *Margins of Philosophy*, trans. Alan Bass, Chicago: University of Chicago Press.

Derrida, Jacques 1988 [1972], *Limited Inc.*, Evanston: Northwestern University Press.

Derrida, Jacques 1994 [1993], *Specters of Marx*, trans. Peggy Kamuf, London: Routledge.

Duménil, Gérard and Dominique Lévy 1998, *Au-delà du capitalisme?*, Paris: Presses Universitaires de France.

Duménil, Gérard and Dominique Lévy 2003, *Économie marxiste du capitalisme*, Paris: La Découverte.

Dunbar, R.I.M. 1996, *Grooming, Gossip, and the Evolution of Language*, Cambridge, MA.: Harvard University Press.

Engels, Frederick 1991, 'The Franconian Dialect', in Marx and Engels, *Collected Works*, Volume 26, London: Lawrence and Wishart.

Engels, Frederick 1976 [1934], *Dialectics of Nature*, trans. Clemens Dutt, Moscow: Progress Publishers.

Fairclough, Norman 1989, *Language and Power*, London: Longman.

Fairclough, Norman 1992, *Discourse and Social Change*, Cambridge: Polity.

Fairclough, Norman 2000, *New Labour, New Language?*, London: Routledge.

Favret-Saada, Jeanne 1977, *Les Mots, la mort, les sorts*, Paris: Gallimard.

Flahault, François 1978, *La Parole intermédiaire*, Paris: Seuil.

Fodor, Jerry 1975, *The Language of Thought*, New York: Thomas Crowell.

Fodor, Jerry 1994, *The Elm and the Expert: Mentalese and its Semantics*, Cambridge, MA.: MIT Press.

Fussell, Paul 2000, *The Great War and Modern Memory*, Oxford: Oxford University Press.

Goldmann, Lucien 1970, *Marxisme et sciences humaines*, Paris: Gallimard.

Goody, Jack 1997, *Representations and Contradictions*, Oxford: Blackwell.

Goux, Jean-Jacques 1973, *Freud, Marx, économie et symbolique*, Paris: Seuil.
Goux, Jean-Jacques 1984, *Les Monnayeurs du langage*, Paris: Galilée.
Gramsci, Antonio 1971, *Selections from the Prison Notebooks*, ed. and trans. Quintin Hoare and Geoffrey Nowell Smith, London: Lawrence and Wishart.
Grice, H.P. 1975, 'Logic and Conversation', in *Essays in the Way of Words*, Cambridge, MA.: Harvard University Press.
Guattari, Félix 1972, 'Machine et structure', in *Psychanalyse et transversalité*, Paris: Maspero.
Habermas, Jürgen 1984 [1981], *The Theory of Communicative Action I: Reason and the Rationalization of Society*, trans. Thomas McCarthy, London: Heinemann.
Habermas, Jürgen 1992 [1988], *Postmetaphysical Thinking: Philosophical Essays*, trans. William Mark Hohengarten, Cambridge, MA.: MIT Press.
Habermas, Jürgen 2003, 'Interpreting the Fall of a Monument', *German Law Journal*, 4, 7: 701–8.
Hardt, Michael and Antonio Negri 2000, *Empire*, Cambridge, MA.: Harvard University Press.
Harpham, Geoffrey 2002, *Language Alone*, New York: Routledge.
Harris, Roy 1998, *An Introduction to Integrational Linguistics*, London: Pergamon.
Harris, Roy and George Wolf (eds.) 1998, *Integrational Linguistics: A First Reader*, London: Pergamon.
Huyghe, François-René 1991, *La Langue de cotton*, Paris: Laffont.
Irigary, Luce 1985, *Parler n'est jamais neutre*, Paris: Minuit.
Jakobson, Roman 1963, *Essais de linguistique générale*, Paris: Minuit.
Jameson, Fredric 1981, *The Political Unconscious*, London: Methuen.
Lafargue, Paul 1936, 'La langue française avant et après la Révolution', in *Critiques littéraires*, Paris: Éditions Sociales Internationales.
Lafont, Robert 1978, *Le Travail et la langue*, Paris: Flammarion.
Lakoff, George and Mark Johnson 1980, *Metaphors We Live By*, Chicago: Chicago University Press.
Lakoff, George and Mark Johnson 1999, *Philosophy in the Flesh*, New York: Basic Books.
Langacker, Ronald W. 1987, *Foundations of Cognitive Grammar*, two vols, Stanford: Stanford University Press.
Langages 1969, no. 15, 'La linguistique en URSS'.
Langages 1977, no. 46, 'Langage et classes sociales: le marrisme'.
Lecercle, Jean-Jacques 1987, 'The Misprision of Pragmatics in Contemporary French Philosophy', in *Contemporary French Philosophy*, edited by A. Phillips Griffiths, Cambridge: Cambridge University Press.
Lecercle, Jean-Jacques 1991, *The Violence of Language*, London: Routledge.
Lecercle, Jean-Jacques 1999a, 'Philosophies du langage analytique et continentale: de la scène de ménage à la méprise créatrice', *L'Aventure humaine*, 9: 11–22.
Lecercle, Jean-Jacques 1999b, *Interpretation as Pragmatics*, London: Macmillan.
Lecercle, Jean-Jacques 2002, *Deleuze and Language*, Basingstoke: Palgrave.
Leclaire, Serge 1968, *Psychanalyser*, Paris: Seuil.
Lecourt, Dominique 1973, *Une crise et son enjeu. Essai sur la position de Lénine en philosophie*, Paris: Maspero.
Lecourt, Dominique 1977 [1976], *Proletarian Science? The Case of Lysenko*, trans. Ben Brewster, London: New Left Books.
Lefebvre, Henri 1966, *Le Langage et la société*, Paris: Gallimard.
Lenin, V. I. 1961 [1929–30], 'Philosophical Notebooks', trans. Clemens Dutt, in *Collected Works*, Volume 38, London: Lawrence and Wishart.
Lenin, V.I. 1964 [1917], 'Letter to the Editors of *Proletarskoye Dyelo* on Slogans', in *Collected Works*, Volume 25, London: Lawrence and Wishart.
L'Hermitte, René 1987, *Marr, marrisme, marristes*, Paris: Istitut d'Études slaves.
Liebermann, Philip 1998, *Eve Spoke: Human Language and Human Evolution*, New York: Norton.

Löwy, Michael 1979 [1976], *Georg Lukács – From Romanticism to Bolshevism*, trans. Patrick Camiller, London: New Left Books.

Lukács, Georg 1981 [1963], *Die Eigenart des Ästhetischen*, two volumes, Berlin: Aufbau-Verlag.

Lyotard, Jean-François 1977, *Instructions païennes*, Paris: Galilée.

McArthur, Tom 1998, *The English Languages*, Cambridge: Cambridge University Press.

McNally, David 2001, *Bodies of Meaning: Studies in Language, Labor and Liberation*, New York: State University of New York Press.

Machery, Pierre 1978 [1966], *A Theory of Literary Production*, trans. Geoffrey Wall, London: Routledge & Kegan Paul.

Marazzi, Christian 1997, *La Place des chaussettes. Le tournant linguistique de l'économie et ses consequences politiques*, Nîmes: Éditions de l'Éclat.

Marcellesi, Jean-Baptiste and Bernard Gardin 1974, *Introduction à la sociolinguistique*, Paris: Larousse.

Marx, Karl 1973 [1939–40], *Grundrisse*, trans. Martin Nicolaus, Harmondsworth: Peguin/*New Left Review*.

Marx, Karl 1975, *Early Writings*, ed. Lucio Colletti and trans. Rodney Livingstone and Gregor Benton, Harmondsworth: Penguin/*New Left Review*.

Marx, Karl 1976 (1867), *Capital*, Volume 1, trans. Ben Fowkes, Harmondsworth: Penguin/*New Left Review*.

Marx, Karl and Frederick Engels 1976 [1932], 'The German Ideology', trans. Clemens Dutt et al., in *Collected Works*, Volume 5, London: Lawrence and Wishart.

Mauss, Marcel 1990 [1923], *The Gift: The Form and Reason for Exchange in Archaic Societies*, trans. W.D. Halls, London: W.W. Norton.

Medvedev, Pavel N. 1978 [1928], *The Formal Method in Literary Scholarship: A Critical Introduction to Sociological Poetics*, trans. A.J. Wehrle, Baltimore: Johns Hopkins University Press.

Merleau-Ponty, Maurice 1968 [1964], *The Visible and the Invisible*, trans. Alphonso Lingis, Evanston: Northwestern University Press.

Merleau-Ponty, Maurice 1973 [1969], *The Prose of the World*, trans. John O'Neill, Evanston: Northwestern University Press.

Milner, Jean-Claude 1978, *L'amour de la langue*, Paris: Seuil.

Milner, Jean-Claude 1989, *Introduction à une science du langage*, Paris: Seuil.

Milner, Jean-Claude 2002, *Le Périple structural*, Paris: Seuil.

Milner, Jean-Claude 2003, *Les Pas philosophiques de Roland Barthes*, Lagrasse: Verdier.

Monod, Jacques 1972 [1970], *Chance and Necessity*, trans. Austryn Wainhouse, London: Collins.

Nettle, Daniel and Suzanne Romaine 2000, *Vanishing Voices*, Oxford: Oxford University Press.

Panaccio, Claude 1999, *Le Discours intérieur*, Paris: Seuil.

Pasolini, Pier P. 1976 [1972], *L'expérience hérétique*, Paris: Payot.

Pêcheux, Michel 1982 [1975], *Language, Semantics and Ideology*, trans. Harbans Nagpal, London: Macmillan.

Perrot, Marie-Dominique 2002, 'Mondialisation du non-sens', *Recherches*, 20: 204–21.

Perfettini, F.M. 2000, *O signore, Cosa ci hè?, ou: Le Corse du bon usage*, Borgu: Mediterranea.

Rossi-Landi, Ferrucio 1983, *Il Linguagio come lavoro e come mercato*, Milan: Bompiani.

Scarry, Elaine 1985, *The Body in Pain*, Oxford: Oxford University Press.

Searle, John 1969, *Speech Acts*, Cambridge: Cambridge University Press.

Shukman, Ann ed. 1983, 'Bakhtin Circle Papers', in *Russian Poetics in Translation*, 10.

Sohn-Rethel, Alfred 1978, *Intellectual and Manual Labour: A Critique of Epistemology*, London: Macmillan.

Sperber, Dan and Deirdre Wilson, 1978, 'Les ironies comme mention', *Poétique*, 36: 399–412.

Stalin, Joseph V. 1973 [1950], 'Marxism and Linguistics', in *The Essential Stalin*, ed., Bruce Franklin, London: Croom Helm.

Steiner, George 1976, *After Babel*, Oxford: Oxford University Press.

Thao, Tran Duc 1951, *Phénoménologie et matérialisme dialectique*, Paris: Éditions Minh-Tân.

Thao, Tran Duc 1973, *Recherches sur l'origine du langage et de la conscience*, Paris: Éditions Sociales.

Venuti, Lawrence 1998, *The Scandals of Translation*, London: Routledge.

Virno, Paolo 2002, *Grammaire de la multitude*, Nîmes: Éditions de l'Éclat.

Voloshinov, Valentin N. 1973 [1930], *Marxism and the Philosophy of Language*, trans. L. Matejka and I.R. Titunik, London: Seminar Press.

Voloshinov, Valentin N. 1976 [1926], *Freudianism: A Marxist Critique*, ed. N.H. Bruss and trans. I.R. Tutinik, New York: Academic Press.

Voloshinov, Valentin N. 1983, 'The Construction of the Utterance', *Russian Poetics in Translation*, 10: 114–38.

Vygotsky, Ler S. 1962 [1934], *Thought and Language*, ed. and trans. Eugenia Hanfmann and Gertrude Vakar, Cambridge, MA.: MIT Press.

Waquet, Françoise 2001 [1998], *Latin, or The Empire of the Sign*, trans. John Howe, London: Verso.

Wallerstein, Immanuel 2003, 'Entering Global Anarchy', *New Left Review*, II, 22: 27–36.

Williams, Raymond 1958, *Culture and Society 1780–1950*, London: Chatto & Windus.

Williams, Raymond 1976, *Keywords*, London: Fontana.

Williams, Raymond 1977, *Marxism and Literature*, Oxford: Oxford University Press.

Wolfson, Louis 1970, *Le Schizo et ses langues*, Paris: Gallimard.

Index

HISTORICAL MATERIALISM BOOK SERIES

ISSN 1570–1522

1. ARTHUR, C.J. The New Dialectic and Marx's *Capital*.
   ISBN 90 04 12798 4 (2002, hardcover), 90 04 13643 6 (2004,
   paperback)
2. LÖWY, M. The Theory of Revolution in the Young Marx. 2003.
   ISBN 90 04 12901 4
3. CALLINICOS, A. Making History. Agency, Structure, and Change
   in Social Theory. 2004. ISBN 90 04 13627 4
4. DAY, R.B. Pavel V. Maksakovsky: The Capitalist Cycle. An Essay
   on the Marxist Theory of the Cycle. Translated with Introduction
   and Commentary. 2004. ISBN 90 04 13824 2
5. BROUÉ, P. The German Revolution, 1917-1923. 2005.
   ISBN 90 04 13940 0
6. MIÉVILLE, C. Between Equal Rights. A Marxist Theory of International Law. 2005. ISBN 90 04 13134 5
7. BEAUMONT, M. Utopia Ltd. Ideologies of Social Dreaming in
   England 1870-1900. 2005. ISBN 90 04 14296 7
8. KIELY, R. The Clash of Globalisations. Neo-Liberalism, the Third
   Way and Anti-Globalisation. 2005. ISBN 90 04 14318 1
9. LIH, L.T. Lenin Rediscovered: *What Is to Be Done?* in Context.
   2005. ISBN 90 04 13120 5
10. SMITH, T. Globalisation. A Systematic Marxian Account. 2006.
    ISBN 90 04 14727 6
11. BURKETT, P. Marxism and Ecological Economics. Toward a Red
    and Green Political Economy. 2006. ISBN 90 04 14810 8
12. LECERCLE, J.J. Marxist Philosophy of Language. 2006.
    ISBN 90 04 14751 9